JOURNEYS, GENERATIONS, AND CRACKED EGGS

Journeys, the Call of God, and the Miraculous

Jim Wheeler

*a couple's journey together in partnership with God through the
valley of cancer as well as on every mountaintop*

- *ONE MAN'S JOURNEY THROUGH LIFE-THREATENING CANCER
  THAT MAY HELP OTHERS FACING THEIR OWN CRISIS*

- *IN THE MIDST OF THAT CANCER SOME HELPFUL GLEANINGS
  FROM PERSONAL EXPERIENCE IN MINISTERING TO OUR NATION'S
  SENIOR ADULT POPULATION AND THE CHALLENGES THEY FACE*

- *A LOOK AT AN AWESOME GOD OF THE MIRACULOUS*

WestBow
PRESS
A DIVISION OF THOMAS NELSON

Scripture taken from the HOLY BIBLE, NEW INTERNATIONAL VERSION ®. Copyright © 1973, 1978, 1984, 2011 by International Bible Society. Used by permission of Zondervan. All rights reserved.

WestBow Press books may be ordered through booksellers or by contacting:

WestBow Press
A Division of Thomas Nelson
1663 Liberty Drive
Bloomington, IN 47403
www.westbowpress.com
1-(866) 928-1240

ISBN: 978-1-4908-0519-1 (sc)
ISBN: 978-1-4908-0520-7 (e)

Library of Congress Control Number: 2013914485

Printed in the United States of America.

WestBow Press rev. date: 8/12/2013

TABLE OF CONTENTS

"I have cancer, but cancer has never had me."(Jim, 2010)

///////////////////////////////////////

"It is my hope this will be a positive, uplifting, faith-filled book to encourage those facing hurdles in their own lives.

It is also my prayer that the ministry to our nation's elderly and the practical helps I share from our experiences may prove inspirational and helpful to those who hear God's call to serve in that or any other mission field or walk of life, especially wherever people face adversity.

Finally, I would desire through this book, to show others what a wondrous, miracle-working God we serve. The God of all creation is interested and concerned in the life of every single human being and the things they face in their everyday life. His love and power is there to tap into and experience."

—Jim

DEDICATION

I dedicate this book to Jesus Christ who saved me by His grace
and allowed me to still be around to write my story.

I further dedicate this book to my sweetheart and wife Sharon
who has stood by my side through my toughest moments,
and to my wonderful family who fill my heart to overflow
with their love and support.

*F*inally, I dedicate this book to all those who suffer and need an
encouraging word of hope and reaffirmation that life is good and
that there are fellow human beings who care. I also hope I can put
a smile on someone's face now and then with the effort at some
occasional bit of light-hearted thoughts contained in these pages.

"I am a man filled with thanks. What a great life!"—Jim 2013

//

INSPIRED TO KEEP UP THE GOOD FIGHT OF THE FAITH

I was especially inspired by something I read in the book *'The Admirals'*, where Admiral Ernest J. King, Commander in chief, U.S. Fleet 1942 talked about how a fighter wins his fight. Along similar lines but not word-for-word, he brought out the idea that the fight is not won by just ducking and protecting yourself from the attacks that come at you from the enemy. To win the fight, one must not quit hitting back. Regardless how many hard blows you have to take, you don't let up on firing back.

//

"When you can't lift it anymore, sit on it."—Jim

(September 22, 2012 Contemplating life's challenges)

ABOUT THE AUTHOR

*J*im Wheeler is an ordained national evangelist with the Assemblies of God and a graduate of the Assemblies of God Global University out of Springfield, Missouri. He was first credentialed to the gospel ministry in 1977. His itinerant preaching ministry has brought him to speaking engagements at many churches, Adult Care Communities meetings, tent revival meetings, and a speaker at a Full Gospel Businessmen's Fellowship International meeting. Along with his wife Sharon, he has brought approximately eight-hundred of their *'Old-Time Gospel Meetings'* to residents in the mission field of those Adult Care Communities in several states and Canada besides the hundreds of preaching engagements in churches. He has ministered in New York, Pennsylvania, Indiana, Kentucky, West Virginia, and several cities in Ontario, Canada. Jim loves preaching, writing and reading. Most of all, he cherishes his family, and is thankful for the God-given gift of life.

ACKNOWLEDGMENTS

I want to express my appreciation to those who encouraged me to put into writing my journey through cancer, especially my sister-in-law Gloria. Others have further affected my decision to also write about the ministry, especially to the mission field of our nation's Adult Care Community which my wife and I have been involved in for several years. Further heart-felt love and thanks to all my family, both my immediate as well as extended family, and to my church family for all their support and prayers as I faced the crisis of cancer. I round out these acknowledgments by especially expressing my thanks to my dear wife Sharon who has kept me going when it seemed the odds were too great to keep going, and who has given all of her heart to be there for me. As someone has said, so I say too: Always choose life.

FOREWORD

Sharon Wheeler

*T*his book is from a man who is especially close to my heart who has a big heart to help others. I speak of course of my husband, Jim Wheeler. To me, he is a brave man demonstrated by all he went through and how he confronted those difficulties that came his way and continues to face those challenges. Within a few years of my marriage to Jim, he had a heart attack, open heart surgery, and several additional heart procedures. I never thought there would be anything else comparable to that crisis we went through. Well, I was wrong. On February 2010, Jim was diagnosed with stage-three esophageal cancer. I could not believe it, but when I looked over his shoulder while he was talking with his doctor on the phone, Jim wrote one word in big letters on a legal pad which I saw: *"CANCER"*. I left the room. I was crying and I felt like this could not be happening. I know that there are great difficulties that come along in life and we are not alone in those times. I believe that whatever God allows into our lives, He will help us through it.

With that said, it is still very hard to take some things. I can remember the exact time we got the news. It was 11:22am. It is a memory that stays with me. God is involved in all aspects of our lives no matter what comes our way. This book will show how two people who did not know from any firsthand experience anything about how to deal with cancer, had to learn fast. I knew from the first two weeks of hectic scheduling of countless diagnostic tests, I would need a day-planner to keep track of all of Jim's appointments. There was so much information from the Veteran's Medical Center coming at us so fast. This book may help someone be a little better prepared for this kind of difficult journey that cancer would prove to be.

The journey continues. We are often on the road, not just going to the doctors. Jim and I have a ministry to Adult Care Communities and churches around New York State and beyond. This ministry is so awesome. I have had the opportunity to meet all kinds of people, and experienced new places to go and see. The seniors at the Adult Care Communities are a generation you can learn so much from. I am blessed so much from talking to these people. We often come out with laughter in our hearts from all of the stories that they can tell you. Some women in the homes wanted to, as they put it *"keep"* Jim, but I would not let them. I have told them he is mine. Then they would have a good laugh at my response. In the year 2000, I was able to be in Louisville, Kentucky where we were doing a worship service at my mom's nursing home. It was a very special experience to have her in one of our services. She sat right up front with us. Jim also ministers at churches. A lot of those times, he introduces me not only as his wife, but his partner in ministry and he gives me the chance to greet the people before he preaches. Sometimes I join him up front for the alter-ministry time to pray for people. The ministry is an eye-opener for me. I have learned so much from Jim doing this ministry.

Well, maybe you can guess why the title is called *'Journeys, Generations and Cracked Eggs'*, although the *"Cracked Eggs"* part might be a little bit of a mystery until you read the book. I hope you can resist the temptation to jump ahead to that part and just let the book take you there through the preceding chapters first. Do that and you will be better prepared for the latter part of this book when you get there. Let me just say that the latter part of the book is about a lot more than cracked eggs. The book takes the reader through this terrible disease called cancer, and then on into the journey of our ministry, and then finally into the subject of a miraculous God. Now let me take you for a moment from our office where I am writing this forward, to a journey through our house to our kitchen. The story of the eggs as seen from my husband's eyes is only a light-hearted catalyst for that part of the book called *'Cracked Eggs'*, to talk not so much about an incident with some eggs, but far more importantly to launch into writing about the God of the miraculous. I know this story will bring a smile to your face or at least it should, and maybe it will even offer a few useful nuggets of spiritual insight to consider. So I would ask you to just sit back and maybe have a cup of coffee with you and think on what my husband Jim is writing here.

This book is from my husband Jim's heart to your heart. I do not know how much this book will help someone. I just know that love and prayers goes into this book. I hope you can pass it along to someone you know that is going through cancer or any other challenges, or to someone who can find from it some fresh inspiration and practical guidance in ministry. Let this book be a source of encouragement. I hope you can be blessed by reading its pages, and may God bless you on your own life's journey.

Keeping on the journey with Jim,
His loving wife, Sharon

INTRODUCTION

Over the course of our lives we travel a lot of different kinds of roads. Some are interstate highways while others may be not much more than a narrow pathway. We may find ourselves traveling rocky roads, or smooth roads, even at times dirt roads.

*A*nd so not in those exact words, but in somewhat more simplistic words I recall a similar line of thinking from the humorous philosophical words that came forth from the mouth of the TV character Barney Fife on one of the Andy Griffith episodes. There good old Barney stood, hands on his hips, offering his words of wisdom. He always gave us a good laugh. I love those old shows that we knew in more innocent times. I will talk about journeys in this book. Indeed it is true what Barney said about life's roads.

February 1, 2010 was no ordinary day for me. The word cancer resounded in my ears and heart like nothing ever before. I was diagnosed with esophageal cancer and confronted with the very real possibility of an early death from this type of cancer. Someone encouraged me when they told me they didn't see any tag on my back saying *'expiration date'*. I think what matters most when we face life-threatening disease is our attitude and how we live whatever time we do have, whether it is only a few more months or many more years. You can hardly get through a few days or weeks without hearing someone talking about cancer on the news. Though I was fully aware of the terrible havoc cancer can bring about in a person's life, it had never touched my own body. Somehow I thought it was never going to happen to me. The idea that one day you might hear your doctor telling you that you have cancer is not something you are ever fully prepared for.

The situation was very serious. Within only two months following my initial diagnosis, having put off surgery in order for Sharon and me to renew our wedding vows, the cancer had progressed from stage 2b to stage 3. From what I was told, by the time of surgery the cancer was precariously close to developing into fourth-stage cancer which would have penetrated the outer wall of my esophagus and quickly spread, leaving me with even less hope of survival. As it was, I already faced the very substantial possibility I might not survive. The cancer involved a substantial portion of my lower esophageal section as well as into part of my stomach and some lymph nodes. I would have to have a radical surgical procedure to remove most of my esophagus, some of my stomach, and ten lymph nodes, some of which tested positive for cancer. My remaining portion of my stomach would then be stretched into a tubular shape and reattached up near my right lung to what little remained of my esophagus. Esophagectomy, also called esophageal resection is what they call it. In chapters to follow in this book, I will go into detail about this ordeal and my journey through cancer in the hope that I may offer an encouraging word to others. You do not have to be a person with cancer to read this book.

This book is intended to be helpful in dealing with any challenge. Do you find life to sometimes be a struggle? For many, that is no doubt an understatement. This book may very well offer you some encouragement. I find my life to be a wonderful, exciting experience regardless of any circumstances. That does not mean I always feel on top of the world. While every day is good because God made each and every day, not everything that happens in the course of a day is good. I do not pretend or deny that life is often very difficult, but I do tend to look for the bright side of things. Sure, like with anyone else, I realize not all days will be easy. Some will be harder than others. Some day's challenges will at times even seem impossible to confront or survive. Quite frankly, some days just do not have a bright side. But I am convinced most days do.

I would like to suggest here that the reader of this book try to constantly be looking out for the positive attitude I sincerely attempt to show throughout my account of the difficulties I faced. It is not intended to be a depressing book or a book of sorrows or complaints, but rather an encouraging upbeat book that brings hope to those who suffer or struggle. My wife Sharon has been on this journey with me, by my side. It would not only be a tough road for me to traverse, but it would take every ounce of energy and emotional stamina for Sharon to see this through with me. And I do not even know what my sons and daughters may have gone through in their private moments as they thought about their dad possibly dying. At one point in my early days of having a rough go of it during a lengthy recovery at home, I was encouraged by a sister-in-law to write a book and tell my story. Over the ensuing months ahead, there were others who voiced the same sentiment. After prayerfully considering it, I came to the conclusion that God did want me to write. As I continued to formulate in my mind what this book would say, I began to think about how God had been with me on this journey as well as in many other aspects of my life. He had been there for me when my first wife Joan had died in 1987. He had been there for me when I had answered the divine calling to be a preacher of the gospel. That was no easy challenge for me to tackle. He had been there with me when I went through the crisis of multiple heart attacks and six heart procedures including open-heart bypass surgery and then heart stents several years later. I like to tell people that I am wired and ready to go! My chest is literally wired together following heart surgery; I have wire stents in my heart arteries; and I have wire meshes from my double-hernia surgeries. I suspect there are a few more wires and other synthetic materials I do not even know about that are inside me from surgeries. God was there now as I faced a dangerous surgical procedure to remove a lot of cancerous tissue and subsequent radiation and chemo therapy. I would need God all the way. He is still bringing me along as I continue to face each new hurdle. My heart was and is overwhelmed with all that God has done in my life.

As I had a lot of time during recovery at home to think about many things, I found myself wanting to not only tell the story of my journey through cancer, but also to speak of what God had done in our ministry and to speak of God who had so often manifested His presence and His miraculous powers. I was on this journey through the crisis of cancer, but I realized it was one part of the overall journey of life. Part of my journey in life has included the itinerant preaching ministry that God first called me to in 1975. As time has gone along God opened wide the doors of ministry to churches and the mission field of our nation's Adult Care Community in several states, and Canada. That ministry has taken us to some sixty cities and hundreds of meetings to thousands of people, with some meetings at the Adult Care Communities approaching eighty to a hundred in attendance. Such response has been nothing less than a miracle of God. Such numbers are not the norm in the Adult Care Community ministry, yet it is what we have seen at these meetings. I share these figures not to say we did anything great, but to remind the reader of what an awesome God we serve and to bring glory to His name. Only God could do these things and bring these results. I will not boast about anything I have done. I will only boast of what God has done. I am with the thinking of the Apostle Paul when he says these words in 2 Corinthians 10:17 *"Let him who boasts, boast in the Lord"*. We have seen the power of God at work in these places as the crowds have come out and people's lives have been touched by the Lord. It was nothing less than phenomenal how we saw the Adult Care Community ministry multiply and bring out a sea of residents, many of them in wheelchairs, who excitedly responded to the gospel meetings. Equally wonderful has been the response in the churches as people experienced God's touch in countless ways. My cancer has all the more increased my heart that I already had, for hurting people in our nation's Adult Care Community as well as in all walks of life.

I have come to know the God of the miraculous. Thus did I find myself wanting to somehow bring all of this together in one book. It is one book with one over-riding thought. That theme is that God has been there with us through every step in our journey, whether it be the story of my cancer, or the calling of God to the ministry, or in the many times I have enjoyed the divine power of God in everyday life. So I attempt to bring this all together here. As you read the pages of this book you will hear me tell of a number of accounts of the miraculous and of divinely orchestrated chains of events as well as amazing instances of hearing from God. For someone who is facing cancer, I pray my story will bring hope and encouragement. Just knowing what others have gone through can often help. Certainly there are many other things besides cancer that people face which is equally difficult and challenging to go through, and even far more difficult. May my effort to encourage others in any difficulty of life be helpful to someone out there who might read this book.

As I write about ministry and the wonderful things God has done in that part of my life, may others be encouraged and helped in whatever calling God may place upon their lives. May those who wonder if God still cares and still manifests His power, be encouraged to know He indeed still is the God of the miraculous and is active in our time, ready to do great things, even the otherwise impossible, if you will but believe and trust Him with your life. May reading this book and the countless times it speaks of God and His love and concern for all of humanity encourage others to place their faith in Jesus Christ. I gave a lot of thought as to whether my book should have just stayed focused solely on how God brought me through cancer and whether the three-fold subject of journeys, generations, and the miraculous could fit appropriately together in one book. I have concluded that it is what God has laid on my heart, so it is what I have run with. All of it has been miraculous, whether talking about coming through the cancer, or how God moved in the ministry He called me to, or in showing me spiritual truths about His miraculous nature.

For me personally, cancer has been a harsh thing to deal with but it has helped me to be more empathetic and sensitive to what others go through. The ministry to the Adult Care Community is a ministry of encouragement and hope for our older generation. With that in mind, I have decided it was fitting to include our story of ministering to these dear souls in the Adult Care Community where we have seen every emotion and so much of the physical suffering they face. Many are lonely, fearful, or depressed, sad, or just plain hurting. There are also many who have demonstrated a great joy for life, and exuberant praise of a good God who loves them. They have so much to offer in life experience, faith, and wisdom. It would be a mistake for the younger generation to not tap into that wisdom. I wish to emphasize the upbeat, optimistic, positive theme of offering hope and encouragement and further emphasizing what a great thing this thing called life is.

I find it is a challenge to re-live and to tell my story of my journey through cancer and at the same time, come across with the genuine positive outlook that I honestly do have. While I speak such positive words, I would add here that I do not mean to gloss over or paint an overly, rosy outlook on life or in any way diminish the reality of difficulties others may face. Cancer is unquestionably ugly and harsh to say the least, and in my writing, I do not try to dress it up as anything less. It is a harsh and rugged, rotten thing to have to face. I share considerable honest detail of the effects and difficulties cancer presented me with. I know if I could have found a book written by a cancer survivor who told it to me straight as to how tough an ordeal cancer could be, I would have appreciated the unpolished truth about what to expect. I would also have wanted such an author to give me reason for fighting the battle and remaining hopeful, no matter how dire the prognosis might be.

With this said, I proceed. If you are going to read this book, let the reader be prepared for its contents. You will probably find what I've written to at times be a rather unusual account of what one Christian has experienced. I tell of extraordinary things God has done, some of which may be hard to believe, and I do so without apology because all of it is true. I tell of a miraculous God and divine experiences in my own life; of possible angelic visitations; of visions, dreams and numerous times of hearing a Word from God. In regard to those angelic visitations, I do not say that I absolutely saw angels, but neither do I totally rule out the possibility. Either way, human or angel on those occasions, they were all part of God's provision and watching over us.

Why do I share these things? I do not share them out of any sense of boasting about those things God has allowed me to see or hear, for indeed I have nothing to boast of accept of what God has done. I tell these things because I choose not to hold these things in that my heart is bursting to tell. I do so because I believe the Lord has directed me to tell these things so that others might be reminded of what a wonderful God we have who rules all of creation. I do so to draw minds and hearts to Almighty God and to bring glory to His Name. May the Lord Jesus Christ bless and keep you close to Him as you read this book and as you continue on in your own journey.

Keeping on the journey,
Jim Wheeler Sr.

PART I

AN UNWELCOME INTRUDER

JOURNEY THROUGH CANCER

1. KEEPING ON THE JOURNEY

"I have been young, and now am old; yet I have not seen the
righteous forsaken." (Psalm 37:25)

Feel like you're growing old? Or maybe you just know full well
that you have grown old. Douglass MacArthur had some thoughts
on this when he suggested people grow old through giving up their
ideas. He talked about how yes, years take a toll on our skin as the
wrinkles begin to appear, but it is important not to lose interest
in life lest even your very soul wrinkles. He went on to talk about
being as young as your faith, self-confidence, and hope, and on the
other hand being as old as your doubts, fears, or despair.

TRUSTING GOD IN THE VALLEYS
AND ON THE MOUNTAIN-TOPS

"When all has been said, may the reader be encouraged to trust
God throughout the journey of life no matter what the situation or
crisis, whether in the valley or on the mountain-top."—Jim

*T*he preceding introduction to this book probably could have fit
nicely as part of this first chapter as it sets the stage for what you
are about to read. With that said I hope you took the time to read
the preliminary things such as the *forward* and *introduction*. In the
words that follow I will take the reader into my world where I was
confronted with a journey through cancer. From there, I will move
into the journey God has taken me on when He got hold of my heart

3

and called me into His service. In the latter chapters I will share some things God has shown me in the area of His divine power as well as talk about eternal life. I am a man full of hope and excitement for life. As God enables me, I have determined not to allow any challenges thrown at me to rule my day. I have seen too many people who have faced far worse things than have ever touched my life, so I will keep my own complaints in check. God rules my day. Part of the intent of this book is to shine a bright light on an otherwise potentially devastating disease or any other dark corner, and to lift the reader's spirit to great heights and confidence in the belief that life is a precious gift from Almighty God. It is a life meant to be lived victoriously as you put your faith in Him. So what if there are difficulties along the way? I do not trivialize life's difficulties, mine or anyone else's, but I do not let my own challenges stand in the way of loving life, and I encourage others to have this same attitude and approach to their own life. Of course, I realize there will be times that is hard to do, more so for some than others. I understand there are some who face horrendous heartache and difficulties in their life, and I know keeping or recapturing a positive outlook will not always come easily.

CHRIST WILL GET RIGHT DOWN THERE WITH YOU

God does not promise to always remove our difficulties and pains, but if we have to live with those things in life that sometimes *seem* like too much to bear, Christ will get right down there with us in our lowest lows. The Bible tells of three men, Shadrach, Meshach and Abednego who placed their faith in God and refused to worship the idle of King Nebuchadnezzar. He had them thrown into a furnace. They were seen walking around in there with a fourth Man in the fire. That fourth Man was the Son of God, the pre-incarnate Christ. The Lord got right in there with these three men and they came out of that fiery ordeal unharmed. When Christ left His heavenly abode and came to earth and hung on the cross, He was getting right down there with you and me. Does life sometimes lay you out flat on your back? It has mine, several times literally and figuratively. Christ will get right down there with you. Are there times when you desperately need God to touch your life and nothing less will do? Jacob in the Bible wrestled with God one night. He refused to let go of God until God blessed him. That is determination. After Jacob's experience with God, he came away with a limp the rest of his life. God changed Jacob's heart that night. Sometimes you have to wrestle with God in order for Him to get *your* attention and change your attitude. Notice I do not say it is about you getting God to change, but rather it is about Him changing you. Your struggle with God may turn out for good and you may be blessed, but you may also have to accept a limp as a permanent part of your life.

Life does leave its scars. It can serve as a reminder of what God brought you through and it can prove useful as you minister to others more effectively from the benefit of your own struggles. Go ahead and have Jacob's kind of determination, even desperation that you will not let go of God in your wrestling with Him until he blesses you. I have argued with God. Of course He always wins. I have wrestled with God over my own sufferings. He wins again. He has blessed me as I have hung in there determined to get His blessing. He has given me what He has determined in His infinite wisdom I need, and He has with-held from me that which He has determined I do not need. I live with life's scars and permanent disabilities that remind me of my times of wrestling with God. He knows what is best and is fully aware of what I deal with. He tells me, *"Jim, I know where you are; what you are facing; how much it hurts; and I know what I am doing. So trust me."* With that assurance from God, I can continue to get up each day and give it my best shot. Someone said *"The Holy Spirit gives us the ability to suffer for a long time."* That thought really speaks to me. I needed to hear that. Maybe someone reading this book needs that encouraging word as well.

TAKING COMFORT THAT OTHERS HAVE BEEN THERE

Most days are very good, regardless of inconveniences or pain. Though I don't fault those that do, I am not one of those that go around saying every day is a good day. It is true that God never makes a bad day per se, but I do not want to mistakenly come across as suggesting every day brings only good things. That would not be truthful or realistic. Some people are, albeit good heartedly, so into declaring every day a good day that they may inadvertently make others who are dealing with some great difficulty feel obligated to hide their real feelings and pain. Then the person having a bad day may end up trying to put on a positive attitude and a smile when they would really rather have the freedom to voice their complaint. Maybe those of us who are so full of optimism should be extra careful to not always go around telling the suffering how good a day every day is. For me personally, I instead, want to try to demonstrate heart towards the hurting by being a little more thoughtful about what I say. My situation or any one of life's difficulties does not singularly determine whether I am having a good day or a not-so-good day. I hope I can encourage others to think likewise.

I just recently heard of a man with no legs climbing twenty-thousand feet up a mountain. Talk about life being hard and the courage and determination of a man. Such a person puts a lot of us to shame in our complaints. For me the continuing array of complications from having had cancer remain an everyday challenge, but I am full of optimism, hope, faith, and joy of living. When I think about courageous men and women who have lost their legs and arms or something worse while fighting in wars, or other people who have suffered quadriplegia such as the author, painter and speaker Joni Eareckson Tada who has inspired so many, or others who have gone through any number of horrendous loses in life, my cancer seems to me to be a small thing by comparison. My wife assures me however, that my cancer has not been any small thing. Still, I know there are always others who face something worse, sometimes even far worse.

I will recount my experience with the end goal to be that of encouraging others that are facing cancer or some other crisis in their own lives. I am inspired by the Apostle Paul in the Bible who wrote in 2 Corinthians 1:8-10 these words: *"We were under great pressure, far beyond our ability to endure, so that we despaired even of life. Indeed, in our hearts we felt the sentence of death. But this happened that we might not rely on ourselves but on God, who raises the dead. He has delivered us from such a deadly peril, and he will deliver us. On him we have set our hope that he will continue to deliver us."* He went on to say more along this line of thought in 2 Corinthians 4:16-18: *"Therefore we do not lose heart. Though outwardly we are wasting away, yet inwardly we are being renewed day by day. For our light and momentary troubles are achieving for us an eternal glory that far outweighs them all. So we fix our eyes not on what is seen, but on what is unseen. For what is seen is temporary, but what is unseen is eternal."*

When all has been said, may the reader be encouraged to trust God throughout the journey of life no matter what the situation or crisis, whether in the valley or on the mountain top. God is there for you. He knows what you are facing. A fellow-minister friend of mine said in one of his sermons that there are things you can do, and there are things only God can do. He is interested in you and He is capable of doing for you what you cannot do on your own and to help you do better those things you can do.

THIS TOO, IS PART OF *"THE CALL OF GOD"*

As I approach my story of what God took me through in part-one of this book, I want to preface what I am about to write with a few thoughts which I hope will help connect all that this book is about. For the bigger portion of my life I have been a preacher of the gospel. I have attempted to be a minister that brings an encouraging word to others. In recent years I began keeping journals of the places God has taken me to in ministry. I always thought that maybe one day I would use those journals to assist me in recounting the experiences along the way in ministry and maybe write a book to re-tell it in hopes it might serve to encourage others to serve God. I look at my life as a journey where everything that happens in that journey is interconnected.

You could say this book is about how God has been there with me in every aspect of my life, and much of it has affected not only my private life but also the calling to be a minister of the gospel. Before February 2010, I would not have ever imagined that part-one of this book would even be a part of my life. But then cancer happened, and for a while, it interrupted my life's calling of preaching Christ. I would come face to face with my own mortality and have to put my preaching schedule on hold for a while. I would go through this new and unwelcome challenge of cancer and would have to learn how to walk a closer walk with God. The cancer could discourage me and leave me permanently knocked off my path with the Lord and His calling upon my life if I let it, or I could trust God and let it make me a stronger man of faith in Him. I chose the latter. I say all this to say that in some ways, struggling through the cancer was just as much a part of my calling into ministry as was my times of getting behind a pulpit to proclaim God's Word. It would be an opportunity to share my faith in new ways, and further draw people's attention to the Lord Jesus Christ.

I will spend eight chapters in part one writing about the journey through cancer. Following that, I will write about our ministry travels and then talk about the miraculous and the way to God. May the reader not see my story of the cancer as separate from the rest of the book, but rather as an important part of where God has taken me in His calling upon my life, whether it was the joy of ministering through the preaching of the gospel or the testing of my faith through the challenge of life-threatening disease. Come with me now on my journey.

"Cancer". ...& SO THE JOURNEY BEGINS

The scribbling of one word on a yellow legal pad, while sitting at our office desk, the phone up to my ear, and taking the call from my gastroenterologist. It was February 1, 2010 at 11:22am. It had been three days since January 29 when I had gone to the Samuel S. Stratton VA Medical Center in Albany, NY for an endoscopy and colonoscopy. Something had been obstructing my swallowing for a long time, maybe as far back as a couple years, but in recent times it had become much worse. It was not a problem with my throat, but a problem further down into the lower part of my esophagus. While of course I knew a malignant tumor was a remote possibility, I went into the hospital only suspecting a minor benign growth of some sort in my esophagus that I anticipated could easily be removed during endoscopy. At no time in my life previous to my diagnosis on that day in 2010 did I ever give it serious thought that I would one day hear the news that I had cancer. I suppose until it touches our own lives, most of us tend to think cancer is something that happens to someone else, but not us. But for Sharon and me, reality came home and there I was with cancer.

ONE WORD

"Cancer". Just one single, simple word jotted down on a piece of paper as I take the first of some notes from the doctor's call. And the tears from my dear wife Sharon begins almost simultaneously as she stands over my shoulder to find out what the doctor has to say regarding the tests results. Was cancer high on mine or her short list of a likely diagnosis? Surely not. Remotely possible, sure, but in our minds, not highly likely. But there it was, that awful word, *"Cancer".* And so comes the shock-wave we least expected and we had no idea or experience on how to handle this somber news. She leaves the room and begins to weep. An otherwise beautiful wintry day has suddenly been shattered by the so often referred to big *"C"* word

9

which has so unceremoniously and cruelly darkened our day. It is as though a dark cloud has blotted out all light and our immediate plans for the normal activities of our lives in the days ahead has totally been altered and derailed, and the news hurts beyond description.

For me, the greatest hurt is seeing and hearing the weeping of my wife and the lost, frightened look in her face. Instantly, she is caught off guard, wondering if her husband will even be around in a few months, and has our life together just been issued a fast approaching expiration date? And what of myself? How did this news hit me? I do not remember the exact words, but the doctor from seventy miles away simply said *(not in these exact words but similar)* something to the effect: *"I have the results of the endoscopy. I initially saw some outgrowth of some tissue in your esophagus. The biopsy results indicate that you do have cancer. I really am taken aback by this. I truly thought it was just some benign tissue we could take care of. I did not expect these results. You have cancer and we will need to begin some scheduling for further tests and set you up with oncology."* No, I was by the grace of God, not shaken to the core, not suddenly crumbling in despair over this thing called *"cancer"* growing inside of me. I simply, quietly and calmly responded: *"OK. Cancer."* My calm, unshaken reaction to this news was possible only because of my strong confidence and faith in my God. And it was just before my saying those words, that upon hearing the diagnosis, I calmly jotted down the single word *"Cancer"*. Was I being a bit careless in casually writing that word in full view of my wife who was standing there hoping for some good news? I don't know. It came to my ears from the doctor and my pen was already in hand, the legal pad lying there, ready to take notes, and the pen just fell to the page and out came the word onto the paper that I heard: *"Cancer"*.

In some ways, God had been preparing me for many years for such a time as this. My journey thus far in my walk with the Lord had been especially close in recent years, and I had long prior to this news of cancer, settled in my heart and mind that no matter what was ever to come my way, I would trust God. I knew my life was *"hidden with Christ"* as the Bible says. I would be here only as long as God determined, and not a moment more or less. I knew from the start that while I had cancer, that cancer never would have me. God had me, and He still does. That truth would soon become a part of my testimony that God would give me the privilege to take to thousands of people over the ensuing months and if he kept me around, the following years.

I did ask Doctor Ashley, my gastroenterologist, an additional question, the question that always inevitably gets asked with the news of cancer. *"How long do you think you can estimate I may have?"* ... or *"How long can people expect to live with this kind of cancer?"* I asked something to that effect anyhow. Up to that point, I had known two friends who had the same type of esophageal cancer, and what a horrendous event that was for them. They had both since passed away from cancer. I was prepared to hear that my prognosis would likely not include my being around very long. I instantly found my mind-set changing to one of anticipating dying soon. Only by God's intervention, could I possibly hope to beat the odds. Dr. Ashley thoughtfully and carefully responded to my question. I cannot recall word for word his answer, but in the end of the conversation, if I remember correctly, he said *"about five years"*. And that was an overly optimistic figure.

Through my own researching of this cancer and from what other doctors told me, I would soon come to discover that my prognosis was more along the line of seventeen months to maybe three years. I had even heard from some sources that there was the possibility I might very well not even survive the surgery, or the treatments and furthermore, if I did survive the eight hour surgery, I might not survive thirty days following the surgery. These are some of the things I heard from varying sources. I would come to find out in 2010 that approximately seventeen-thousand new cases of esophageal cancer was diagnosed annually at that time and there were approximately fifteen-thousand deaths from esophageal cancer annually. By the time this book is published those figures may be different. Long-term survival rate *(past five years)* is not terribly high. Only about fifteen percent. Some thirteen percent do not survive more than a few months to three years. When I heard or read the facts and figures about esophageal cancer, I did not let it scare me or rule the day. I knew full well that there is a God of all the universe who does not let so-called odds and numbers determine His desired outcome. If God chooses to keep me around a lot longer than those time spans, He can and will. Life is indeed as the saying goes, for the living. News of possible imminent death must not determine our attitude or approach to life while we are still living.

"THERE IS A TIME TO CRY"

The writer of Ecclesiastes points this out quite clearly. There is a time for everything, even tears. While this type of cancer is not rare to an extreme extent like some exotic disease, it is actually not one of the more common cancers compared to some types. No matter how you cut it, we were in for a long, incredibly difficult road ahead of us. At times, it would seem like it was almost going to get the best of us. Only the Lord kept us going. That is not to take anything away from excellent doctors and medical science. I had top-notch doctors and a top-notch medical center to get me through. But ultimately my life was and is in God's hands. Upon seeing me jot down *"five years"*, Sharon left the room further weeping and seemingly suddenly lost in her own world for that brief moment. The call from the doctor would end. The scene changed as I met my wife in the living room and we hugged and quietly wept together. Tough guys cry too. I do not have to work up any picture of an overly-dramatic, emotional scene here in this book. I am simply telling it how it was. There is enough real emotion in the real thing. If it pulls at a reader's heart-strings, I pray my story of this real life story and our testimony of how God brought us through will draw others to a saving faith in Jesus Christ.

I am still here, able to write these words because I serve a great God and Savior, and because He saw fit to keep me around a while longer to tell others of His saving grace. Certainly there are many others whose lives are equally committed to Christ, and still cancer takes their lives. Only God knows why my life was spared and I was blessed with more years.

A VERY SPECIAL LUNCH DATE

Earlier that day, at around 10am, two of our dear long-time friends, Waylen and Cherilyn, had called and said they would be in town and they invited us out for lunch. What amazing timing of God. Now here we were, fresh from receiving this news from my doctor. We had not told anyone yet. The weeping, the hug, and the myriad of thoughts racing through our minds about what our future would hold had to be temporarily subdued as we needed to head out to meet our friends for lunch. We were blessed to be able to go out and spend time with them in that difficult time. The timing of God could not have been better. Upon hearing this dreadful news, the best thing that could happen at the moment, would be to be with our friends.

Waylen befriended me in 1968 and his witness eventually played a huge part in leading me to give my life to Christ that year. Though I initially often let God *(and some people)* down as I struggled in the earlier years to walk rightly with the Lord, this dear friend and man of God never let me down, but faithfully loved me in the Lord and played a huge part in making me the man I am today. We had our lunch. It was a wonderful time with our friends. God used that lunch moment to help us catch our breath and to kind of reset our overloaded emotional circuits. We were now ready to tell someone else. We broke the news to them at that table in the restaurant that day. There we were sitting and sharing our heavy hearts. There I was, telling two of my best friends that I have ever had, what was happening in my body. They prayed for us that day at that table. It would be the first of many times where God would bring a word of encouragement that we would need in the months ahead. We would depart from our God-sent friends and head back home to begin the long journey of facing the unknown. How would we do it? What would be next? How would it all turn out? Would I soon be saying my final goodbyes to my wife, my family, and my friends? Would I suffer terribly as the cancer progressed? Could I be strong enough to tolerate the side effects and lengthy ordeal of chemotherapy and radiation treatments? How would my wife face losing me to death from cancer? And what of my sons and daughters, and the rest of my family? How would they handle what might lie ahead? Would I get to preach again? Would I suffer greatly? All these and so many other questions would come to mind.

MANY JOURNEYS WITHIN ONE JOURNEY

As I have previously mentioned in my introduction, I had traversed other journeys, whether it was the grief over losing my first wife to a premature death, or me going through a series of heart attacks. Now here I was, facing another seemingly insurmountable mountain to climb. When I had faced God abruptly taking my first wife Joanie home to be with Him in 1987, I had no chance to say our goodbyes. She was just suddenly gone, and I was ill-prepared to handle that loss. That journey of grief and pain would torment me so greatly. I had so many regrets that I had not done more to show her my love, even simple things such as buying her more flowers, or somehow giving her a better life with more of the things that might have made her life easier, or just telling her more often how much I loved her.

I remember how in the month or so just before she got ill, she had said she wanted the two of us to start spending time each day in the Bible and prayer together. We had recently drifted away from doing that and she sensed the need for us to get a fresh start with God and draw closer to Him again. I look back at it now and I sense that she knew in her spirit that time was growing short. I never got around to doing this as we let the business of life take precedence in our daily routine. Oh how I wish I had not delayed in my response to her desire that day. I recall what she wrote to me in a card on our twentieth anniversary. She said: *"We have very special feelings for each other and I know they will last forever."* As I recall those priceless words, I take some comfort in realizing it was not so much about needing to regret that I had not given her more things that life affords. Those special feelings matter immeasurably more than any material possession I could ever have provided her.

The time of grieving of course has long since subsided, but she will always be missed not only by me but by her family whom she loved so much. Many do not just *"get over"* the departure of loved ones and you do not need to. You do move on with life and you treasure those wonderful memories of the time you had together. But *"no wallowing in grief"* as someone advised me long ago. As for my regrets I mentioned, I do encourage people to do those special things for those you love while you can, paying more attention to what is on their heart, or maybe it's a visit of someone you know who is hurting or in need, and you can take the time to go out of your way for someone by a visit or helping meet a need. One moment an opportunity is there, and the next moment it can be too late. Maybe it is a relationship that has been strained and harsh words have been exchanged. Do not hold onto those grudges or let a broken relationship linger when you can mend those fences. Be willing to forgive and be forgiven.

We are not guaranteed a single additional minute with our loved ones or any other human being. We must make the most of the time we do have with others lest we find ourselves full of regrets when they are suddenly gone from us. With that said, I have long since re-married and I am blessed with a wonderful, loving wife who is a gift from God. We have a beautiful relationship and we both go the extra distance to make sure neither of us will ever need to have any regrets when the time of our departure comes and one of us steps into eternity.

There have been other journeys God has sent me out there to take. Some of those journeys have been difficult ones to travel. Some have been glorious and full of great joy. There is the journey of God's initial call upon my life in 1975 to the gospel ministry that has taken me up to many mountain-tops and also down into some low valleys. It is a journey that has taken me to the pulpits of many churches as well as into the specialized mission field of our nation's Adult Care Community, ministering to one of America's greatest generations. I will get into this journey of ministry later in this book. But for now, back to this journey called cancer. I mention these journeys to say that no matter what the journey, no matter how much comes our way, we can continue to love life and keep going. For me, and for most people that I know, the good days far outnumber any difficult days. I also realize that for some, that is not the case.

BACK HOME

So back home we went that day from our luncheon date with our friends. Upon getting back home that afternoon, we had another call from the hospital. I would need to have a CAT scan for starters, which would prove to be the first of many scans of all types, as well as countless lab work-ups, more endoscopies and colonoscopies, and so many other tests. Eventually the sheer volume of appointments and doctors and tests would overwhelm us and bring my wife to tears as she tried to keep track of all my appointments. That afternoon, knowing much of my time and energies would be at the medical center for months to come, I resigned from a small job I had been doing for some eighteen years as a school crossing guard. My primary full-time work and vocation was that of an itinerant preaching evangelist, but I subsidized my income from preaching with a few other small jobs including this school crossing guard job.

After resigning from that job for the school, I would never return, and would take early retirement and begin collecting Social Security at sixty-two. For all I knew, there was a high likelihood I would not even be here to wait and collect my full Social Security at sixty-five so it made good sense to collect social security at this earlier age. Besides that, the ensuing days and months ahead would put me out of commission and I would be too ill to work. I did go to my school crossing guard job one final time that afternoon on February 1. Sharon went with me. As we sat in the car, I recalled how Sharon had been trying to get me to renew our wedding vows the past few years, but I had always put it off, saying maybe we would do it someday. We had married in 1988. Due to the fact that I had lost my first wife in 1987, I had felt our wedding ceremony should be kept low-key. Therefore, we were married by a Justice of the Peace. No wedding party. No formal wedding dress or any of the things that normally come with a wedding. Sharon had a desire to experience all of that and in a church.

Now in 2010, on a cold wintry day, sitting in our car, knowing the statistical odds with this cancer, there was every reason to expect that I was likely dying of what would turn out to be third-stage esophageal / stomach / lymph node cancer. Time was suddenly at a premium. I looked at my wife who was heart-broken over the day's news and I told her we would renew our vows. She cried of course. It was a very special moment in our lives. Her mind quickly filled with all that this would mean. We would go all-out with this renewal of our vows which we did on April 3, 2010 with a full complement of a wedding party including a maid of honor, bridesmaid, best man, groomsman *(our son Chris)* who also would give her away, ring-bearer, flower-girl, preacher, a church wedding, reception, photographer, the works. She was so thrilled in the moment even though at the same time dealing with the emotions of the cancer diagnosis. This event would become one of the highest points in hers as well as my life during the difficult days ahead. By the way, it is no small thing that as it turned out, that cancer did not take my life. I have no hesitation in saying it is a miracle from God that I survived and am alive to tell about it.

A CHAIR, A WORD, AND A FAMILY GATHERING

Home. What a day thus far. There was a quietness that would come over our spirits and our home. God was quieting our hearts and minds. I had Sharon get on the phone and tell the family they need to drop whatever they are planning for the next evening on February 2. They need to plan on coming to our house. We have something of immediate importance to break to the whole family together. They had all been aware that I had a swallowing problem manifested by discomfort in my mid-chest area and was awaiting some tests results. But very likely, no one had given serious thought to it being cancer. Until cancer is a confirmed reality, it is hard for anyone who has not been touched by this disease to imagine the possibility that it is actually intruding upon their lives. Sharon and I had already been smacked hard with the reality that cancer had reached its ugly unwelcome presence into our lives. Now it would be time for the family to experience this reality. We would come together the following evening at 7pm and break it to them.

Meanwhile, as Sharon retreated to the office and proceeded to begin the hard task of making those phone calls, I felt like I was in a daze as I had more time for this crisis to sink in. I went to my favorite recliner in the living room. As I sat there, I gave thought to what was happening and I found myself talking to God. I said to God: *"OK Lord. Years ago in the midst of one of those times I was despairing of life over my first wife Joanie's death, you gave me a Word from Psalm 118:17 and that Word became the catalyst that I needed to get up and face life and live again. That Word was this: 'I will not die but live, and will proclaim what the Lord has done.' That Word has sustained me these past many years since then. I have taken your Word and my testimony to thousands of people. Now Lord, I have cancer and my life is hanging in the balance. I need a fresh Word from you, Lord."* I no sooner said that prayer than I clearly heard the Lord speak. Yes, God does speak today, and yes, He did speak to me in my spirit. He said: *"Jim, read the next verse."* I asked Sharon for my Bible. Alone again with just my Bible, the Lord and me having a moment together, there in my recliner in the cozy corner of our living room, I read from Psalm 118:18 which reads: *'The Lord has chastened me severely, but he has not given me over to death.'*

The short account of this moment with the Lord is that I latched onto that Word and it became my sustaining new, fresh Word from God that would see me through the coming trials. God would give me a message from this entire Psalm 118 which I would take to several churches and Adult Care Communities all around central NY, and beyond. I would share this news of cancer to my home church brothers and sisters, and share this Word that God gave me. Over the ensuing months ahead, time and time again, God would send someone in my pathway to tell me almost the identical statement: *"Jim, the Lord has said this cancer will not end in death."* Even people who had not heard of my testimony of receiving this Word from God would come up to me and tell me this, almost word for word. From day one, even from the very moment my Doctor uttered the word cancer, I knew beyond a doubt that cancer never owned me or had me, even if it resulted in my death, but God had me, and none of this was out of His control. Come what may, I settled it in my mind from the get-go, that I was OK with however God would so choose to have things turn out. I could say with the Apostle Paul: *"...now as always Christ will be exalted in my body, whether by life or by death. For me to live is Christ and to die is gain."* (Philippians 1:20b-21) I would now prepare to tell my family the news.

A SOMBER EVENING

Tuesday evening came so quickly. I could not draw from any previous life experience that would adequately equip me to tell my family the news. It was a somber evening as one after another came to the door and we gathered around in our living room. There I took my seat in my recliner that only the day before I had sat in and heard from God. Now I was there for my family to hear from me. I cannot now recall much detail about that evening. I just proceeded to tell them the news. There were probably some concealed emotions as well as there were some obvious emotions. I do recall my own voice cracking in emotion somewhat as I spoke to my family. I felt like I was preparing them early on for the likelihood of soon saying my final goodbyes. That is not a pessimistic attitude. It was just being realistic. If this type and advanced stage of cancer were to take its usual course, I should not very likely be around long. It is not a type of cancer that has a high survival rate, especially at the late stage I was at. I did not have throat cancer as so many people have mistakenly thought it was. That type of cancer is a whole different thing, often caused by smoking, but can have other causes. I had esophageal cancer which is a cancer deeper in the esophagus than the throat.

I had first noticed a problem a couple years earlier when sticking a fork in left-over pasta or other cold foods in the refrigerator, and enjoying that extra mouthful of food in the evening or mid-day that we'd had for a meal earlier. I don't know the exact first time it happened, but one of those times, the cold pasta got stuck half-way down my esophagus and extreme discomfort ensued. I nearly panicked as I paced the kitchen desperately trying to get relief. The relief would come after a few scary minutes. Then over a long period of time, this same scenario would happen again and again, only worsen each time. I just figured I was probably eating too fast or too big a mouthful, and that for whatever reason, maybe I needed to get out of that habit of raiding the refrigerator between meals. At some point, the problem progressed to having difficulty swallowing large pills.

At the same period of time all this was going on, I began to have increasingly unusually severe bouts of acid reflux at night. It would come on suddenly and I would awake, sit up fast, and experience an extraordinary and terrible burning from the acid coming up my throat. Again, I paid little attention to this, thinking I just needed to cut back on evening snacks. What I did not realize at the time was that acid reflux can progress into very serious problems which in my case it had, including doing damage to the inner lining of the esophagus which if left untreated, can turn into cancer. I have discovered since then that many people are not aware just how serious acid reflux can be. It is not something to treat lightly. We live in a culture that promotes poor eating habits, whether it is the advertisements on TV showing the sports fans gobbling down over-sized subs or over-indulging on five-topping pizzas, beer, extra-hot chicken wings, and having a big burp-in, etc., or restaurants dishing up servings to their patrons that is enough to feed three people.

The medical profession is falling short in speaking out on the seriousness of acid reflux. It can kill. I know. It nearly did me. Anyhow, this is what went on with me as I unknowingly was racing towards the development of cancerous tissue in my digestive system. It became a very great crisis. I could not any longer enjoy a double-cheeseburger or French fries, or much of any kind of food. Meats, bread, and pasta became nearly off limits as it would take me an hour to eat a normally fifteen-minute meal. Time and again, Sharon would have to pound my back to rescue me from the discomfort of food trapped half-way down my esophagus. One particular time we had gone out for dinner at a local Italian restaurant. Suddenly, I was in serious trouble. We had to leave our meal, pay the check, and exit the building quickly. That day, out in the parking lot, we both thought I was going to die on the spot. It was the worst episode I had ever experienced with this problem. I survived, but it was a close call as my breathing was strained for a prolonged length of time. It would not be long before I would face surgery. This crisis outside that restaurant happened on a Saturday and my surgery was the following Friday. It truly was a difficult and scary time in our lives. Sharon was living with the constant fear that she was losing her husband to a cruel and tormenting disease that had unexpectedly encroached upon our lives.

FAMILY GATHERED

Now here we were on February 2, with the family gathered, and I was telling them something that they clearly understood could very possibly take my life, and maybe very quickly. That evening different ones shared their thoughts. We talked in heart-felt ways of course. I expressed my love of my family and how much they all meant to me. They all assured me of their love for me. I wish I could recall more detail, but suffice it to say that it was a very special heart-felt intimate time together as the family was drawn closer that evening, ready to get through this together. I am a very blessed man. God has blessed me with a wonderful family. They all would prove to be a great part of my inspiration to fight the coming battle that this cancer would bring. At no time would this coming battle be easy. I would have to fight every inch of the way to deal with what was to come. Thankfully, the battle is really the Lord's, not mine, and He would ultimately be my strength. My family, my wife, my praying friends and fellow pastors would also strengthen me.

Perhaps the most precious part of that evening with my family was what happened as they prepared to leave. My daughter Vickie initiated the idea of us as a family, joining together in prayer. She had us form a circle. She prayed. Some of us had tears. I have never been more moved in my heart than I was at that moment. Cancer was a demon who thought it could rule the moment. God ruled instead. I have also never had a moment where I was more proud of my family than I was that evening. My heart swelled with pride and with hope. I knew right then, all the more so, that with prayer we had nipped this crisis in the bud from the start. God was in control and He, not cancer, would have His way in life or in death.

Soon it was just Sharon and me in the living room. What had just happened? Something wonderful had taken place in our lives, our family, and our home. I have hanging over our TV a large framed painting of Christ sitting on the mountainside looking over the city below. I keep that painting there as a reminder that Jesus Christ is the head of my home, and I say with Joshua of the old testament, *"... choose for yourselves this day whom you will serve, ...as for me and my household, we will serve the LORD."* (Joshua 24:15) We would now commit the future to God. The Lord was looking upon us and He would be with us in the journey that lay ahead. With that assurance, we could go to bed that evening and sleep a restful sleep, knowing we were in good hands. Another day was done. Only God would know what tomorrow and all our tomorrows would bring. That was and is always good enough for me.

2. "WE'RE OFF TO SEE THE WIZZARD..."?

"Be strong and very courageous ...have I not commanded you? Be strong and courageous. Do not be terrified; do not be discouraged, for the Lord your God will be with you wherever you go."
(Joshua 1:7a; 9)

Thomas Jefferson said something along the line of it taking just one person who has courage to be a majority.

'ONCOLOGY'. NEW TO ME

*O*ncology. I hesitate to admit it, but in the spirit of being totally honest, I do admit I was ignorant in regard to what that word referred to or at least I admit I had only a limited, somewhat vague knowledge or familiarity with that medical term. I had never needed to know until now. That afternoon of February 1, 2010 after we had returned home from our lunch date, we received the second phone call of the day from the medical center. It was a receptionist from the Oncology clinic. They said I needed blood work and an appointment with an Oncologist. We would be heading for Albany, about seventy miles away for a Thursday morning appointment, February 4. Also I was scheduled for a CAT scan for Monday, February 8. The wheels were already quickly turning. These appointments and tests would only be the initial beginning of countless tests, scans, a multitude of doctors, and rapid-fire appointments. It seems we were facing a near future that would have us spending more time in the medical center than at home. At least it seemed that way.

We would rack up easily a few thousand miles during the coming months traveling to Albany, and twice to West Haven VA Medical Center in Connecticut. Oncology? Oncologist? Maybe not entirely new words to me, but up until then, those words had never before held any significance in my life because cancer had never before so directly touched or intruded upon my own life. I think I am a fairly well educated man, but somehow I had never had the occasion to need to know anything about Oncology. Now that clinic and that word would take on a major role and significance in our lives. You may notice I often refer to this cancer business as being something faced in the plural sense. We, our, us. Though I was the one with cancer, I was not alone in this event. Sharon was affected by every facet of this cancer. It would rock her world to the core as well as affect my family too. We would have a few days to mull over what was in store. As we learned that the Oncology clinic was about dealing with cancer, we prepared ourselves to go to a place we had never been before.

My journey was about to take us into the dark forest of the unknown. When I say *"dark forest of the unknown"*, I cannot help but think of the movie, *'The Wizard of Oz'*, and how the four main characters, Dorothy, the straw man, the tin man, and the lion, all headed off on a great journey towards Emerald City to meet the Wizard of OZ. Surely he would grant them their wishes. Dorothy, to get back home to Kansas; the straw man, to have a brain; the tin man, a heart; and the lion, courage. They would follow the yellow brick road that would take them on a precarious and uncertain trouble-laden journey into the unknown. Now I was heading off on a journey that would seem a lot like their fictional journey, only my journey was all too real. I would meet up with scarier things than witches, mean-spirited apple-throwing talking trees, dark forests, or flying monkeys. Death was trying to have its way before it's time. I know

now it was trying to arrive prematurely because here I am, still kicking and hanging around to write this book. This tent, my body, in which I temporarily dwell, will not be lying in the grave before God says it is time. And when that day does come, I will not be in the ground, only this temporary tent we call the body, will be there. As for me, I will be meeting Jesus face to face in Heaven. I have already acquired my reservations for heaven when I chose to accept God's invitation to give my heart to Jesus in 1969. Never-the-less, for the moment, a difficult journey had begun.

ONCOLOGY WAITING ROOM

Thursday came all too soon. There we were, in this huge, intimidating major medical center, entering for the first time into the Oncology clinic. I had been to this hospital many times before for my primary care and for Sharon's appointments. Sharon is the veteran. She has Veteran's disability status from three injuries suffered in her three years-plus stint in the US Army. I qualified for a one-hundred percent health care coverage under her health care, no doubt all part of the plan of an omniscient God. Though I had been in this Medical Center many times before, this time in the Oncology clinic, it seemed like this medical center was bigger and more intimidating than ever before, probably because I knew my life would either be preserved or lost in this facility. Would I lie in a hospital bed in the coming days or on a surgical table, breathing my last breath? I honestly had to think about these possibilities. Yet I must be quick to say here that I am not intimidated by much, and if I ever am, that intimidation is short-lived because I always come back to remembering that God is bigger than any of this. As I center on my trust in Him, the great big medical center begins to shrink in size and I find myself secure in a quiet place with my Heavenly Father. With Him, the fears are vanquished and I feel like I can confidently face anything. Of course there remains a lot of the unknown. What will we hear from my Oncologist? Will I face the dreaded radiation and chemo-therapy treatments? That was pretty much a certainty. And what lies down the hallway from the waiting room where I am now sitting? And what lies around the corner at the end of that hallway in the infusion room where I have come to realize the chemotherapy is administered? I tried to picture that scene, but later would discover that what I pictured was not even close to what it would be.

First we would go in together and see the Oncologist for the first time. As I sat in the waiting room, I realized I was in the company of several other cancer patients. Why were they able to sit there looking fairly normal and not throwing up? They had been through numerous chemotherapy and radiation treatments. Didn't that mean that they were constantly looking for the nearest toilet or bucket to handle the effects of the treatment? That is what I expected to see. But such was not the case, and that was encouraging to me. Yes, many showed obvious signs of being ill and worn down. Some had obviously lost a lot of weight and moved about in their extraordinarily gaunt frames from all they had gone through. But they were alive and fighting the fight of their lives. Many did not show any outward signs of their illness. This gave me hope. I am a fighter. I too, will put up a good fight. They are. So will I. That day, I was suddenly a member of a segment of humanity that was in the same battle. I felt camaraderie with these folks. I had to. I was in the same boat. They had cancer. I did too.

MY TURN

Finally, the wait was over. It was my turn to enter the door into the Oncologist's small room. So much that I did not know what to expect. But there she was, a smile on her face which somehow quickly took the edge off and made us feel a little less anxious. Yes, even God's people get anxious. The ideal is to not be anxious. But even those writers in the Bible who encouraged us not to be anxious about anything, were themselves, at times anxious. In we went and had a seat. We began to get a more detailed education on what my condition

27

was and what was ahead of us. I again cannot recall in detail what that first meeting entailed, but probably of greatest significance was the subject of my life expectancy. I recall her saying almost with a sense of it being positive news, that in the best scenario I might have as much as five years.

Now in my mind at that moment, five years was not something to get overly thrilled about. Tell me fifteen to twenty years and I might stand up and do some happy shouting. But five years? Maybe when you are young like she was, telling a man in his sixties that he might have five more years seems like a pretty good deal. After all, to her, I probably seemed old, and being around for five more years should be great news to my ears. Wrong. At least it was not five months. But I must be fair in speaking of her. She would prove to be a wonderful person and an excellent doctor who deeply did care about the both of us. Her title and name is Dr. Thalody. As time would go by, coupled with my extensive own research along with what some of my other doctors would tell me, it would become clear my prognosis could very well be that my life expectancy was much less than the five years. Perhaps seventeen months to three years if I survived surgery and treatments. Not a rosy outlook. Sharon and I came to peace with the possibility and we were prepared for me to die if that was God's plan. Also, when you are faced with no choice but to accept the possibility that you may soon die, it is not so hard to go ahead and make peace with that possibility. Maybe it is still hard for someone who does not have an assurance of eternal life through faith in Christ, but I did have that, and my relationship with God has kept me strong.

OH YEAH, …I STILL HAVE A PREACHING ENGAGEMENT

In the midst of all that was going on, I remembered all too well that life goes on and I am a minister of the gospel with a busy schedule and I still had a preaching engagement at a church Sunday. Greene Assembly of God, in Greene, NY. Could I still go there and preach only days after hearing I have cancer? I sure could! That was never in doubt. I would be there, and like any other preaching engagement, I would be there loaded for bear to preach the Word of God. The devil could not interfere with that. God gave me the appointment and I was still standing. Off to Greene we would go. It would especially be a joy to go there and do something I love instead of thinking about cancer. It was one of those *"times of refreshing"* that God gives.

That Sunday I preached a message titled *'The Triumphant Church'*. I was a bit physically and emotionally weak that day. I told the people of my cancer. One person afterwards, said to me *"You have an anointing"*. As I heard those words of encouragement, I knew any anointing and empowerment in my message or upon me was from God. I had opportunity to pray for a few that day in response to alter ministry time. The church encouraged us and they all gathered around us at the altar area and prayed over us. It was so special. Once again, we were blessed with people coming together to pray, this time, the family of God, His Church. We were in good hands.

A PRAYER

As I recall this preaching engagement in Green, NY on February 7, I look into my journal where I keep a record of all my preaching dates. I notice on February 1, I had recorded a prayer of mine and it seems fitting to include it here, so the following is what I wrote in my journal on that date:

"Today I found out I have esophageal cancer. I trust God. I do feel sad about this diagnosis. I do not know what will happen. I love my wife and family so much. I also want to preach a lot more. Dear God bring us through this journey that is ahead. May I be strong and courageous, and bring glory to your name. May all my family be saved. May I live my life and face this trial in a way that shows my family how a man of God faces the valleys of life. Amen."

It would be six weeks before I would preach again, as a multitude of hospital appointments would keep me too busy. I would later get in six more preaching dates before my major surgery on May 7, 2010. After surgery, I would not preach again for four months and would do that only minimally while in the midst of undergoing radiation and chemotherapy. There would be long intervals where I would be too ill to preach. The one thing I loved to do so much was now becoming so hard to do. But when I could muster the strength with God's help, I would be behind a pulpit some place pressing on and preaching the gospel. Cancer could not diminish my God-given passion to preach.

3. UNWELCOME DETOUR

"Commit your way to the Lord." (Psalm 37:5)

Barbara Bush spoke of roadblocks and how upon being faced with one, the solution was simply to detour around it.

A SUSPICIOUS SPOT

I find the detour quote catchy but I do not like roadblocks or detours. They are both equally annoying and interruptive of where I am heading. I may mention detours a couple more times or even several times in this book when I may get off on some rabbit trails or something comes up in the midst of what I am writing about that takes me briefly off the primary subject at hand. I think it is only appropriate that if I am writing a book about journeys, I should include those detours that may come along as I traverse this journey of writing my story. Some destinations you just want to get done with. Get there; do what has to be done; and get back home. I figured cancer was enough on my plate. No extra stops along the way needed or wanted. February 7, following my preaching date in Greene, NY we headed for Albany. We would stay the night at Best Western Motel, a favorite motel that we would frequent many times in the days ahead.

Upon arriving at the motel, I recall suddenly having terrible chills and weakness. Sharon was checking us in while I took a seat in the lobby, feeling like I would fall if I did not sit. I did not have any idea what was coming over me. I figured it would pass. As I mentioned in the last chapter, I had felt weak during preaching. We checked in and relaxed. Then dinner hour came and we went to the motel's restaurant and ordered up a nice meal. Barely into it, I could not eat. As usual, food would not go down my esophagus smoothly. I also got the chills again, and I just felt terrible all over. I went back to our room without finishing my meal. Monday came and I had the CAT scan. By lunch time at the medical center's cafeteria, I started with the chills again. We went home. By Tuesday I had chills and a fever of 104 late in the evening. The ER *(Emergency Room) 'tell-care nurse'* said come in right away. It was 11:30pm. We waited until morning and on Wednesday at 8am, we got a call from Oncology. They wanted me to come in. Before we could leave, they called again at 8:30am and said with some urgency that I needed to get there soon. There was a spot on my lung that the CAT scan had revealed. They did not know what it was. Of course this only sounded further alarm for us. What was this? Was it more cancer maybe? That was the first thought of my oncologist.

We arrived at the hospital after lunch and after a lengthy time in the ER I was diagnosed with a full-blown serious case of pneumonia. Boy was I ever sick. I could barely sit up. I would spend the next four days in the hospital, throwing up, breathing shallow, terribly weak, and just feeling awful. The third day there, a representative from the bereavement department of the hospital came into my room. Her name was Nancy. Sharon was there with me when she showed up. Nancy talked to us about what the bereavement office does for patients. She let Sharon know she was available for her *"if something happened"* to me. Of course they were well aware of my recently being diagnosed with third-stage esophageal cancer and the fact that there was a high possibility of death from it, maybe even within only a few months. When she left, my wife Sharon looked at me with concern and apprehension and said: *"Do they think you are going to die?"* It was obvious they were thinking along that line and they were there to help prepare us for that very distinct possibility. You can well imagine what thoughts naturally raced through Sharon's mind at that moment after the hospital sent someone from their bereavement department to talk to us.

We got past that moment and thankfully I recovered sufficiently from the pneumonia to be able to be discharged and finish my recovery at home. What was the big idea of pneumonia showing up when we were still trying to come to grips with cancer? Pneumonia would be a detour along the journey we were on. We are to *"commit"* our *"way to God"* as the Psalmist says, and here we were on our way, on our journey, and come what may along the way, even these detours, we must fully commit it all to God, and we did. I do not know any other way to live life if one wants to make it through the maze of life's roadblocks and hurdles. Many try to go the journey on their own and then they wonder why their lives are so complicated and frustrating. My journey was not without life's difficulties, but it was bearable and full of hope and security as I let God be my guide and bring me along on the journey.

ONE OF MANY

That hospital stay would be the first of five hospitalization admissions over the next several months and several visits to the ER. It seems to have been a chaotic time. There were the falls: I had taken a hard fall outside just a few weeks earlier when I fell on my driveway and landed on my back. For reasons I am uncertain, my legs had begun to become very weak and unstable. Was it related to my health having been deteriorating leading up to the cancer diagnosis? Maybe. I'm not sure. Then I took another hard fall next to my truck on January 19, 2010 as my legs again gave way and I slid under the truck, unable to get up. My knees had twisted during the fall and a neighbor happened by to help me. I ended up in the ER for that incident as I could hardly stand up. The doctor reset something in my leg as he made a fist behind the bend of my leg and suddenly without warning me, with a quick motion he yanked my lower leg into a bend which corrected something. I did end up on crutches for a week. Just prior to this fall, I had recently written a column in the religion section of our local newspaper that dealt with the subject of sexual immorality which in these days of sexual perversion can be a touchy subject. Then this fall happened.

When I showed up at church on crutches, one brother in Christ at our home church said something to the effect that I *"must be making the devil mad"*, suggesting that my recent health calamities might be by the devil's hands as he does not like the things I have been preaching and writing. I also began coming under attack by unbelievers who were expressing their displeasure with me for preaching the gospel. I cannot say for certain whether the devil had a hand in my fall and injury or any of the other health problems that were hitting me, but I certainly do know that when you take a strong stand for Christ and a stand against evil, you do anger the devil with what you do and say. At the same time I must add here that as a believer I am not subject to whatever Satan wants to do to me. I am under the blood of Christ and nothing will happen to me unless God permits it. I'm about to go off on a rabbit trail as I think about this.

There is a concern among many leaders in the Lord's Church these days that too many believers, and even too some ministers of the gospel today may be hesitant and maybe even fearful to preach too strong a message because one, they do not want to rock the boat and lose any of their people whom God has placed under their pastoral care, and two, they do not want to have to deal with the uncomfortable position of being criticized by unbelievers. I only mention that to encourage fellow ministers to *"fearlessly make known the gospel of Christ"* as the Apostle Paul in the Bible said, and I hope and pray that they likewise keep me on my toes by reminding me to preach fearlessly as I share the message of the gospel. There are plenty of unbelievers in my community that make it clear how much they despise me writing a column in the newspaper and taking a stand against the evils of today's society. These same people no doubt come against other Christian writers of that column. I have received what can only be perceived as threatening post cards from local atheists, including a couple of them from one man with various colored and different size letters cut out of magazine articles and spelling out evil, critical sentences haphazardly pasted on the post cards. Now that is just plain creepy and evil.

I have had others accuse me of being *"intellectually dishonest"* just because I spoke about faith in God and I make the claim that you can know Him on a personal level. These are just a couple samplings, but there have been plenty of harsher reactions to my writings on the Christian faith. It is not a popular stance to speak honestly and straight-forward about sin and repentance these days. Preaching the Bible without compromise can be hazardous to your health. Some years ago during a conversation with an angry man in which I was trying to maintain a Christ-like spirit, the man responded with words that were clearly a threat on my life. I hope no minister holds back from writing or preaching a strong message out of fearing negative responses. In such a time as we now live it is no time to write a milk-toast column that doesn't preach too strong. Choosing to preach a watered-down version of the gospel just to insure you will not be attacked for your words is a poor decision and one that fails to speak the truth.

The Assembly of God evangelist Steve Hill in his book *'Spiritual Avalanche'* said it even stronger than I have just said it. Without directly quoting him, he very correctly indicated that there are Pastors today who used to be preaching with evidence of themselves and their message being Spirit-empowered but now they are delivering very weak, sometimes even non-sense type sermons to Christians that apparently haven't matured and are more like babies in their bassinets. Such timid, weak preaching will not cut it in today's messed up world. I'm glad Jesus and the writers of the Bible did not retreat but spoke boldly regardless of what the response might be. I have no doubt at times angered a very real devil, and some of the public. I plead the blood of Jesus Christ as my protection against the devil's or people's attacks. I am with the Apostle Paul of the Bible who asked believers to pray that he would *"fearlessly make known with boldness the mystery of the gospel"*; that in proclaiming it, he may speak boldly, as he *"ought to speak". (Ephesians 6:19-20)* I should add here that most responses to the columns I've written are supportive and encouraging, and most of the fellow ministers who contribute to that column write strong messages without compromising God's Word.

I guess I've kind of strayed from my subject of talking about taking some falls and have gotten into meddling and preaching. I have a tendency to do that and probably will a few more times in this book. I'll try to get back to the subject of my falls now.

I'M FALLING ... BUT I "*CAN*" GET UP

There used to be an ad on TV where an elderly woman fell in her home and she says: *"I've fallen and I can't get up."* My heading of this section is a little different. As of mid-2013 I had fallen eight times since cancer weakened my body, but accept for two of those incidences where I needed a little assistance to get back on my feet, most of those times I have been able to get back up on my own. It was beginning to feel like an unseen force was giving me a beating. My bones are not what they used to be. Sometimes I feel like a stick man or as though I was on shaky stilts. Well, bad bones are the least of my problems. I find myself laughing about my falls. Of course I say that with compassion for others who may get seriously injured from falls. It is not really a laughing matter, but somehow I laugh at myself. Am I just getting clumsy as I age or do I need to learn yet more about how to put the brakes on and be more cautious with my movements and steps?

Many years ago in my youthful days I used to give my friends a pretty good fight back when I played football and refused to go down when I had the ball. That was all attitude. I admit I did not have some of the athleticism others had, but I played with a lot of hard-hitting passion. I don't know if I was necessarily all that tough, but it was more about an attitude I had. I just had an attitude that said I refuse to be beaten. One of the keys to keeping moving forward is to be determined to keep your feet moving. Of course sometimes I still got beat. I still do though, have that attitude. One time I had tackled a three-hundred and fifty pound man in a football game and he was the one who got hurt in that collision. Actually I just hid my own pain, but after that tackle I most definitely was feeling it. Truth be told, part of me wished I hadn't tackled him after it was over. No doubt the parts that hurt. He landed on top of me. But again, I had an attitude and foolish or not, I wasn't going to shy away from the challenge of bringing him down. That attitude has come in handy as I faced cancer. I guess I still think I have those legs of my youthful days, and down I go for another fall. I also still have that determined attitude that keeps me fighting all challenges thrown at me. It came in handy again when I was determined to get my education and accomplish the challenge of becoming an ordained minister. As for running again like those youthful days in sports, someday I am going to run again when God gives me new legs on the other side of eternity.

ER AND OTHER HOSPITAL VISITS

Before getting into more careful detail in chapters to follow, I offer a preliminary brief summary of hospital experiences and scans, etc. There were the additional ER visits and admissions to the hospital. I have already mentioned the January 2010 and January 2011 falls. There was also the February 10, 2010 ER visit, and subsequent hospitalization for pneumonia. Following the initial cancer diagnosis, I was hospitalized February 22-24, 2010 at the VA Connecticut Healthcare System Medical Center in West Haven, Connecticut, an even bigger complex than the one in Albany, NY for more complex cancer tests. May 7-21, 2010 was the biggie. I was hospitalized at the VA Medical Center in Albany for the extremely complicated surgery to remove most of my cancerous esophagus, about a third of my cancerous stomach, and ten lymph nodes two of which also were cancerous. I will get into that whole ordeal in some following chapters.

Only a week after my discharge, I was back in the ER on May 28, 2010 for staph infection which I caught from my stay there following the surgery, and subsequently hospitalized for three days. June 2, 2010 I was back in the ER with staph infection again. Yes, hospitals can make you sick. October 25, 2010 I was back in the ER with a life-threatening low white blood cell count, the medical term being *'leucopenia'*. November 24, 2010 I was back to the ER with even more seriously low white blood cell count which it turns out according to one doctor, brought me very close to dying. Actually, he was more blunt than that as he let us know it was a wonder that I even was still alive. Then there was the big bleeding event. It all happened so unexpectedly. All these medical events just seem to cascade upon me like a domino effect following the cancer diagnosis. I was going through a period of time when it was one thing after another, all of it related to the cancer or complications from cancer and my treatments. As much as three years later in April of 2013 I would go through another stretch of time where complications from cancer would disrupt my life and come upon me like an overwhelming flood.

But getting back to that year of 2010. Physically, I was tumbling steadily into ever so weaker a state. This time with the bleeding event I was suddenly swallowing copious amounts of blood. There was no warning. I was watching TV when out of the blue I began choking on blood. Running to the bathroom, blood gushed out my nose and mouth. There was so much blood I ended up swallowing a great deal of it as well. Sharon came in. I had blood going every which way especially due to the unexpectedness of it. I was not prepared for this as I had never before in my life experienced uncontrollable bleeding like this, and now it had become something extraordinary, way beyond a common nose bleed. We thought something in my body from the cancer treatments or surgeries must have gone haywire. In fact, it turns out that it was indeed related to my cancer and medications. Blood was ending up on the sink, toilet, and floor as well as several other areas. It was filling my throat faster than I could handle it. We could not get it stopped. I was gagging, losing my balance partly due to my already weakened state that I was in from treatments and now losing blood, and getting very sickened from swallowing blood.

I was ambulanced away to the local hospital ER. It took them about four hours to stop the bleeding. My blood was extremely thin due to medications and blood just started flowing. It was a result of my health being compromised due to the chemo and radiation treatments I had gone through. I lost a couple pints of blood that day. Not an exaggeration. In some cases that can be enough to go into shock but I only got somewhat weakened and lightheaded. Also I was in a bed for the four hours at the E.R. which probably helped keep me from anything worse happening. I remained very weakened for a while. In May, I almost did not make it to a preaching engagement because of another less severe bleeding episode. I would have a couple more lesser episodes of this later.

To add to all this for good measure, I was hospitalized for the fifth time with double-hernia surgery which happened due to my groin muscles being so weakened from the cancer surgery putting me out of commission and being unable to do much to keep my muscles strong. Between heart surgeries in previous years and more recently cancer surgery and then double-hernia surgery, I have been cut wide open with a continuous scar running along approximately a twelve-inch length from the top of my chest, on down my abdominal area, and multiple incisions at the bottom of that incision running across my lower abdomen area, plus a lengthy incision on my right side, and several lesser incisions and drainage punctures on chest, side and back. Pirates in the movies with all their battle scars don't have anything on me. I say that in jest of course. So much for speaking of all my battle scars. The fact is I would much prefer to not have any scars to tell of. It is truly amazing though, how much the human body can take. Each of those scars represents the wonder of modern-day medicine that God has gifted mankind with.

As I look back and go over all that went on just during my journey through cancer, I wonder how Sharon and I made it through it all. But I also know it is largely God that brought us through. Otherwise

39

we would not have gotten through it. At this point I may sound like a compulsive ER visitor running to the hospital with every little thing, but such was not the case. None of it was avoidable or just a little thing. I would sooner avoid an ER like the plague, but all of these visits, before, during and after the cancer diagnosis were related. Before I had even known about the cancer, I suspect it had been taking its toll on me and weakening my body for quite some time. All this left me feeling like I had been taken in a back alley and been beaten up by a street gang.

"But we have this treasure in jars of clay to show that this all-surpassing power is from God and not from us. We are hard pressed on every side, but not crushed; perplexed, but not in despair; persecuted, but not abandoned; struck down, but not destroyed." ...
"Therefore we do not lose heart. Though outwardly we are wasting away, yet inwardly we are being renewed day by day. For our light and momentary troubles are achieving for us an eternal glory that far outweighs them all. So we fix our eyes not on what is seen, but on what is unseen. For what is seen is temporary, but what is unseen is eternal." (2 Corinthians 4:7-9; 16-18)

"SPOCK, ...SCAN FOR ALIENS, AND BLIZZARDS?"

I loved the Star Trek series and movies. Captain Kirk would often tell his science officer Dr. Spock, to check his instrument panels and scan for any possible inhabitants on a planet they might be visiting. They could also scan for geological and other natural events on the planet. My life for the better part of the past few years had been about scanning for *"alien"* suspicious spots and growths in my body. And the ones they spotted were about as welcome as an evil invading alien from outer space. And it was a lot more than the many scans done on my body. There were also the multiple colonoscopies and endoscopies. The only thing welcome about the endoscopies was the experience of being heavily sedated when they injected the sedative. I confess that I actually enjoyed that part of the procedure. I can see where drug addicts so easily get addicted to their highs. But their highs come with too high of a price as they put their very lives and minds on the line. I had never known there were so many types of body scans used to examine the body. In the lead-up to my surgery, they ran me through a gamut of scans and other tests. Just keeping up with the multitude of appointments was a challenge.

IF I MAY TAKE A MOMENT TO THANK MY WIFE AND EVEN BRAG ON HER A LITTLE BIT...

Who better to brag on their wife than her husband? She of course would never lift herself up or trumpet her own accomplishments, but I can and will. She is a God-given treasure and that is part of what drives me to talk about her here. What a tremendous help-mate she has been and was during my most difficult days. Sharon handled the scheduling and took notes throughout all that we went through. Thanks to her work of meticulously keeping her notes, I can access those journals for information to assist me in writing this book. Sharon is one gal who knows how to get things done, and is highly gifted in organizing and coordinating things. She gives of herself in so many ways. She is also a fighter and that helps get things done as well as helps her get through a lot of the more challenging times. She has quite a resume of accomplishments if I may brag a little on her here. She went through four years of ROTC, served three years in the Army and promoted to Corporal-level ranking, and earned sharp-shooter status on the rifle range; rose to the level of Senior Vice Commander of the local Disabled American Veterans association; successfully graduated a course in nurse's aide training; successfully led two diabetes support groups including establishing one from ground up; led the way in organizing several major health fairs; served many times as a featured public speaker at diabetes education meetings in several cities and at various community organizations; is a well-informed person in diabetes-related subject matter through attending countless conferences and educational formats on the subject; she and her diabetes support group was high-lighted in a photo article in a major nationally-distributed diabetic magazine, *'Diabetic Living'*; took a course in signing for the deaf; preached the gospel a couple of times; headed up a local Christmas box collection sight for Samaritan's Purse collecting almost fourteen-hundred boxes at our home; led a women's ministry group; appointed to serve on a special local town council as secretary; and in just so many countless ways has been there to help people in need.

I realize this book is not centered around her accomplishments, but without her, I doubt I could have survived the cancer. She has been a blessing to many people and has been a blessing to me. Many people have often called upon her for her skills when they were faced with some complicated situations and they know she has a reputation for getting things done. She does not give up until all avenues have been exhausted to try to solve a problem. She also has the ability to bounce back when disappointments have come her way. I say to her: *"Way to go my dear wife!"*

MOVING FORWARD

Moving forward with those scans and various other diagnostic procedures, my initial colonoscopy was January 29, 2010 which revealed some trouble spots. A second colonoscopy to check out a suspicious spot seen on a PET scan was done April 22, 2010. That one was most unpleasant and involved some uncomfortable removal of suspicious tissue. My first endoscopy was January 29, 2010, which revealed the cancer in my esophagus. February 24, 2010, I had another endoscopy with an ultrasound camera to determine how deep into the lining of my esophagus the cancer had gone. It revealed I was borderline stage-three level of cancer. One more level deeper and it would have penetrated the outer wall and cancer could have run rampant all over the place. February 27, 2010, I had my third endoscopy to stretch my esophagus. That one gave me a sore throat for a week. I had my first CAT scan on February 8, 2010. Since then

I have had many more CAT scans and at this writing I continue to be scheduled for more periodic CAT and PET scans.

CONNECTICUT

CAT scans are limited and I would need more complex scans. They sent me to Connecticut for my first PET scan on February 23, 2010. What a trip that was. We would do it again on June 29, 2010 for another PET scan. Due to the radioactive injection for the PET scan, I had to avoid being close to people for ten hours, especially pregnant women. I had been to the medical center in Connecticut one other time before all this business with cancer. June 12, 2008, I had stents put in my heart there. The next day in our motel room before heading home, we heard the sad news that NBC correspondent Tim Russert had died. It was so sad. We loved him. He was one of the gentlest of men in the media. The day before that, following my stents procedure, I had severe heart pain and was held in the hospital recovery room until they could be sure I was OK. Blood work revealed I had a high level of enzymes which can mean heart attack. If the pain did not stop, they might have to keep me in the hospital and I might be facing another heart procedure.

A priest *(or an angel?)* appeared seemingly out of nowhere and I asked God to have him notice me and pray for me. He came in. He prayed. He left. I was instantly well. Miraculous healing? I think so. I cannot imagine any other explanation. And this priest? There was just something about him that I cannot put my finger on it. I had the distinct sense that there was something going on in that moment of time beyond the natural realm. It was as if Sharon and I were the only ones aware of his presence in that room and that no one else was seeing him. We asked some staff there what his name was and how we might contact him so we could thank him. They had no record or knowledge of that man being there or on staff or in that area that day. To this day, we are not sure if he was a man or an angel. I suspect the latter. The notion that it may have been an angel might be hard for some to swallow, but not for me. It would not be the first time I had experienced what I suspect were angelic visitations in my life.

MORE ON *"ANGELIC"* VISITS
(& some undesirable spirits too?)

I feel I can hardly mention those additional angelic visitations in my life without offering the reader some details. So here I go again, off subject, this time to talk briefly about some special times of experiencing God sending help our way. In 1971, while driving through Mississippi with my wife and children, we ran into a furious storm with torrential rain and wind. I blew a tire and pulled over into a parking lot. The lightning and thunder was upon us in full force. A man showed up and offered to change the tire for me while I get back in the car with my family and calm them down. He changed the tire and offered us money. We did not take him up on that offer. One moment he had shown up out of the blue, and following his offer of money, he walked away. We never did see where he went. He was there and then he was not there. An *"angel"*? My wife and I always suspected there to at least be the possibility he could have indeed been an angel, one of those *"ministering spirits"* the Bible mentions, sent from God to minister to God's people. Sure, he may have just been a man, but in my spirit, I suspect otherwise or at the very least I do not count that possibility out.

On another occasion in 1995, while Sharon was driving us home following my open-heart surgery, we ran into a blinding snow storm. The windshield became iced over and dirty. There was no windshield washer left so Sharon pulled over to the side of the interstate highway. We were not near any highway access or exit ramp. We were smack in a desolate stretch of mountainous highway with nothing and no one in sight. Sharon got out of the car to grab hold of some snow on the ground to wash the windshield. Due to the heart surgery, I was helplessly unable to do anything as I was wrapped in a blanket with a protective pillow over my still raw chest incision. A man instantly showed up when only seconds before there had not been another vehicle in sight, and filled our windshield washer reserve. Sharon started the car and turned on the wipers. She turned to thank the man, but he had simply left already. She never saw where he came from or when or where he left to. An *"angel"*? I don't know, but it's not out of the realm of possibility. We always had the distinct feeling in our spirit that we had just experienced something special from God, possibly an angelic encounter.

I know that sort of claim, or any of the other accounts I give of possible angelic visitations must seem to some reading this to be just too much to believe. But you would have had to be there at these times to really appreciate the possibility. No doubt, in accordance with the Biblical promise, there have likely been many times angels unaware to us have ministered in our lives. Most of the time such visitations go unseen, but the Bible assures us that angels do minister to God's people. Even if these instances I mention were possibly not angels, although I really do suspect they were, they were at least someone that God arranged to come along when they did to help us. I don't know why there have been so many spiritual experiences in my life and why some people seem to never have any such experiences to tell of. Only God knows the answer to that. I'm certainly not unique or special in this respect. I have known several other Christians who have had a number of spiritual experiences in their walk with the Lord. I should add here that there are also spiritual entities from the demonic side.

On one occasion, I sensed in my spirit a nearby presence of a demonic spirit. I called a pastor friend and asked for prayer and that presence left. Why its presence was evident that day I may never know. But we are not to live in fear of such evil spirits. God's Holy Spirit is in us who believe in Him. The Bible speaks of the gift of spiritual discernment. That may very well include among other things, the tendency to occasionally see into or sense things in the spirit world in a Biblically acceptable way such as seeing angels or even sensing an evil spirit. This should not be confused with so-called psychics talking with the dead which is absolutely an evil practice and false. More often, Biblical spiritual discernment is about discerning of good from evil rather than actually seeing something. Like many Christians, I have many times been given spiritual discernment. When representatives of cultish religions have approached our home, I have often sensed an evil spiritual presence just before or immediately after seeing them in our neighborhood. Before they could tell me who they were, I would tell them who they were. When that has happened, I have tried to be gracious and share with them a brief version of the gospel message. Upon doing so, they always quickly retreat and leave.

On another occasion, following my message I had preached in a church, a man interrupted the service with some evil ranting and after I realized what he was doing, I gently stopped him in his tracks. After the service, he proceeded to approach me and entered into a verbal attack aimed at me while I was standing on the platform. I immediately confronted him sternly and stopped his attack. He turned and walked out of the auditorium. Upon trusting in God's power and asserting God-given authority, it was as though God had closed his mouth and sent him into retreat. Clearly that day I sensed an evil presence around that man and the Holy Spirit took over the situation. So yes, I confidently assert that there have likely been a number of angelic visitations in my life, a few of which I've been aware of, and also there have been a few encounters with evil spirits.

BACK TO THE SCANS

A PET scan had showed another suspicious spot in the rectal area. They did a Procoloscopy on March 2, 2011 for that. That day at lunch, Sharon broke down over so many things going on. We got past that time, but it was hard. On March 3, 2010, I had a MUGA Heart scan. March 18, 2010, I had an MRI for a full-body scan. I also had a Bone scan two weeks later. I also had a brain scan and another brain scan some time later. I had more suspicious spots in the groin area and had ultrasound to check that out. Every time a test showed a suspicious spot, doctors naturally had to consider the possibility that it might very well be more cancer. All this made for a stressful period of time. It was beginning to look like *alien* spots were showing up all over the place and this was of course very unsettling for us to say the least. Whew! Just recounting all these procedures is exhausting, but I feel it is important to try and tell the whole story of what my journey with cancer entailed.

"LET IT SNOW—LET IT SNOW—LET IT SNOW"

I mentioned blizzards a little ways back in a sub-heading. Twice in our travels to medical centers during this time period in 2010, we managed to narrowly escape getting caught in nor'easter blizzards. In the week of February 23-25, 2010 during travels to Albany, NY and West Haven, Connecticut, blizzard conditions were happening all around us but never exactly at the place where we were until after we had moved on. Similarly, this scenario happened again in the week of January 12, 2011. We kept finding ourselves one step ahead of blizzard conditions. God had spared us both times. Being on the road in the blizzards would have been a bad situation. We know blizzards are dangerous and they can cost people's lives sometimes or cause accidents and hardships on people. But the adventurous side of us comes out when we hear of huge snowfalls approaching. There is just something amazing about watching nature's awesome power in snow storms. Truth be told, meteorologists, from the scientific standpoint, love this stuff. They eat it up.

The adventure of a big snow storm slowing everything down and keeping everyone snowed in has a certain thrill to it. Maybe *"thrill"* is a poor choice of words. There is just something about hunkering down during such meteorological events and riding out the big snow storm. I should say here however that we do not really think of big snow storms as something to be desired, especially in light of the fact that some severe nor'easters have hit the U.S. eastern seaboard, some as recently as in 2012 leaving behind some horrible devastation. But if not for such potential harm, nature's ability to put on a display of its power could at times hold a certain amount of awe. Out of respect and sensitivity towards those who have faced extreme storms, especially worse things like floods, hurricanes or tornados, and suffered great loss, I temper my thoughts on suggesting there is anything desirable about blizzards. Certainly skiers and other winter outdoors enthusiasts love the big snowfalls. For us the big thing is how God watched over us and we didn't get caught in the midst of blizzards while traveling to medical centers. Now on two occasions over two years, we would get back home after blizzards had hit our home town. But the best thing of course was that we were safe and spared anything like getting stranded in the Catskills Mountains or off the road some place. Scanning for aliens *and* blizzards … enough already.

$4.$ MAIN EVENT

(SURGERY / ICU)

"Even though I walk through the darkest valley,
I will fear no evil, for you are with me;
your rod and your staff, they comfort me."—(Psalm 23:4)

"And now for the big show!" Yikes! It was somewhere around 2002, give or take a year or so. It was an occasion where our home church was honoring the Pastor and his wife for their years of service there. My wife was the leader of the Women's Ministry at the time and was taking part in introductory segments of the special service. Several things were planned for the occasion, including the NY District Assemblies of God Secretary / Treasurer, Mearle Grossglass speaking, and also myself bringing a message. As my wife Sharon was finishing what she had to say, she then kind of briefly got her thoughts a little mixed up and said: *"And now for the big show!"* Sounds like the ring-master for a three-ringed circus. Those were not quite the words she intended to say, but it just kind of popped out that way. Quite humorous at the time I suppose, but not quite the best or most appropriate words. Admittedly, I cringed in my seat as I heard her put it in those words for what I saw as a sacred assembly. While it was not quite the best way to word it for that particular occasion, later we joked about it. I think of those words even now as I prepare to write this chapter.

The main event in my life in 2010 was about to get underway. I would finally after months of tests, be coming down to the day

49

for the big surgery and what would turn out to initially be sixteen straight days in the hospital. This would indeed be the *"big show"*. I was looking at eight hours of surgery. I had met with the thoracic surgeon, Dr. Fabian, a few times. He had spent time going over exactly what I was in for, even drawing a picture on paper in his office to try and show me what the surgery would involve. It would be a complex surgery. In response to my asking him about how rough my recovery would be, he let me know quite clearly that it would certainly not be a cake-walk. He is considered to be one of the best around the northeast to do this surgery. That is what I heard anyhow, and I tend to believe it is most likely true. At this point in my book, I must take a moment to speak more of Dr. Fabian. I have known several very good doctors who have had a part in my health care. I have already mentioned my oncologist and gastroentologist. They proved to be wonderful doctors in the care they gave me. Dr. Fabian was easily one of the best doctors I ever had the privilege of knowing. There is something about him that seemed to always put myself and my wife at ease. He always brightened our day whenever I saw him. He still did when I saw him for continued visits.

One time at a follow-up visit my wife showed him pictures from of our family and he then showed us his. I am certain that God arranged for him to be my surgeon for this monumental operation that I was about to face. The surgery involved first giving me an epidural before putting me under, in order to help my body be less traumatized by the kind of major pain this type of radical surgery would cause. If I understood correctly, my brain would register the trauma of this surgery at a lower level by the epidural blocking some of the trauma signals. They would go in through my chest and abdominal cavity and begin the process of removing a large segment of my esophagus, stomach and some lymph nodes. Four hours into the surgery they would begin the complicated process of turning me onto my side to make additional incisions in my right side by my ribs to get at some of the more complicated maneuvers in rearranging my remaining stomach and what was left of my esophagus. It would take an hour just to get me turned and set up for that next phase of the surgery. They would stretch my stomach into a tube shape and move it up by my right lung to reattach it to the small amount of esophagus that remained. I will get more into this later.

For a while following the surgery there would be the possibility of this reattachment springing leaks. If that happened, he would have to go back in and repair it. Not a pleasant prospect.

ALL THE WAY FROM FLORIDA

Here I was, only a few days away from surgery which was scheduled for May 7, 2010. On May 4, our younger son Chris asked if he could stay with his mom Sharon on the night of May 7. Her heart was touched by his desire to be with her that first night. She would be staying at the Fisher House for the duration of my hospital stay, a residential setting provided through the VA Hospital. She cried when he indicated he wanted to be there for her. On May 5, my brother Doug and his wife Gail came to our home in Oneonta to visit and said they would see us at the Fisher House before surgery. They had come up from Florida. We were so moved by their coming to be with us at this time. May 6, we left for Albany. I would stay with Sharon that night at the Fisher House. We arrived at about 3:30pm. At 4:30pm, much to my surprise, as I went to the door, there was my sister Joyce whom I had not had any idea was coming. She too, had come up from Florida. I was totally caught off guard when I saw her. The feelings that rushed over me cannot be adequately described. Doug and Gail were there too. I was thrilled beyond description over my brother and sister and Gail being there for us. It was a good shot in the arm for me that day. I am blessed to have been part of a wonderful family. They made themselves comfortable as they sat around the beds and we all just had a casual time visiting. I felt like we were back in time to when we all were just kids at 2 Endicott Avenue in Johnson City, NY where my siblings and I had been brought up. This moment in the Fisher House was one of the richest moments in my life. I will always treasure it.

BIG DAY ARRIVES

Friday, May 7, 2010. There's a date we are not likely to forget, although actually who am I kidding? These days my memory often depends on my wife recalling dates and other details. Anyhow, that day was an early morning rise for Sharon and me, as well as for family. I was told I would be the only surgery on my surgeon's schedule that day, and it would be an early start. There was too much at stake for him to have any other surgery on his schedule that day. He would need to be at his best. My sons and daughters wanted to be there by 6:15am to see me before surgery. Jimmy, Patty, Vickie, Chris, as well as Chris' girl friend Heather and their daughter Desiree were there. My brother Doug and sister-in-law Gail and sister Joyce got there by 6:30am and my oldest *(boy is he old)* brother Bill and sister-in-law Gloria got there by 7am. I was due to go back to pre-op by 7am. The family got together in that waiting room, in a circle again for prayer, and again like another time, it was Vickie that led the prayer.

An important note to insert here is that from day one of my diagnosis, we had saturated this whole matter with prayer, and we never did let up on keeping every aspect of what was coming in prayer. It had always been totally committed over to the Lord. So Vickie prayed. Another powerful moment. Oh, and by the way, Bill is not really so old. We often seem to have a lot of fun with each other that way. All my siblings are great. I am blessed to have them in my life. I add here a little insert about an exchange my brother Bill and I had in 2012. I had been dealing with a problem going on in my head and I had a brain scan to check it out. I told my brother what the doctor had said about the scan. The doctor told me I had an *"old-age brain"*. Now I am about nine to ten years younger than Bill. He emailed me back in response to this by saying: *"Now my question is....If you have an old-age brain, then where does that put me!"* That is funny. I emailed him back with the response that maybe he had an *"antique"* brain, but *(I continued) "antiques are usually of high value"*. And so the fun goes on between my *"old"* brother and me.

NO FEAR ... READY FOR WHATEVER HAPPENS

As Sharon and I left the waiting room, she of course was filled with emotions. I was filled with emotions too, but not about any fear of surgery. The cancer and the surgery never gave me any apprehension. My emotions were over what a great and loving family I had, and a wonderful wife in Sharon, and especially over a wonderful God who had everything under control. If it was my time, I was prepared to wake up in heaven if that was God's plan.

THE RING

In pre-op, a lot was soon going on. Sharon had to go back to the waiting room for a while, and then she came back with me until it would be time. There we were, only five minutes away from the moment I would be rolled away on my gurney to surgery. There was no guarantee my body would survive the coming surgical trauma or that I would wake up again this side of eternity. It really was that dangerous and complex of a surgery. Before going to surgery I had to take off my ring, glasses, etc. As I lay there with Sharon standing by the side of my gurney, I took my wedding ring and put it on a necklace we had previously purchased for this time and I put the necklace around Sharon's neck. It was a very special moment. If I did not see her again or if I did not survive the initial days following the surgery, she wanted to have this moment in pre-op to cherish. That necklace with my ring would be some comfort to her and a treasure she could hold close to her heart. We hugged and kissed each other. Sharon cried. I would not have that ring back on my finger for quite a while. My wife would wear the necklace with the ring on it for the next seven weeks. It would be mid-June before I would have the ring back.

IT WAS TIME

Finally at 8:20, it was time to go to surgery. When they wheeled me away, Sharon cried as she paused in the hallway watching me disappear beyond some doors. Before she came back into the waiting room, our son Chris met her and hugged her and told her that dad was *"going to be alright"*. I am so glad he was there for her like that. In the waiting room, as I was later told, our family had practically taken up all the room. Much of what I will write about at this juncture will be a recounting by Sharon of what transpired. The surgical team would keep Sharon informed periodically during the lengthy surgery.

A PRECARIOUS JOURNEY

Never before can I recall any one single thing being prayed about by so many people. Throughout this ordeal from day one of my diagnosis of cancer in February 2010 all the way well into 2011 and even beyond to this very day, literally hundreds and more likely thousands of people were praying for me and many indicate they continue to do so. My name and my request for prayer went out across the entire NY District of Assemblies of God. That meant the potential of hundreds of pastors and whole churches praying for me. During the first year or so beyond my surgery, I received almost weekly notes from the staff and leaders in the offices of the NY District Assemblies of God letting me know they prayed for me during their chapel time and several who prayed would sign their names on the cards. Not only that, but some people in Africa and China were keeping me in prayer, as well as people in several states across the nation. Family, friends, ministers, churches, health care professionals, various organizations such as my wife's diabetes support group, the Disabled American Veterans, Bible study groups, and on and on and on. It was just amazing. As I write and continue to be alive today, I cannot help but realize that while I have been spared and given an extension on my life, although actually my days were already numbered by God before I was even born, there are countless others who did not get to survive their cancer. It makes me all the more appreciate my life.

God did not keep me around because I was better than anyone else. I am far from being that. I am here because God is not finished with me yet. Only God knows the reason I survived cancer. I have known better men than me who haven't. What it does do to me is it causes me to want to be certain that I do not waste the privilege of still being here. I am driven all the more to be carrying out God's call upon my life. I will keep preaching the gospel as long as God allows. With God's help I will be the best husband, dad, brother, grandfather, friend, minister, citizen, man, and Christian I can be.

OPERATING ROOM

Now back to May 7, 2010, there I was, heading into the operation room. Before being put to sleep, the surgical team would insert the epidermal needle into my spine after three tries. It never did go in quite right. Then it was time to be put to sleep. I was completely at peace about whatever would happen. There was the very distinct possibility I might never wake up again to see my wife and family on this side of eternity. Any number of things could have gone wrong. Not only was this a very complicated and dangerous surgery, I also have heart-trouble history. I went forward knowing there was a higher chance with this surgery than some other surgeries, to die on the operating table. I was expected to survive it, but that possibility of not doing so was very much there. Sharon watched me be wheeled away down the hall and out of her sight that day, knowing full well the gravity of the situation. I was about to get underway on a very precarious journey that would begin from the moment I went under and would continue not only through the long surgery, but on into the initial days and weeks ahead. I try to take some time here as I recount those sixteen days in the hospital.

This event would prove to be far more intense and complicated than when I had gone through my open heart surgery years earlier. That is not to diminish the seriousness of heart surgery. That was a critical event and for anyone who goes through heart surgery, it is no walk in the park. But having been there, done that, this time around with the cancer surgery would put me through the ringer like nothing I had ever experienced before.

IS IT REALLY ACCURATE TO SAY THIS ?...

"God will never give you more than you can handle" ?

While I recount this time in my life, and I tell in some detail the difficulty and pain of it all, I write this book with others in mind who may face such a crisis or something far worse in their own lives. It can be helpful to others if they realize they are not alone in the various kinds of challenges life may throw at them. Knowing others have faced similar difficulties can help. My desire in writing this is not to parade before anyone my own sufferings. My life has been about far more good times than bad times. I want to encourage others out there as they face whatever comes at them. I would not have wanted to face this time in my life on my own. I am thankful for the support of family and friends, and mostly I wanted to keep close to God as I traversed this journey. With God's abiding presence, I really did face this crisis in my life with no fear whatsoever, and with absolute assurance that God would help me through it.

I remember telling one of my neighbors about my cancer. He seemed to almost get panicky over my cancer as he thought about the possible prospect of himself ever receiving such a diagnosis. He let me know that if he ever got cancer, he would just crumble in terror and be unable to deal with it. Hearing that from this otherwise confident stable man made me realize all the more how fears can control a person's life if they do not have faith in God. At this point in this book I want to discuss something that is a favorite thing for God-fearing people to say, and that is that *"God will never give you more than you can handle."* I certainly heard this statement directed towards me a number of times. It has such a nice sound to it and some end up thinking it is word-for-word, a verse in the Bible. It is not. Even though I am a student of the Bible, I found myself wrestling with this statement. A person who gets to hurting bad enough may have difficulty finding solace in the statement that God will not give them more than they can handle. The fact is, there is no Bible verse that specifically says that. There are verses that intimate it or are misapplied to that thought.

People tell others this statement from a good heart as they only want to encourage one-another. However there are a couple problems with saying it. One, when you tell that to people who are going through a great suffering, it puts additional stress on them when they are going through something that quite frankly just does *seem* at the time to be too much. Imagine a soldier who has just had a leg blown off and someone putting their hand on that person's shoulder and saying: *"Well, at least you can know that God will never let anything happen to you that is more than you can handle"* or telling that to someone who has just lost everything including loved ones in a tornado. Such a casual statement might only add to that person's anxiety and suffering which in the midst of their ordeal does *seem* very intolerable. More careful thought needs to go into how we talk to those who are in such terrifying pain. Two, actually the Bible does not specifically say in so many words that God will never let more suffering come into our lives than we can endure. That may come as a surprise to a lot of good folks. A lot of well-meaning people, myself included, have often and incorrectly came across as giving the impression that a certain verse in the Bible says God will not give us more than we can endure, misapplying some scripture beyond what it was intended to say. In fact, there was one time where the Apostle Paul spoke about some especially difficult things he was going through, and he said concerning those times that for him and others with him it was *"far beyond their ability to endure, so that they despaired even of life"*.

Endure? Beyond their ability? So great a challenge that they *"despaired even of life"*? That does not sound like a man who thinks God never gives us more than we can handle, at least in our own ability. With God's help, yes, but even then when Paul knew God was there for him, he still made it clear it *seemed* like it was too much for him to endure.

In recent times, especially when I have considered the terrible suffering some people face, I have taken a more careful look at what God actually does say or does not say about this. What the Bible does tell us is that there is no *temptation* that comes our way which God will not enable us to endure. (1 Corinthians 10:13NIV). Yes, according to that, we can resist any and all temptation because God promises He will not allow us to be tempted beyond what we are able to endure, and He will provide a way out of that temptation. That has to do with giving in to the temptation to sin. But as for God not allowing more than we can endure regarding suffering, He does not make such a promise in those exact words, and certainly not in that verse of scripture.

The suffering of a victim of rape, or the grief over the murder of a loved one, or the horror of an automobile accident, or any other terrible experience in life can certainly *seem* like too much to handle at the time. Job, a man in the Bible from ancient times, went through sufferings that *seemed* like too much for him to endure. While going through his sufferings there were no doubt times he would have preferred death rather than try to endure his sufferings any further. Note that I emphasize what *"seems"* like too much to endure. As it turns out, Job came through his sufferings and one might want to conclude that he did indeed endure it. I can admit here that there were many times during my recovery from cancer surgery when due to my severely altered digestive system I found myself curled up in bed in so much pain that I welcomed death. I did not sin in feeling that way.

God totally understood. Sure, I survived it, but that does not mean that I ever felt like it was tolerable. I think I am a fairly tough guy and can handle considerable pain, but there were times it seemed like too much for me. For something to be *"tolerable"*, it has to be something that is by definition *"not too unpleasant to put up with or accept"*. The fact is people often do face things that are too unpleasant to put up with or accept.

MORE ON BEING ABLE TO ENDURE

I can well imagine that my pain was never close to the severity of what some cancer patients have gone through who have never gotten relief in this life and who agonized until their final breath. I fully realize this. I have been blessed to thus far not have to go through that level of suffering. There are general principles we find in the Bible that cause us to believe God will not give us more than we can endure. We do have the assurance that God is with us and that He strengthens and helps us believe we can come through any difficulty. The Bible tells us in Philippians 4:13(NIV) that we can do all things through God's strengthening us. Does that mean we can after all, endure any level of suffering? Truth be told, there will be times when a person faces a level of suffering which he cannot endure *in his own strength*. In fact, yes God does sometimes allow you to face more than you can endure *on your own*.

God calls on us to be very courageous, but He knows such courage is only possible by Him giving us that courage. My wife says I have been brave in how I have faced my cancer. I do not know how accurate her assessment of me is in that regard, but I am not a man easily given to fear either. I have known the faithfulness of my God too long to live a life of fear. I see a great God who, while he may not give me a free pass from terrible pain, can and will strengthen me to face whatever happens. The Bible does tell us that in Christ we do have a High Priest who sympathizes with all our sufferings. While it does not mean that God does not allow *seemingly* unbearable difficulties to enter into our lives to go through, it does tell us that Jesus totally is able to feel our pain and care about what we face. He suffered way beyond anything we will ever be confronted with having to endure. A recent president of our times said something to the effect that he feels your pain. But truth be told, no he does not. Ultimately only Jesus can make such a claim.

GET TOUGH OR DIE ???
(or ..."So you think you are a tough guy eh?")

Before continuing on here, I pause to go off on one of my little rabbit trails again. As I write about human suffering and challenges of everyday life, I am reminded of an encounter I had some time back with a man who was struggling with a myriad of problems. This person was feeling overwhelmed with life's difficulties. The list of things he was facing included a health problem, finances, relationships in his life, and some other matters that he just could not seem to work out. While I got into talking to him about the Lord as I often do with a lot of my encounters with people, this person indicated he thought he really would not be needing Jesus all that much. Though he was facing a very rough time in his life, his attitude was that given a few more years of his own hard work and the passing of time, he could handle whatever life threw at him on his own. It seemed as though the very notion that he might *need* Christ was an offense to his manhood. I guess he was of that popular but flawed mentality that sees Jesus as little more than a crutch. Tough guys sometimes foolishly think it would not be manly to admit to needing Christ, as though to do so would somehow be a sign of weakness.

As I thought about that, I recalled something I had written in another format some years ago in which I stated that *"I am tough and I cry."* At the time of that writing, I had recently suffered the loss of my first wife who died so young. I admitted to shedding many tears in my process of grief, but I never was in doubt as to my manhood. I would remind any man who might think being a

Christian is for wimps that number one, you can maintain your manhood and toughness while at the same time admitting your need of the Savior, Jesus Christ, and number two, you can maintain your manhood and toughness while admitting you cannot always handle every difficulty that comes at you. Sooner or later you may discover that you do indeed need Christ. Johnny Cash sang some words about having to get tough or die in the song about a boy being named sue. The song was a fun song, but that is all it was. In truth, there are times when it will take more than just getting tough to make it through life's greatest challenges. Even Johnny Cash often testified to this being true in his own life, and they do not come any tougher than Johnny who confessed Jesus as Lord and Savior of his own life and is today with Jesus.

I like the old bumper sticker that says *"Real men love Jesus"*. Tough men would do well to be aware that Jesus was one tough, rugged man. We are told he grew in stature among men and we know he was the son of a carpenter and therefore no doubt also a hard-working skilled carpenter Himself. This same tough Jesus is the same one who with a whip in His hand, overturned the tables in the temple when religious folks were defiling the temple with their evil practices. He showed no fear as he dared to boldly and even violently with *righteous indignation (that's what some people like to so handily call their anger)* cause a ruckus and raise his voice of displeasure. This same tough Jesus slept under the stars with rocks or less for a pillow, climbed mountains, and was a rugged seafaring sailor at times. Above all this, lest there be any doubt to his toughness, he bore the torture of being whipped, punched, a crown of thorns placed on his head, spikes hammered into his hands and feet and a horrifying death on a cross. He even turned down a drink that was offered which could have numbed his pain on that cross. Jesus knows all about toughness, and by the way, Jesus on a number of occasions wept.

Anyone too tough to need Jesus? I do not think so. I needed Him, and at times, rather desperately, and I still maintained my manhood through it all. To such men or women that may think they can go it alone and do not need Christ, I say you could not be more mistaken. Let Him help you. You do need Him, and you always will. There is a popular two-word phrase I hear frequently these days that goes simply like this: *"MAN UP!"* I believe that says it well. To men out there who have any doubt about the manliness of being a follower of Christ, I say kindly but assertively, *"MAN UP."* Christianity is not for wimps. God told Job to *"brace yourself like a man."* The famous evangelist Billy Sunday of the early 1900s believed a man is not completely a man until he gives his heart to Christ and becomes a Christian. I agree and I reiterate, Christianity is not for wimps. Rather, to have the courage to turn your life over to Christ and be bold enough to unashamedly call yourself a Christian and live the Christ-like life does not diminish your manhood, but in fact adds to it and makes you a complete man.

Dare to be a man of God. To women out there, dare to be a woman who loves Jesus. He brought me through the toughest times and without Him, I am sure I would not have made it as well as I did, if at all.

TIME FOR A LONG NAP

Getting back on track, I now return to the subject of my surgery. During the time I was asleep for the surgery, they kept Sharon informed as to how things were going. What a long difficult day it was for her. Four hours into the surgery, they began the hour-long process of turning me onto my side and then going through my right rib area. Years later to this day, I continue to deal with extreme chronic pain in the right side and thoracic area *(upper-right flank)* from the trauma of what they did to my insides there and I still have to take a strong narcotic several times a day to keep it manageable. But with that said, the pain's affects are diminished when I realize I have life. I can tolerate the inconvenience. Chronic pain need not ruin a person's life, and it doesn't mine. But then I really cannot know what others may be going through. Yes, it adversely affects my life at times, but it does not rule my life. I do not waste anyone's time by complaining about it. If I mention my pain, it is not to complain. Everyone has their difficulties. I keep people informed about how I am doing if they ask or if I feel they need to know.

At 4:20pm, the surgery was done. It had been over an eight hour operation. Dr. Fabian, the lead surgeon, came out to see my wife at 4:40pm to tell her that I was in the recovery room. Every thirty minutes Sharon kept checking with ICU to find out if I was there yet. They said they were waking me up slowly due to other complications. I did not wake up until 7:20pm in the recovery room. They got me to the ICU at 9:10pm. After such a long ordeal, Sharon was allowed only two minutes to see me. Things got a little scary for her. They told her to leave because I was not doing well. My blood pressure was way out of whack and my heart was seriously, even critically acting up. Sharon anxiously kept checking with ICU to see how I was doing. She still could not see me. At 10:15pm, she saw me for ten minutes and again had to leave. What a hard day it must have been for her. They told her to go to the Fisher House and get some rest. Thankfully Chris and his girl friend Heather and their daughter were there to keep her company that night. At 2:30am, and again at 4:15am, Sharon got phone calls from ICU telling her that my heart and BP were acting up again.

ONIONS

A side note here: I just stepped into our kitchen as I was going over some notes for my book that Sharon provided me about this time. She is in the kitchen. It is 8:45pm on November 23, 2011, the evening before Thanksgiving. Tomorrow we will have the family over for the holiday dinner. Sharon is preparing some things for tomorrow. I walk over to her and ask her to clarify some of these notes she gave me, and as I go over those events of May 2010, I notice Sharon getting teary-eyed and at first I think, *"Oh, bringing back memories of that time is causing her to cry"*. Ah, but then I realize it is the onions she is peeling. Oh well. I can hardly wait for tomorrow when my family will be here for the holiday.

BACK TO MY STORY

Back to my story, the anesthesiologist Daniel, was on call that night. He stayed on that whole night to keep an eye on me. How's that for caring, personal attention? It does not get better than that. I am so thankful for the highest quality care I received at the VA Hospital. At 5:55am, ICU called Sharon again and told her to get over there right away. I was not doing well and the situation was reaching another critical point. At 6:30am, they removed the epidural that had remained in my spine since surgery because it was causing my body to have an adverse reaction. I have vague, scary flash-backs to that night. I was semi-aware of things going on and ICU personnel moving quickly to do a lot of different things as they tried to stabilize me. Sharon tells me I sometimes was waving my hands in mid-air and talking delusional. Since that critical time of my heart going way out of whack, I have had occasion to look back over my medical records and what went on that day. I have seen the EKG readouts. Just looking at them and reading what went on at that time is enough to startle me and to be amazed that I am still here.

As I was looking over the EKG, Sharon filled me in on some more details of that event. She had been called in to see me briefly and was told that if I had a minister, that it would be a good time to contact him because there was a chance I was not going to survive, and that I may very well die. Talk about ominous words. My heart was in severe tachycardia during this time and then atrial fibrillation. Looking at my EKG graphs, the readouts were all over the place. I was right on the verge of a myocardial infarction *(heart attack)* if things did not settle down. This would happen on at least two occasions where Sharon would be called in because the possibility of death was real and perhaps potentially imminent. I would like to think that maybe some of the staff on duty that day were just over-reacting as to the level of seriousness of that event.

Whatever the case, they would finally get me stabilized and Sharon could come in. My body had been radically traumatized from a complex surgery and a multitude of both large and smaller incisions. Thank God for morphine. I felt like my whole body was tightly stapled together, and I had absolutely no control of what was going on with me. I often went off into a deep, even weird sleep from all the medications. Much of the time, I did not fully understand where I was. At one point, I remember a couple of people cleaning me up and in my drugged-up mind it seemed like I was in a small room upstairs above an old western saloon, and these two people were tending to my wounds like you might see in an old western where the cowboy had been shot up. I guess I watch too many old westerns. I just wanted them to leave me alone and let me fall off into a sleep where I could escape the whole event.

Having gone through all this, I now realize that we humans can make it through a lot more than we might think we can. I certainly hated that time in my life when I was going through it, but I always kept the faith and today, I suspect that I no doubt am the better for it. God has given me a deeper appreciation for what others go through. God has a way of bringing forth something good from the worst situations. His Word says it best in that old faithful verse: *"And we know that in all things God works for the good of those who love him, who have been called according to his purpose."* (Romans 8:28)

ELEVEN DAYS IN ICU

I began my time in ICU that Friday evening of May 7. Then it progressed into the early hours of May 8 which I have just described. What a long night, both for me and for Sharon. As Saturday wore on, it would prove to be a very rough day. My heart continued to act up frequently. At one point, my BP was 288 over 230. I have heard that there was concern my heart would fail. Although I was heavily sedated, I do have vague recollection of that time. I was helpless and my life was totally in theirs and God's hands. It gave Sharon considerable alarm and stress of course. It was not long into mid-day Saturday before they were recruiting Sharon to help in various ways, such as watching machines to let them know how my BP was doing. For a while the machine would go off and alert them that my BP was seriously out of whack. That would happen about every forty-five minutes.

As is the norm, many tubes and various things were hooked up to me and it must have presented quite a sight. It was more than usual for what I had had done to me. My heart surgery years before had a lot of things hooked up to me, but much less than this time around. I could not have anything by mouth, not even a sip of water. It would be eleven days before I could have just a sip of water. That is a long stretch of time. Sharon helped moisten my mouth and lips with wet swabs which I did hundreds of times. I became very familiar with those swabs and got to the point where I was using them every few minutes when awake. Not getting a drink of water for eleven days certainly became an experience I would not wish upon anyone. I never did get hungry though, as I was nourished via tubes.

My time in ICU would become a memory I doubt I can ever shake or forget. It was the strangest of times and so much went on there. Repeatedly, there were portable chest x-rays, and just a host of so many exams and tests and procedures. There were the strange dreams induced by my morphine. There were the times I just felt so sick or confused. Physical therapy of walking was strenuous and became one of those things I particularly dreaded. The therapists had to be firm with me when I did not put forth the level of effort they knew I needed to. Bathing in bed, and all the other inconveniences became a burden that I grew so tired of.

DEVELOPING AN UNHEALTHY FONDNESS
FOR OPIATES

Morphine and some other opiate through I.V. became my friends. I was kept loaded up on these two narcotics. I would often fall off into a deep sleep which was a welcome break from dealing with pain and all the activities going on around me. I have often had to ask Sharon who all visited me there. My memory is foggy on that. Turns out I did have many visitors including Pastors, family, etc. At one point Sharon tells me that with no one around I was reaching my arms upwards and saying *"Here they come!"* I have no recollection of what that may have been about. She tells me there were many instances where I talked about things that were not really there or really happening. During much of my time there, I was living in another world created by the drugs.

It would turn out in the months ahead, long after going home, that my pain would continue to require morphine and also oxycodone. It was necessary to stay on these medications for a prolonged period of time, but the negative side to it was that it kept me in a weak, sleepy state and later would prove to have caused my body to depend on it. I would eventually have to get off the morphine, cut back on the oxycodone, and also discontinue several other addictive medications. When that time would come, I would experience serious withdrawal symptoms that would prove to be very scary. I will get back to that later. But for my time in the hospital, and for many months afterwards, morphine, oxycodone, and some other addictive medications would continue to be a part of my daily routine.

The pain from this kind of surgery, at least in my case, would not be letting up soon, or completely. To this day as I write here, I remain on oxycodone, albeit at a much reduced rate, but never-the-less, very necessary to manage the chronic pain that has never fully ceased. My insides have been seriously altered which is the reason for the continued pain. But I should point out here that the pain is something that can be tolerated and I encourage anyone reading these words to not be discouraged or fearful if you may be facing similar surgery. You can live through a lot more than you might think you can. I did. I still do, and it has not at all taken away my passion and joy of life.

A NEW CHALLENGE

Swallowing. Now there is something most people just take for granted. It was now May 11. Still in ICU. No drink, no food since May 6 before my date for surgery. Like most people, I love food. The pleasure of eating is a blessing from God. I suppose a lot of people never actually look at it that way. They just eat with little thought about it being a privilege and blessing. But it is, and when for one reason or another, you cannot exercise that blessing of life, you become keenly aware of how wonderful it is to quench your thirst or enjoy a tasty meal. It was now time to get a good look at what remained of my upper digestive track. Off I was to the x-ray department to attempt to do a barium swallow so they could see if and how well my swallowing capability was as well as examining the interior surgical work that had been done on me. It was an anxious time. If the barium swallow revealed any leaks in the area where they reconstructed and connected my now tubular-shaped stomach to my shortened esophagus, it would mean going back in to surgically repair the leaks. Such a possibility was for me, a terrible thought, but it had to be checked.

I lay flat on an x-ray table with my feet against a short platform at the end of the table. They then rose up the table to bring me to a standing position tucked into very close quarters between the table and the x-ray machine. I barely had an inch or so of space in front of my face and body to spare. It would not have been a good or tolerable situation for anyone with severe claustrophobia. I was instructed to turn my head to the side and when the technician says to, I was to carefully in ever so tiny amount, try to swallow some barium. Mind you, I had not swallowed anything since before surgery many days earlier. The plan was to examine it as it goes down my throat, through my shortened esophagus, into my remaining stomach and into the lower digestive track. I tried. My throat had been raw and dry ever since surgery. As I barely managed to get it past my upper throat, upon entering my esophagus, I gagged horribly and could not get it to go down without great difficulty. Also the pain was like a razor blade as I tried, although I admit I have of course never swallowed a razor blade, so that may be a considerable exaggeration. But it was a very sharp, painful experience. After a couple attempts, they gave up.

May 14, it was time to try again. Again, my esophagus did not function sufficiently and I could not do it. By this point there was arising the concern of the potential possibility that the surgery may have permanently altered my esophagus to where I might never take nourishment through my mouth again. The prospects of having to be on a feeding tube the rest of my life was not something I cared to think about. Now they had to find out if a scan might reveal the problem, so I had another CAT scan. Dr. Fabian said the scan indicated no unexpected problems, but he also said if I cannot swallow by May 17, he would have to open me up again and see what is going on. Another very unpleasant prospect. It was a very serious situation. Dr. Fabian was clearly treating this very seriously. He told us he would give it the weekend to see how things go. When he left, I told Sharon we needed to make this critical situation a matter of prayer immediately. We prayed in my room. Sharon then contacted two churches and explained the urgent need for prayer. The Pastors put the prayer request out on the church prayer chains. She also contacted family and let them know the situation. We knew prayer was just as important as anything else, and actually most important.

So May 17 came and it was another go at it. Praise God, this time it worked! I had dodged a bullet. The weeks and months ahead would present me with a long, difficult challenge of learning how to eat and drink again. I would for a long time, be only a nibbler and have to carefully and thoroughly chew my food in order to swallow it. To this day, I eat very small portions of food and fill up quickly. I lost a full sixty pounds in those first few weeks, and went from 207 pounds down to 147 pounds. I would look in the mirror, undressed, and almost come to tears over my gaunt appearance. It was a shock to my eyes. I never did gain much back. Maybe 18 pounds after two years, bringing me to a weight of 165 pounds. I have come to the point where I am OK with that, and I actually like being the thinner man. But on the negative side of the coin, I am in a precarious situation because there is not much room for going through another event that might cause further weight loss. Meanwhile, being on the thin side is good for my heart and no doubt is better than being over-weight like I used to be.

I cannot in this book, recount a lot more detail about my time in ICU. Much was lost due to my being so sedated. I recall the visits of so many wonderful people, the tremendous almost super-human care and efforts of my wife who wore her own self down to help me through, and my God who never left me stranded, all of which brought me through to the next step and beyond. It was time to move forward.

5. 7TH FLOOR

THE 7TH FLOOR ... TIME-TRAVEL
BACK TO ANOTHER SETTING

*I*t was 11am, May 17. After eleven hectic, intense, strange days in ICU, it was time to move into the next phase of my journey during that sixteen-day hospital stay. I would be leaving what had become familiar surroundings in my little corner of the ICU unit. Actually, after being there so long, I had gotten somewhat comfortable with my room there. There was a certain kind of secure feeling that I had come to appreciate. There I was, in the best equipped, cleanest, most efficient unit in the medical center for top-notch care. It was a safe place with constant care. Now I would leave there and head for some place I was not familiar with.

As I think about this, I cannot help but think about our relationship with God. He is our safe place. It is much easier to always just stay in one comfortable place in our walk with God, yet there are times He asks us to take steps into uncertain territories. He tells us to step out from the safety of the shoreline and launch out into the deep. Someone said *"you cannot get to the other side unless you leave the shore"*. How true. Years ago God had given me a vision as I sat in my office looking at a map of NY State. I told God I wanted to travel to many places in all directions outward from my home town of Oneonta, NY, to preach the gospel. At the time, I could not see how that would ever happen. Then God gave me a vision of a spider-like web of lines reaching out from Oneonta in all directions to places He would take me to preach. One thing led to another over the years and now many years since that vision in my office, I have a map

71

with spider-like lines reaching out to about 50-60 cities in several states and Canada where God has taken me to preach. But at some point back when He gave me that vision, He told me I would have to take some steps of faith and leave my comfortable place. Soon after that, God enabled me to enter into full time ministry, traveling as an evangelist to hold nearly a thousand evangelistic meetings since then, in many churches and in our nation's Adult Care Communities which God gave Sharon and me a specialized calling to do. Again, I get ahead of myself here. More on that calling later.

NEW PLACES

But there I was, leaving behind what had become a safe haven, the ICU, as well as all the wonderful staff that took care of me there. The 7[th.] floor? What would lie ahead for me there? It did not take long to find out. They wheeled me into a large multi-bed room and got me settled down in my little corner that would become my new place and experience for the next several days. The room and for that matter the whole wing of that part of the hospital was drab, depressing, cluttered, smelly, downright looking like, in my mind, an injury ward out of the World War II period. I had seen a few war stories to recognize this looked a little like what the movies had shown. At least that was my perception in my still drugged state. It probably was not quite nearly that dismal, but it was not the *Ritz* or anything remotely as nice as where I had just come from. It felt like veterans crowded together in VA hospitals to recover from their battle wounds. Unpleasant surroundings, short-tempered over-worked staff, grumpy patients, sounds of groaning over pain, and just an all-around negative environment. Thin, thread-worn, discolored sheets looked like something out of another time in history as did the rest of the surroundings. I guess in retrospect, it probably was not as bad as my first impressions. The nurses and other staff were hard-working, caring people who were doing their best to make us comfortable and get us through our own ordeals.

I had been spoiled by the extraordinary high-tech, super-clean environment of ICU. Now I was in just a semi-regular room. Here I would progress to where I could go home in a few days as soon as I was up to it. But my first couple of days in there really did have me feeling like I had gone back through time-travel to the days of WW II and it felt like I was among the war's injured like I had seen in the movies. Of course, in actuality, I was in a room with war veterans from WW II, Korea, and Viet Nam. My time there had its own share of experiences. It would prove to still be a tough time to go through. The 7th floor, my new place.

TUBES AND OTHER EXPERIENCES

By the time I had left ICU, a majority of tubes and various machines had been removed or disconnected. I was now in a normal hospital bed and room. Well, semi-normal anyhow. Much less intense care, but never-the-less, it was a place where very sick or recovering patients were kept a close eye on. I had survived thus far, a very serious surgery and lengthy time in ICU. Now I would hopefully progress enough in my recovery to go home soon. I still had a gastric feeding tube called a *"G-tube"* attached to me, going through an incision into my small intestine to feed me. I still could not eat food through my mouth. It was now the eleventh day with this tube and no food or water by mouth. I also had a tube running up my nose and down my throat into my elongated stomach for gastric fluids to flow back up and out of my body into a container which had been there since surgery.

On May 17 at 2pm, that tube was finally removed and I had my first try at eating some soft foods like jell-o and applesauce. My throat pain was like a knife *(no doubt another exaggeration)* cutting me and my first effort at eating did not work. That tube that had gone down my throat for eleven days, was part of the cause of my extreme throat pain and that pain lasted many days even past the day of my hospital discharge. During my stay on the 7$^{th.}$ floor, one guy opposite the end of my bed on the other side of the room exercised his bit of humor. Every time a doctor or nurse would come in to check on him or do some procedure on him and they would say his name, he would point them in my direction and tell them I was him. I guess he wanted me to get stuck with needles in his place. But I was getting my share of poking and prodding already, so I was quick to let the staff know I was not him. It was all in fun of course and he made me laugh a little in the midst of my pain. There was also another preacher in one of the beds besides me, but he was very sick most of the time and so we did not get the chance to talk much. I was glad to finally be rid of the tube that went in my nose and at least now I could begin trying to get back to eating and drinking something. Hopefully I would soon begin to have success in that effort. But on the other hand, as I have already said, there was the possibility my newly constructed digestive system might never function sufficiently again and therefore there was the distinct possibility I would never be able to swallow food and I could be facing receiving my nourishment through a tube the rest of my life. Not a big likelihood, but I was told it might possibly be the case. It was a tricky operation that did not guarantee anything.

On May 19, I had another tube removed that had been there since May 7. They removed the chest tube that had been there for drainage of blood. During my time in both the ICU and now on the 7th. floor unit, I went through physical therapy two or more times per day. The first time I did P.T. was on my fourth day in ICU. It was my first time of leaving my ICU room with Dan, my Physical Therapist. He would guide me in a slow, shaky walk in the halls of ICU. I remember how groggy and weak I was that first time. Medications made it difficult for me to move or keep my eyes open, let alone, go for a walk. He had to tell me to lift my head up and open my eyes. It was never an easy time on those walks. Now on the 7th. floor unit, he would continue my P.T. Little by little, I did better. Sharon often helped me in my evening walks as well, and I gradually could go more distance. The G-Tube was still in place and would remain attached to me until June 15 due to complications.

Long after I went home, Sharon would tend to my care including flushing my G-Tube twice a day and cleaning up the area. It was something they had to teach her how to do before leaving the hospital. During that time span, there were some tense moments such as when a nurse gave Sharon a hard time about some things related to my care. She was already stressed out from everything, so she did not have much left in her to tangle with medical staff. A period of her and this nurse being at odds with one-another went on for a while, but eventually they got back to being on good terms. This G-tube cleaning was only one of many things she had to do in caring for me at home. They also taught her how to operate a feeding-tube machine in case it turned out that I had to survive by use of a feeding tube. As it turned out, she did not have to feed me that way. I progressed to where I could manage to get some soft food down my throat. But it would turn out to be a very long haul in the coming months as I struggled to enjoy a meal.

SOME THINGS YOU JUST NEVER DO GET COMFORTABLE WITH

I never did get to where I felt very comfortable in my corner of that 7[th.] floor room. It was a unit that just seemed to have a depressing atmosphere to it. I guess it was because it was a place of suffering and sickness, and there was not a lot of smiling faces there among the guys who were patients or among the staff who had so many concerns in caring for them. But even with that somewhat depressed atmosphere, I met a number of nurses and doctors and other staff that were a source of encouragement to me in my time there. They were always very professional and caring. I found night time to be especially difficult and long. By now I was getting sick of being in the hospital. I wanted to go home but I knew I needed to be further along in my recovery first.

I got lonely in those night hours. It was always a helpful moment when a night nurse would stop by to see how I was doing, and maybe talk a few minutes. From the beginning back when I first got the diagnosis of the cancer, Sharon and me had resigned ourselves to the strong possibility that I would not be around very long. The prognosis for surviving was not very positive. Even though we committed everything over to God, we knew how serious things were. While walking in faith that God could and might bring us through to have many more years together, we at the same time prepared our minds and hearts for the real possibility we might have only a few months together. If God chose to keep me around, it would be a pleasant surprise and blessing. Needless to say, my present writing of this book reveals God has indeed blessed us and lengthened my stay here longer than it first seemed like He would. Those days on the 7th. floor were difficult and at times I felt like I was headed for an early exit from life here. Some days were better than others. I treasure the fact that my wife was there for me. I also especially treasure the fact that through every moment, I always had complete trust in God and I knew he was there with me, even in my most difficult times. As a Christian, you can still experience sadness and for some, even depression. God does not hold that against us. He fully understands and He is there to help and bring us through the worst of times.

BY THE WAY, …WHAT ABOUT DEPRESSION?

Since I've mentioned depression, I want to say here just a few thoughts on depression. If anyone reading this is going through that kind of difficulty, you can take comfort in knowing you are in good company as many of God's leading men of the Bible as well as many famous leaders of secular history experienced depression. There should not be any stigma to depression any more than there would be to having heart disease or a belly ache. Out of a lack of knowledge about depression, there are some well-meaning people who mistakenly think depression is a choice. Also, some incorrectly think it indicates a lack of faith in God. Wrong again. Such conclusions could not be further from the truth. Much of depression is due to chemical imbalances in the brain. One example is serotonin imbalance which is believed to contribute to it. No one is at fault for being depressed. No one can just snap out of it and choose not to be depressed.

Now genuine full-blown depression is much more than just feeling low. There are medications to counter the causes of depression and each individual must make their own decision about the use of those. Sometimes even lifestyle changes such as diet and other factors, including God's miraculous healing powers, can help bring people out of depression. Sadly due to lack of knowledge on the subject, there is still a stigma attached to depression and people suffering from it are often viewed as either mentally ill or just choosing to be depressed. Depression is not about just feeling blue or sad. It is not about being a negative-thinking person versus being a positive-thinking person or being a pessimist versus being an optimist. It is so much more than any of that. In the most severe cases, it can be a very dark place for those suffering it, like living under a dark cloud. It can be a torturous place to be and finding someone to talk to who really understands and cares can be very difficult. It would be disastrous if a depressed person sought council from a pastor or some other person and was treated as though he or she ought to be ashamed for being depressed. That person would go away feeling ashamed and lost in a dark cloud of depression that could potentially take years to fully recover from such an experience.

As a minister myself, I especially pray that God's ministers become more informed and educated to where they can improve their counseling skills in such sensitive areas. Many simply do not have the tools or the capacity to relate to the depressed person's experience. Casual, flippant remarks to those who are depressed only worsens the battle they are going through. If you tell that person to just have more faith in God or to shake it off and be happy, you have not helped or shown any compassion. You instead have put that person in an impossible spot because the depressed then thinks they are at fault for how they are feeling and they have no way out.

King David is thought by some Bible commentators to have experienced depression. The Apostle Paul experienced depression which he spoke of in his second letter to the Corinthians in 2 Corinthians 7:6. After speaking about himself and his companions, he said that God comforts the depressed. Abraham Lincoln apparently had severe bouts of depression. Napoleon, Winston Churchill, England's great preacher Charles Spurgeon are some others. A well-known popular late-night talk-show host who delivers his nightly humorous monologue is said to be a very depressed person when not on stage. The list of famous people who dealt with personal depression goes on and on. Now let's go back to that 7th. floor.

FURTHER MEMORIES FROM MY 7TH. FLOOR EXPERIENCE

One other thing I fondly recall from my stay on the 7th floor is one day when my friend, John who was the Pastor of our home church showed up and said he just decided kind of spontaneously to drive the seventy miles and visit me. That meant a lot to me. It was an especially good surprise for me and I was encouraged by that visit.

NOW I SEE, ... NOW I DON'T ...NOW I DO!

One event that gave Sharon and me a scare while there on the 7th. floor was while she was sitting by my bedside. There was activity all around us as other patients in the room were visiting or watching TV. Suddenly out of nowhere, everything around me began to appear blurry. I tried to focus but then it progressed to where I was seeing double and even triple vision, and before I knew it, all was beginning to go dark and I was going blind. That is not one of those exaggerations. The button to call the nurse's station was right next to my hand and so I grabbed it and told the nurse I was going blind. One second everything was normal, the next moment, I was blind. As soon as I told the nurse what was happening, my room quickly filled with several of the staff immediately rushing to my bedside. The doctor on the floor and others quickly attended to me. I do not recall clearly all that went on in those few moments. I thought I was having a stroke or that some sort of complication was transpiring and in those brief moments, thoughts of blindness and even death raced through my mind. Any of that could have indeed been happening, and certainly I was having some sort of complication from surgery or medications or something going very wrong.

After about an hour, things got back to normal and this event was past. But for a brief moment in time, there was a lot of uncertainty as to what was going to happen. Thankfully this event was never again repeated. The cause of it was never determined. Somehow as I recount this event, the line from the Bible comes to mind where it says: *"I was blind but now I see"*. (John 9:25) Just as I was physically blind for those few moments in that hospital room, but came to see again when the medical staff attended to me, so too, I was once spiritually blind until God came into my life and I saw the light of His glorious gospel. Once I was dead in trespasses and sin, but praise the Lord through faith in Jesus Christ, I am spiritually alive and saved by His grace.

GOING HOME

May 21 was a day I had looked forward to. I was finally going home. It had been a long sixteen-day stretch that began at the Fisher House on May 6, followed by surgery May 7. I was discharged at noon May 21, and headed home with a lot of our near future very uncertain. I would be here at the hospital many times for treatments, tests, and multiple doctor appointments over the next few years and beyond. I would even be readmitted a week later for several days of hospitalization. The day before I was discharged, they told us I would need a hospital bed at home for the rest of my life. That came as shock to both of us but at the same time I was glad to hear they would provide me the special bed. My digestive track did not allow me to sleep flat. That never has changed. Years later it still doesn't. I would continue to need a bed that I could raise up at either end, depending on the need. Knowing my wife and I could possibly never again sleep together in our queen size bed was hard to take for both of us, and it brought Sharon to tears.

At arriving home, we bought a temporary wedge for raising my upper body and head in bed until they got the hospital bed delivered which came on June 3. I could not lay flat without serious digestive problems. I still can't. When we stay at motels, I have to use several extra pillows to elevate my upper body. We went out right away and purchased a twin sleigh-bed style bed for Sharon and moved her new bed side-by-side to my new hospital bed. Our queen size bed stayed unassembled in the attic in hopes that one day I would improve sufficiently to where we could once again sleep in it occasionally. We did eventually assemble it again, in another room as a guest bed. I am thankful they provided the hospital bed. It has proved to be very necessary. Also immediately upon getting home, I discovered that my recliner was insufficient for my very much needed comfort while recovering at home in the months ahead. I dealt with tremendous pain and illness, and would need to have access not only to my hospital bed much of the time, but also a very comfortable large recliner.

This surgery and recovery would prove to not be anything remotely similar to most surgeries, but would be something so radical that a full recovery never did take place. We purchased a nice recliner and had it delivered right away. This chapter of the main event in the hospital that month of May in 2010 was now behind me and at home we settled in and prepared for the next leg of our journey.

6. "HOME-SWEET-HOME"?

… NOT SO FAST!

"Now to him who is able to do immeasurably more than all we ask or imagine, according to his power that is at work within us, to him be glory." (Ephesians 3:21-22)

I was so glad to be in the comfort of our own home. Summer would soon be here and I looked forward to those days of hot sun where I could set outside with my shirt off and just let the heat of the sun bring relief and healing to my body that had been so traumatized and cut up. It would also turn out that I would be unable to mow my lawn, work outside, or plow my driveway when it snowed. For most of that first year, I could not even take out the garbage or help bring in the groceries. I would be facing chemotherapy and radiation treatments and continued pain and increasing weakness. Sharon would handle all the shopping, the garbage, laundry, house cleaning, etc., besides being my main health care provider in the home. My sons would take care of all the outdoors work. They were really there for me and continue to be there for me when I cannot handle things.

A man loves to take care of his own home and be the heavy lifter in the home. For me to have to relinquish the entire work load to my wife and sons was hard for me to do. When I did attempt to do anything physical, or even just be on my feet for more than a few minutes, the pain in my right side and my entire upper torso especially to the right side, front and back, would hurt to the point that I could not stand up. This improved minimally over the first year but even today as I have previously stated, I continue to deal with a great deal of pain years later and cannot stand for long. An hour's worth of any kind of work is all I can handle.

RE-ADMITTED

I was home only six days when I began to run a fever and became very ill. I was re-admitted to the hospital on May 28 for three days. This was now my third hospitalization in 2010, and this one barely after I had just finished with the sixteen-day stay there. It was not long before I found myself feeling quite low and frustrated. I kept close to God but I needed some encouragement. It was all beginning to become too much for me after all I had been through and now hospitalized again. As what is probably typical of most men, I hesitate to admit that I broke down in front of my wife while I lay ill in the bed. Being tough does not always require keeping one's eyes dry. Hard as I tried to be strong, I could no longer contain my emotions. It would not be the last or only time this would happen. Later while Sharon was out taking care of some business, unbeknown to me, she was calling some people to let them know I was feeling really low. I received three phone calls in fairly close order from my son Jimmy, my friend in ministry John, and my long-time friend Waylen. Their calls were so timely and helpful and it helped get me through my immediate crisis.

It is so vital to have family as well as brothers and sisters in the Lord who you can count on in those dark moments of life. After three tough days there, this time on the 8th. floor unit which was far better than my environment on the 7th. floor, and a private room, I was discharged on May 30. I could go home again for a little while. On June 1, I saw Dr. Fabien my surgeon. Much to my disappointment he left my G-Tube in. It would have come out that day if I had not been hospitalized that third time just a few days earlier. At home, Sharon continued the regimen of flushing my G-Tube twice daily. I felt quite helpless during this ordeal. I had to lay flat on my back and just let her tend to the matter of doing this necessary twice-daily procedure for twenty-four days straight. It involved several steps and was an unpleasant and messy procedure. I could not do anything to help her with this. In times like this, in addition to being my wife, she was my nurse and I was very dependent upon her taking care of my health needs. She prepared me mushy pureed food, crushed ice for my still hurting throat, and even had to crush all my medications in order for me to swallow. That I can say emphatically was not a tasty cocktail. Yuk! I was and still am on anywhere from as few as 30 on up to as many as 40 medications and a few non-meds products, most of them daily, to manage my health and keep me alive and to deal with an ongoing myriad of health issues.

On June 2, I was back to the ER in Albany for complications in my gut. I had staph infection again, also called C-Diff, which in severe cases such as mine was can cause death, and I required fluids and meds. On June 7, I began receiving Meals-On-Wheels for the next ten days. I am thankful for that. It helped Sharon a lot. But the mushy food was really yucky to swallow. *"Yucky"* seems to be a word that is frequently the prominent and adequate adjective to describe a lot of things in my experience during those times. Meals-on-wheels. I always thought that was for *"old"* people. Well, depending on who you are talking too, some think I am an old geezer. But not really. Not at this writing anyhow. June 15, I went to see Dr. Fabien again. Finally after forty days of having the G-Tube in, he removed it. From there forward, I gradually was able to improve on what I could eat, but I still had to stick with soft food and my appetite was minimal. I ate very small helpings and lost more weight. Nothing tasted good, not even coffee. It would not be until almost a year before my taste and appetite returned. At least for a while, I could again get a chance to try and enjoy home-sweet-home.

HEADING INTO A VERY WELCOME SUMMER

Time to see my Oncologist again, Dr. Thialody June 16. I was not at all happy to hear she wanted me to have another PET scan.

But off we were again, heading for West Haven, Connecticut on June 28 to have the scan the next day. We dreaded the long trip, but it had to be. We got back home June 30 and continued my journey through cancer. The July 4th. holiday was soon upon us and our family got together at our place for our annual picnic that we usually had on Memorial Day but this year of 2010, we had to move it to this later date. It was the first time we had all gathered together since the surgery back in May. It was a very special time for me. I was still very weak and going through a great deal of difficulties in my lengthy recovery. I could not eat much more than a part of one hotdog and just a few baby-size helpings of salad, etc. My son-in-law Kevin sitting next to me in our yard invited me to come out to his family's lake and spend some peaceful time on their boat, do a little fishing, and just get a chance to enjoy a quiet, restful time with him there. I appreciated the thoughtfulness of Kevin in offering me that opportunity and I wish I had been more up to accepting that offer, but I was just too ill still. Though I did not get to do it, I am so thankful for the invitation. I often pictured that serene scene and time on the lake even though I had not gone there. It was a year filled with frequent doctor and clinic appointments. I would have to be scheduled for another surgical procedure to implant a port into my chest for chemotherapy access.

July 26, I was wheeled back into a surgical room where they proceeded with the port-implant procedure. I did not get to go to sleep for this one. They gave me some medication to block the pain as they made the incision and placement of the port. Supposedly the medication was intended to sedate me enough to where I would not feel any pain, but I frequently have not sedated very well, and that occasion was no exception. I kept asking the anesthesiologist if he had given me enough sedative because I was still feeling the pain. Later he told me he had given me the maximum he could and was surprised I still felt the pain. Obviously I did not feel the full extent of the potential pain of them cutting into me. That would have been unbearable, but I did feel more than I should have. From what I hear from most people who go through such procedures awake, the sedative works and I was just an exception to the norm.

We headed home and much to my surprise, the port incision began to hurt terribly as the sedative wore off. By now though, with having gone through so much in the past few months, I was at a point where I could deal with discomfort and pain which had become so much a normal part of my life now. All the difficulties only served to all-the-more build up my fighting spirit and determination that with God's help, I would come out on the other side of all this and God willing, beat the cancer. There is the well known saying that says *"when the going gets tough, the tough get going"*. I have always been one to believe that outlook is true, and I am determined to get going every time I am challenged. For me personally, I do not know any other way to approach my life. My mom at the funeral service of my first wife in 1987, said to me that I *"come from strong stock"* and I will get through my grief. She was right. I still and always will miss Joan my first wife of twenty years, and I never get over her, but the season of grief has long since passed.

My prayer is that this book you are now reading here will help someone somewhere who may be facing cancer or who is in need of some encouragement in some other aspect of their life's journey. As I write and tell of how difficult it was, I do not do so to scare anyone who might be facing similar crisis in their own lives. I do not write about the details of my painful experiences in order to whine about my sufferings or to have people feel sorry for me. From what I have seen, most everyone faces their own great trials in life and many hurt far worse than I have. Rather I again reiterate here as I have previously pointed out in this book, that my goal is to show to anyone out there that you can meet your cancer or whatever you are facing, head on and if you will give it to God, you can go through anything life dishes out to you, even if it is death its self. I was prepared to trust God in life or in death, and that is still true for me now. I do not believe in trying to soften up the hard things life throws at you. Pretending that pain and hardship is somehow not really so bad when it really is, only makes it harder to deal with when that pain hits home. I have been wonderfully surprised to discover how much more difficulty God has enabled me to tolerate and go through than what I thought I could handle. He is an amazing God and He is right there with me every step of the way. I am never alone.

NO MATTER WHAT THE CHALLENGE IS

Even as I write these words, horrid events have ceased our nation as it deals with the massacre of some seventy-one movie-goers in a crowded theater in Colorado. The new Batman movie has just debuted and a crazed gunman has opened fire on the people, leaving several dead and many wounded. A few months later the news comes across the airwaves that almost thirty people have been murdered in an elementary school in a small community in Connecticut including twenty children. And the list of tragic events add up whether it is natural disasters or something else. As I attempt to write words of encouragement in this book, I feel like some may find my words to be hollow at such times as this and of little consolation as they deal with the pain of these real life tragedies. There seems to be a never-ending parade of new horrific tragedies nearly every other day or so someplace in our troubled world. Once again such painful human tragedies remind me that there are always greater trials and more heart-wrenching experiences others face than anything I have had to go through. With that said, and recognizing the horrendous suffering and terrible trauma people face in life, I stay with the assertion that no matter what the challenge is, God is still there and with Him, anyone can make it through the maze of their pain and keep going forward. Somehow, some way if we look to God, He gets us through.

"WHY ANOTHER SCAN?"

My thoracic surgeon, Dr. Fabian, was not pleased when he found out on one of my appointments with him on August 3, 2010 that oncology had sent me all the way to Connecticut for another PET scan. He felt it was not necessary because he was quite confident he had removed all the cancer. I too, would have been quite content to not have to make another trek back to Connecticut to go through that ordeal again. But at any rate, it was concluded by all parties concerned, that in the long run it was best that I'd had the scan. There would for a long time, remain the very distinct possibility that some cancer might yet be in my body. And it was not my final PET scan. There would prove to be more in the months and years ahead. I of course do not care to be bothered with having to go through all these scans and other diagnostic and varied medical procedures, but at the same time I am thankful for the science and all the medical marvels and technology that is available today. It no doubt saves lives. It has saved my life repeatedly.

NOW IT WAS TIME TO BEGIN THE NEXT PHASE

With the diagnosis of cancer, the prospect of chemotherapy and radiation always brings some dread to any cancer patient. Many have seen the movies and TV shows about people going through cancer treatments, and the effects of treatment, whether it is hair loss, vomiting, weight loss, extreme weakness, emotional drain, etc., and so often, the story ends with the patient after all the suffering, dying anyway. If those stories are meant to scare the heck out of us, and depress us, they have the potential to do a pretty good job of that. But the truth is, cancer treatment and survival rates have improved dramatically in recent years and the medications to stave off or minimize a lot of the treatment's effects have shown great improvement.

From the get-go when I first made it known that I had cancer, I cannot tell you how many people tried to convince me that there were better alternatives to treatment than chemotherapy or radiation. It was certainly tempting to listen to them and to opt not to have treatments. Those who offered other *"remedies"* to me were of course good-hearted, often God-loving people who truly only meant well. Some so-called remedies were truly very strange ideas that I will not get much into here. I do however express my serious doubts that soaking in a bathtub full of hydrogen-peroxide or drinking a daily dose of a tomato-based cocktail will *guarantee* a cure of cancer as some have actually suggested to me. Suffice it to say, I believe God has given man knowledge to come up with sound medical science and I trust proven medical treatments over unproven, far-fetched strange concoctions and seemingly absurd home-grown remedies. I should however also say that I realize some alternative remedies may very well actually have some legitimate healing powers.

I have discovered that a lot of well-meaning fellow Christians think that if one has chemotherapy or radiation treatments, he is showing a lack of faith in the healing powers of God. I know of a few who took that attitude and chose to forgo such treatment, only to shortly thereafter, die of their cancer. Of course in all fairness, even with the treatment, there is no guarantee against dying of the cancer, and in many instances the cancer-survivor cannot be certain as to whether the treatments did or did not have anything to do with their surviving or cure. I also do not judge anyone's decision about this. I myself before I had cancer, had always believed I would refuse chemotherapy and radiation if I ever did get cancer, and that I would put my faith in God. When I did get cancer, I still took time to pray and to do research before deciding whether or not to have the treatments. God spoke to my heart and said I must trust Him. That faith in God did not necessitate my refusing sound scientifically proven medical treatment.

One thing I do often see among my fellow God-fearing brothers and sisters is that some demonstrate an unwarranted disdain for science, especially medical science. That is an ill-advised attitude. In recent times we are seeing a coming together of science and faith which is a positive step in the right direction. It could well be said that God himself is the Master Scientist. He is also a mathematician, a biologist, a physician, an environmentalist, and on and on. He has given us modern science. Of course some far-fetched scientific conclusions and theories are nonsense, especially when it comes to how ultimately the universe came to be. But much of science is very compatible with the beliefs of the community of faith. I chose the cancer treatments after much agonizing consideration, and it is that very faith in my God that enabled me to choose to have the treatment. I knew that there is solid scientific medical evidence that chemotherapy and radiation gives the patient a better chance of survival even if it means going through some suffering in the process. I chose to trust God to help me get through the dread and potential suffering of the treatments.

I hate throwing up more than just about anything. So anyhow, it took me a big step of faith in God to have the treatments. I like what one preacher had to say about people who think it is a lack of faith to seek medical care. He said that *"not taking care of your body or avoiding sound medical help demonstrates a spirit of stupidity."* I have faith in God and that includes trusting the knowledge He has given doctors and the medical community to treat diseases. With that confidence and faith in God, I went forward with the treatments for cancer. I get a flu shot every year for the same reason. It is just plain wise to do so and it is an expression of my faith in God who has given humanity the knowledge to combat illness.

NO NEED TO TRY TO GO IT ALONE … LET OTHERS IN

I need to add another thing here about this matter of choosing for or against the treatments. My wife, my family, my sister Joyce, and some others all assured me that they supported me in whatever decision I chose. It is in the end, your decision, not anyone else's. Even the doctors assured me it is up to me and they would continue to be there for me regardless what I decided. Of course the oncologist is going to strongly recommend the treatments. It was a very freeing thing to know those that loved me were not pressuring me to choose the treatments. In the future if I were to face cancer again, depending on the circumstances I might very well choose to forgo treatments. We do not know what we will decide or how we will react to such things until it happens to us.

My sisters and brothers all proved to be a great source of encouragement and support during this whole event in my life. My sister Joyce had fairly recently gone through cancer herself and she and I communicated more during this time. She kept in frequent contact with me to see how I was doing and offered helpful advice along the way. I never kept the news of my cancer to myself. From the start, I knew I had a wonderful family, and I wanted all the moral support I could get. I would encourage anyone going through similar crisis in their lives to let family be aware and involve them in what you are going through. Family is so important. For many people, their family ties might not be so close as I have been blessed to enjoy, and so it is harder to bring family into your situation, but I believe that in most cases, if you give them the chance, they will care and old differences and problems between family members can fade away in such times and relationships can be renewed where needed. To try and go it alone is just asking for things to be all the more difficult. There is nothing weak or wrong in needing others as you go through tough things in your life.

KEEPING MY WITNESS UP FRONT

I also kept my Christian witness active throughout my ordeal. My wife and I never hesitated to share our faith in Christ, whether it was to say to my oncologist that I have faith in the Lord, or to tell a nurse in pre-op about my faith in Christ. I shared Christ in my days of hospitalization, at clinic appointments, in hospital lobbies and hallways, in the chemotherapy room, and whenever, wherever the opportunity presented its self. I was never obnoxious about my testimony. I just gently shared in small ways when the clear opportunity presented its self. While my regular preaching ministry was on hold due to recovery, we found God was planting one-on-one opportunities to minister to others in the hospital, whether it was patients or staff.

Not only did I share my faith in God by my words, but also by my attitude and actions as I was determined to handle what I was going through in a manner that would demonstrate how God's people face life's adversities. It was not always easy to do, and in the midst of pain and trouble, I probably sometimes came up short of my goal to live out my faith without weak moments surfacing, but I was committed to do my best with God's help upon whom all my efforts were totally dependent on. If any effectual good has ever come from my testimony, it has been possible only by the grace of God. In myself, I am not capable to do any of this, but in the strength of God, it is possible. As I have spoken here about maintaining a strong evidence of my faith in God, I think of something my wife Sharon did during the ordeal of chemo and radiation treatments and her own expression of faith. Following a program our home church had started, she made a commitment to read the entire Bible through in ninety days. That is no small challenge. It would require real commitment. She read it during treatments, as well as in our room we stayed in overnight at the medical center, and also on weekends at home. She stayed the course and succeeded in her endeavor.

TAKING THAT JOURNEY AROUND THE CORNER

August 9 came. I would for the first time, take that right-hand turn down the hallway that would lead me through the doors into a world where I had never been before. I would now find out what lie ahead in the world of chemotherapy. I would begin my first round of chemo that would be for the next five days. Over the months ahead there would be several additional rounds that consisted of several days each. In my mind up until that moment, I had pictured two or three of us cancer patients sitting in a recliner in a hallway with a line running from a chemo bag into my port for a half-hour or so, and getting sicker and sicker as the chemo dripped slowly into my body.

I had seen some picture in a flier that had given me that impression. I figured everyone on chemo gets horribly nauseous and would be throwing up in a container as they sat there.

None of this turned out to be the case. I instead was led through a double door into a huge room with nurses and technicians scattered around the room either tending to patients or otherwise busy at their work areas. There were three walls lined with patients receiving their treatments by way of injections through their ports. As I was first hit with this sight before my eyes, I felt overwhelmed and out of place. It just did not seem like I should have to be there among these people. What was I doing here? This could not be for me. In my mind, I wanted to just turn around and leave back down that hallway and go home. But at this stage of my life, I knew better. It was not time to run from any potential fears or challenges. Again, I want to assert here that I never did have any fear during any of this event in my life. God dispelled any potential fear from the first day I received my diagnosis. As much as I did not want to believe that I was in the same boat as the rest of those folks there, the fact was undeniable. This was where I had to be, just as much as it was for the others there.

I think that even though I had already been through the cancer surgery and all the rest that I had gone through the past many months, it was only now in that chemo infusion room that the reality of my cancer fully hit me. I perhaps had been in denial all this time to some degree. Now the harsh reality of needing that dreaded treatment to try and save my life hit home. First I was weighed in which became a part of the routine at each chemo session, and then I was directed to a chair. There must have been about a dozen others in there for chemo treatments. I would discover over time that some were doing better than others. Some would live and some would not have so much hope of surviving. I was soon attended to and the process of learning and becoming acquainted with the procedure of chemotherapy began. There were several steps involved including pre-medicating to help lessen the nausea effects of the chemo, and three or so injections into the port preparatory to giving me the actual chemo medication.

The process took two to three hours at each session. I watched TV, read books, socialized with patients and did a lot of waiting and sitting. Sharon did word-search puzzles and played hand-held electronic games. Before long, the preacher in me realized this was also a *mission field*, a place with hurting, even frightened people who needed ministry, not just the chemo infusion room. It was not so bad after all, with all things considered in light of so many unknowns, what to expect, and the concerns of how I would handle it.

While I know there are various types and doses of chemo depending on each patient's need, and no doubt many do experience varying degrees of side effects, I never did throw up, either there or afterwards. I had occasional minimal nausea, but the pills for that worked great. I hope that encourages someone. My hair over time from chemo and radiation did thin a little, but not too much. My fingernails shriveled up which is one of the things chemo can cause. Mostly my treatments did make me very extremely weak and affected my mental alertness some. I had not driven a car since May when I had surgery, and I would not be able to drive for the better part of seven more months.

MORE JOURNEYS TO THE UNKNOWN

Chemo was only half of what I was going to have to confront in this world of cancer treatment that was so new to me. There was also the same initial sense of dread as to what to expect as my wife and I made our way through the maze of corridors, down into the basement level of the Medical Center to find the Radiation department. I again as with Chemo-therapy, had very little knowledge about this treatment where they send radiation into your body to attack cancer cells. As with chemotherapy, I had researched and gathered as much information as I could on radiation treatments. Nothing about what I discovered in my research gave me any reason to feel good about what I was soon going to undergo. Just the very idea that we had to go into the lower levels of the hospital was disturbing enough. What was this going to be like? I most certainly was very uncomfortable with the prospect of it all. But we kept moving forward. It was something that simply needed to be faced. As we sat in the waiting room, I kept wondering what I would find when they called me back into one of several rooms down some more hallways.

After consultations with two radiation doctors, I was mapped out under an x-ray machine to determine precisely the area they would be giving me the radiation treatments. Now I am not the tattoo-type of guy. I actually am repulsed by today's over-the-top obsession with tattooing and body piercing too. No offense intended towards anyone with tattoos. Like a lot of folks, I just find tattooing, as well as the current explosion of excessive body-piercing, to be actually a rather unhealthy, unattractive thing and many of the younger generation seems to be obsessed with it. They may regret all that when they mature with age. But to each his own. The Bible tells believers that their bodies are the temple of the Holy Spirit. It also tells believers to present their bodies as living sacrifices to God, holy and pleasing to Him. With these truths in view, I personally prefer to not deliberately mar up my body. Therefore abstaining from the current popular so-called *body-art* fade is my preference. But guess what? I am officially the owner of five genuine tattoos. For real, yes I jest as it is not much to brag on, but I do have five blue spots permanently tattooed on my chest and abdominal area. They are about one-eighth inch each in diameter, but they are the real deal.

Part of the radiation mapping process includes these laser-beamed tattoos for guiding the precise line up of the radiation machine to accurately target the correct area. Those tattoo marks are a constant reminder of what I went through. Maybe I should have asked the technician who was administering the laser tattoos to have added a little extra body-art tattooing across my chest, something like maybe along the line of the science-fiction starship Enterprise from the Star Trek series which I am a big fan of.

7. AND SO IT BEGINS...

*God will help us if we'll let Him. He wants to do so much for us.
I'm talking about Him who saved us and cleansed us by His blood.
He has given us His Spirit to indwell and empower us through
the fullness of His Holy Spirit. He is there for us in times of every
temptation and we can count on His presence and help in any and
all moments of crisis or whatever the situation may be. No evil can
prevail against us with Christ at the center of our life.—Jim*

September 7, I started my radiation treatments, twenty-five of
them over a five-week period. When I was first told this, it seemed
overwhelming to contemplate going through all that. We would have
to stay away from home for five weeks during the weekdays, and
only be home on the weekends. It was one hectic time packing every
Monday to head up to Albany to stay in the hospital for five days
and then go back home every Friday, only to do this same routine
for five long weeks. At the same time I started radiation, I began
my second round of chemo. I would have a third time in October
where I would have chemo and radiation the same week. Those were
especially rough times. Chemo or radiation, by its self is a rugged
enough experience, but doing both in the same week really took a
toll on my body and mind.

During all this time in our lives from day one back in May for
surgery on up through the many months of recovery, appointments,
procedures and treatments, we would rack up thousands of miles in
travel, countless hours and weeks away from home, many stays at
motels, eating out at restaurants, buying needed extra clothing as

I lost weight from week to week and many other expenses, facing monumental financial costs. It would put a drain on our savings and be a major time of stress. Thankful beyond adequate words that we can express, my brothers and sisters, and family and friends sent us money to help defray the expenses we faced, to the tune of a couple thousand dollars. My health care plan covered one-hundred percent of my medical costs. Between medical expenses for heart surgeries, cancer-related expenses and other medical expenses in the recent years, without exaggeration the costs easily approached or topped a million dollars. But there were plenty of other expenses incurred during my cancer treatments as I have mentioned here. While we were never in any dire straits financially during this time, never-the-less it was a welcome chunk of financial help, enabling us to avoid having to dip into our needed savings too much. It greatly helped. We still did have to spend a lot of additional money beyond that help, but that is a couple thousand we did not have to take out of our own resources.

I think also before going any further, that here would be a good place to express my thanks to those who visited me during my recovery at home. So often when a person has gone through a major surgery or illness and has been hospitalized, people do tend to show their concern by visiting at the hospital, and that is so very crucial to and appreciated by the patient in helping to face the crisis he or she is dealing with. At least it was for me. Jesus certainly encourages us in the Bible to visit the sick. He knows how important it is in the healing process, and that healing process does not end at the hospital. It continues at home. My long time friends, the Brays whom I have previously mentioned, visited me at my home in those days following hospitalization. There was a couple, Ernie and Cheryl and his mom Emma, who took the time to drop by and visit me at home. My friend John, the Pastor of our home church came by regularly several times during my long recuperation when I was mostly house-bound and unable to get out to church. We had wonderful times of fellowship, encouragement and prayer for one-another. At least one time, his wife Robin also came by at our home. There was a brother in Christ, Don C. who more than a couple times encouraged me along the way. There were two brothers from the church, Denny *(his wife Diane also came once with him)* and Ed our church's Men's Ministry leader, who came by a number of times to minister to me. There was Len and Ellie too.

I recall a time another brother from church, Joe who was on our church's worship team as lead guitarist, vocalist and sound man, came by when my wife had to hurry home because I had called her to say I was having a problem. He followed her home and came in to check on my status. Another time I recall that Joe while he was in Albany for work-related matters, heard I was in the ER at the VA Hospital and he went out of his way to come there to see how I was doing. A long time acquaintance and friend, Larry W. whom I had known from my years of secular employment came to our home to visit me during those difficult days. I recently spent some time with him on his 90th. birthday and his love of life and strength of character has always been a source of encouragement to me.

Additionally some of our nearby neighbors, Gary and Linda T. stopped in during my difficult days of recovery, and Gary as well as my next-door neighbor Kevin M. on occasion helped in carrying in some groceries when I was out of commission and my wife needed the help. I enjoyed the visits to our home following my surgery from family members such as my brother Bill and Gloria, or my sister Cindy and Andy. As previously mentioned, my bother Doug and his wife Gail had visited us at home just before my surgery date. There was my immediate family as well as others from the church and neighborhood, etc., too many to recount here, who took the time to drop by and build my faith up and help me in my healing process by their visits. I surely have no doubt left some names out, but they know who they are. As Jesus instructed, they visited the sick, and I am sure it helped me greatly.

My home church gave me a huge poster-board size home-made get well card signed by nearly all the members of the church, with kind and encouraging words. Wow! What a heart-felt and heart-warming thing that was. In addition to the visits, there were the countless cards and phone calls from so many who cared. To those who would visit the sick, I say to them, do not be worrying about what to say when you visit. Such concerns too often hold people back from visiting or making a phone call to those in need of an encouraging word or visit. Just make that phone call. Visit that person if you know it is OK to do so. There is no need to have it all planned out as to what to say. Just the thought and the action of calling or visiting is enough even if you do not know what to say. The same principle applies for showing that kind of concern for the grieving who has lost a loved one.

DANCING IN A PARKING LOT

I couldn't leave my account of the radiation treatments without sharing another personal and very special moment in the journey my wife Sharon and me were on. This special moment is no less important than any of the other experiences we shared during the journey through cancer. It is just as important as any other part of my story in the sense of precious memories as well as in the sense of vital steps along the way to recovery. Here we were at the medical center in Albany during one of those twenty-five days of radiation treatments. I'd had my daily morning radiation treatment and we had arrived back to the hospital parking lot following an early evening meal out.

Each week of radiation involved five straight days of the treatment and staying at the hospital those five days. It was early fall on a September evening. The weather was a balmy, perfect evening. As we pulled into our parking space, we were listening to the great rock and roll oldies from the 1950s. We could have done as usual and just head across the lot to the hospital, but this particular evening we got another plan in our heads and hearts. We left the music on, in fact cranking the sound up, and lowering the windows as we got out and we proceeded to dance in the parking lot. No one else was around, and even if they had been, it wouldn't have mattered. We were oblivious to anything else going on around us. We were for those few brief moments in time caught up in our own private world. A hundred people could have been looking on and we still would have danced. Come to think of it, there must have been potentially dozens or more who may have watched us from the vantage point of the hundreds of hospital windows facing the parking lot. Perhaps a few patients or weary staff had their day lightened at the sight of this couple dancing below.

It was an otherwise quiet time of day outside the hospital. As the gentle breeze filled the air and the evening sun was soon to be setting, I took my wife into my arms and we danced to a slow song. What a special moment it was. For those few brief moments it seemed like we were the only two people in the world and as though God was looking down from above and blessing us, maybe even smiling. That may sound a little on the mushy side for me as that is not how I usually talk. But I don't know a more accurate way to describe the moment than this. It was one of those bright spots during an otherwise very difficult time in our lives. That one single moment lightened one of our days and not only serves as a cherished memory but was one wonderful step forward towards seeing better days to come. Sharon and I could not exactly dance up a storm. I was at that time in a very weakened condition myself from the cancer treatments and Sharon being a disabled veteran has her limits.

Yes, Sharon and I dance. No, we don't hang out at dance halls. But many times we have danced in our living room, usually to the old country classics. Her bad knee and foot from her Army injuries do present some challenges of course, but I try to help her as we dance. I cannot imagine a marriage that leaves dancing out of the picture. Are you married? If you haven't already done so, for the sake of love for your partner and because God will bless your marriage, go ahead and take your wife or husband as the case may be, into your arms and dance. Dance my friend. It is good for the heart and good for the soul. Don't waste a good marriage by letting the romance die out. Feed that part of your marriage and keep dancing.

A *"GRADUATION"* DIPLOMA

During those twenty-five radiation treatments, I was on the table receiving my radiation dosage for about twenty minutes or so each time as the machine slowly moved and aimed the radiation along the route that had been mapped out on my body. I would learn how many times a specific sound from the process would take place, close my eyes and begin counting down the number of times the session was pre-scheduled to repeat, and so I would know when it was almost done. You do not feel anything from the radiation. You just patiently keep showing up for the treatments and trust the technicians and doctors as they do their potentially life-saving work on you. At the end of my twenty-fifth treatment, they light-heartedly gave me a customary *'diploma'* congratulating me for accomplishing my challenge of getting through the treatments. It offered a little bright spot in an otherwise unpleasant process one must face with cancer.

Truth be known, receiving that light-hearted diploma did give me a sense of having faced down a difficult challenge and being able to feel good about myself for having succeeded. Sharon jokingly asked the staff: *"Where is my diploma?"*, referring to hers. They laughed about it and told her she *"didn't get any tattoos or radiation"*. Of course in reality she had indeed gone through this experience with me throughout the whole ordeal of radiation treatments with it always weighing heavy on her heart and mind as to how everything would turn out. She had seen my strength and health deteriorate week after week as the chemo and radiation treatments took their toll on my body and mind. It had to be a trying time for her as we day after day made that journey down into the lower level of the medical center and she watched me be taken behind closed doors for more radiation. Would all of this risky treatment do more harm than good? Would I recover from its effects in the months ahead and would it accomplish the goal of ridding my body of cancer? As I finished my final treatment that day with the reward of a *'diploma'* and Sharon had some fun with the staff about her diploma, it was a special, light-hearted moment to cap off an otherwise unpleasant experience the past couple months.

TAKING YOUR *"POISON"*

These combinations of treatments do take a substantial toll on the body. Chemo is poison. It cannot just single out the cancerous cells and destroy them without harming good cells. That is the big downside of chemotherapy. The alternative however, is to forgo the treatment at the risk of the cancer having a greater potential of spreading and resulting in death. Even at this writing, there are some very promising advances and discoveries being made to zero in on better treatment with fewer side effects. Maybe by the time someone is reading these words there will be some break-through towards curing cancer. I chose chemo as giving me my best shot at defeating the cancer. Well, not my best exactly. Most important was my faith in God. But as for medical treatments, chemo did offer some crucial hope towards stopping the cancer and maybe reversing it totally. I am still here today and able to talk about it. But there is no guarantee. Some will survive without treatment. Some will die even with the treatment. It again, must be a personal, individual decision as to which way to go.

The chemo and radiation does cause extreme weakness and tiredness. It is a run-down, weak feeling that cannot adequately be described. I got to the point to where I could barely hold a cup of coffee or even turn a bottle cap. Holding my head upright or walking a short hallway became a hard, tiring challenge. All I wanted to do was go to bed and sleep. This level of weakness worsened as I went through the treatments, and for several months after I had completed my treatments, I remained in a state of terrible weakness. Still, even with going through that and a lot more, I continue to affirm that the treatments were the best choice for me. I am a firm believer in putting up a heck of a fight in the face of everything that life throws at me. When God makes it clear that I have done enough and it is time to stop putting forth the effort to fight on, then as far as it is within my power, I will let my body take its final breath without further effort. There is as the Bible says, a time for everything. There is a time to fight too, and there is a time to retire from the ring and fight no more. But that timing is up to God.

UNINTENTIONAL DANGEROUS OVERDOSE

Treatments seemed to be running right along quite smoothly. Aside from the expected side effects of weakness and just generally feeling lousy, nothing especially alarming had happened for a while. I felt quite good about the fact that I had faced these scary treatments and I was holding up well. I was not fearful and I was meeting the challenge of getting it completed. Then things began to happen. At one point, I discovered that due to some mix-up in communications, I had unintentionally been taking way too much oxycodone, the opiate for my pain. At an ER visit, upon learning of my overdosing, I was informed that it was a wonder that I was even alive. I knew I had been getting increasingly drowsy all the time, and could not think clearly. I had been downing as many as four times the dosage of this narcotic as was intended. I need not go into details as to how this was happening. Suffice it to say, there was some misinformation somewhere and it happened. I had never knowingly or intentionally over-dosed. I was simply following my prescription's instructions. Obviously that situation was quickly corrected and I got back to a more appropriate dosage.

One thing I have learned in all this is that you the patient must always be on top of what is going on and realize you are a part of your health-care team. Be vigilant to being aware of your needs and healthcare. Be involved. Sometimes you may even have to keep your health care providers on their toes. They are only human.

BACK TO THE ER WITH COMPLICATIONS

On October 17, following a recent round of chemo, I began getting even weaker than what had been normal lately, and then fever and chills. Now that I had cancer, I just figured it was supposed to be like this and that I was expected to accept the fact that I would have to be very sick and not make a fuss about it. I was trying to put off going to the ER. I did not want to keep running to the hospital. I was like this on and off for the next nine days. Nine days I just took no action because I found it embarrassing to run repeatedly to the ER. Nine days! Clearly with all the medications and being so sick, I was not thinking right. Finally at my wife's wise insistence, *("wise" insistence ... she'll like that)* I went to the ER, albeit way past the time I should have done so. I just did not want to have a reputation of running to the ER over every little thing, and it was becoming hard to figure out what was a little thing and what was serious. Of course this was no little thing and none of my trips to the ER were unnecessary. Quite the opposite, dealing with any of the complications and events related to my cancer was serious business and I should not have concerned myself with how my frequent trips to the ER might be perceived by anyone else.

As it turned out on a number of occasions, I was sicker than even I realized and a few of those times my life was actually at risk. Frequently running to the ER when you are going through cancer treatments is not all that unusual. Chemo messes up your system and can frequently result in various problems. They ran tests and discovered my white blood count was way down. As I have pointed out, I should never have hesitated about coming to the ER. Turns out from what the Doctor told me that night, I could have died if the white blood count had dipped any lower. I was down to a bare minimal level. I was one very sick man that night. With some fluids through an I.V. drip, I was able to dodge another life-threatening incident and go home.

Word to the wise: Do not take chances or try to be the tough guy or gal when you are dealing with serious disease or medical treatments. Get to where you need to be to receive medical care, even if it means running to the ER frequently. I guess the bottom line is, know how sick you are. Cancer is big-time serious and I had to repeatedly keep coming back to grips with the reality that I was a sick man with a long ways to go.

HAVING ANOTHER ROUND

There's a line from a country song by Allen Jackson referring to having another beer with the old pop-tops. But another round for me was not a shot of whisky or a beer, although I admit a shot of Jack Daniels would have been tempting. Sorry if saying that disappoints any of my fellow non-imbibing Christian brethren, but yes, as sick as I was, if I thought for a moment that I could have had God's approval, a shot of whiskey really did have a nice sound to it. The biggest things that kept me from that is my commitment to God and my commitment I made as an ordained minister to abstain. I do not drink alcohol. I know its dangers from my more foolish early years. But I was in for another round of a different sort.

November 15, I began my fourth round of chemo. More time away from home, staying in a motel in Albany for a week. Between chemo and radiation, my body was getting to the point where I might not be able to handle much more. November 24, I was sick again. This time I went to the ER right away. I had learned my lesson. It was the day before Thanksgiving. My abdominal area was in great pain. I had C-Diff again. More I.V. drips. Somehow, I still made it back to Oneonta and able to spend Thanksgiving with family at my son Jimmy's home, and though I was not well, I was so thankful for life and family.

On December 2, it was discovered that my white blood count was seriously down again. All my doctors conferred together and concluded I could not have my fifth five-day chemotherapy round due to its effect on my white blood cells. It was proving to be life-threatening. I still, even in the light of this threat, believe it was the best decision for me, to give chemo a shot. What chemo I did manage to tolerate may very well have played a part in saving my life. I was given a white-count shot. Now as an adult, I have no qualms about getting shots. But this one was a doozy! It really, really hurt afterwards on the way home and for days. It had such a powerful effect on my body that shortly after getting home, I could not walk. It is a particularly potent type of injection which the medical staff told us could adversely affect my extremities, especially my legs. It had an almost crippling affect. I could not get from the car to the house on my own. Sharon had to physically assist me as I placed my arm around her shoulders. It was with considerable difficulty that she succeeded in doing this. I was already in a very weakened state from chemo and radiation and this shot just pushed me to the brink of collapse. Jimmy, my older son, came over and brought up a wheelchair from our cellar so I could use it to get to the bathroom and to my bed.

By now, if you are reading this, you know what my attitude is. If something saves my life, it is worth it, no matter the discomfort. I guess that's a given for most anyone. That shot and the resulting discomfort was necessary but I hope I never need it again. I never knew a simple shot could cause so much trouble. Admittedly, as I will write about later, there would be times when my level of pain would border on being too much for me to willingly tolerate, and I would find myself at times, honestly coming close to wanting death rather than the pain. But even in those times, I look back now with some surprise at just how much fight God gave me and how much He enabled me to handle. There is no shame in sometimes preferring to just say to God that you have had enough and would prefer going home to be with Him. But I still had plenty of fight left in me during those times.

Wife, family, God, ministry, it all means so much to me. I could not easily give up. Looking back, yes, those things make it all worth it. Sharon called the hospital and was told this was normal. The effects of the shot could last up to seventy-two hours. I was bed-ridden until the shot got fully into my system. By December 16, my white-blood count returned to better levels, but it would be a long time before it returned to normal levels. What a year 2010 was. The surgery and treatments radically altered my eating habits. I lost my taste for my favorite drink, coffee. Many months later, it did return, thank God. We coffee lovers do look forward to imbibing. Most of my favorite foods no longer tasted good. I was still in the process of being able to swallow better. As I mentioned earlier, there were many times where I was confronted with terrible episodes that landed me in bed. Eating often resulted in abdominal pain beyond anything I had ever experienced before all this. It still does today, but not quite so often, and I have learned how to prevent it to some extent and how to treat it better.

Some of those early months following my surgery and treatments left me curling up in the fetal position in my hospital bed at home, at times feeling total despair at how I could handle it any further. There is no shame in that. It happens. Sharon knew how much it hurt and on a few occasions she let me know that I did not have to try and hang on just to be here for her, but that it was *"OK"* if I could not stand it anymore and if I chose to just let myself give up the fight and go home to be with the Lord. That was a hard, but unselfish, even courageous thing she did. Of course she did not want me to leave her in death, or to encourage me to give up. Out of love, she was willing to make it easier on me if I knew I had gotten to where I did not feel I could fight it any longer. But that unselfish expression of her love only gave me all the more impetus to fight on. I may at times sound overly dramatic, but I have not exaggerated things here. It was that rough a time and if anything, I have probably tried watering down how tough it was. We did face some very dark days.

THE NIGHTMARE OF DRUGS WITHDRAWAL

I did face another complication that I was totally not anticipating. Withdrawal from narcotics and other medications. I remained on morphine, oxycodone, and a couple other addictive drugs in addition to several other daily medications. One day, without consulting my doctors or pain-management clinic, I decided I would take myself off of these narcotics and some other prescribed addictive medications. I have never been one to want to be on mind-altering drugs or artificial highs from opiates. By the way, that stuff did not give me a high. It just helped in managing pain. Alcohol is the worst drug I ever got into in my early years, and thanks to God and to some faithful Christians leading me to faith in Christ in 1968, I was eventually delivered and rescued from alcoholism. I thought that just through sheer self-determination, I very simply could abruptly discontinue these pain medications cold-turkey all at once.

I had no idea how much of a crisis withdrawal could be. Seeing it portrayed in the movies or reading stories about it was not enough. Very soon after stopping four medications cold, I began quickly to experience changes in my thought processes as well as physiological symptoms. Within just a few hours into the night hours in bed, I found myself slipping into a state of mental panic. It was terrifying. My body cringed and shook. I began to experience strange, confusing thoughts. In my withdrawal-induced mental state, I felt like I was losing my mind even though I really wasn't. I became uneasy as I had a sense of something ominous foreboding which is not anything that I normally experience. I felt thoughts of wanting to despair which nearly overwhelmed me. I was never suicidal, but I had this terrible feeling of just wanting to escape this dark moment. Keep in mind that all of this was strictly related to withdrawal from powerful prescription drugs which my body had become dependent on. Due to the extraordinarily extreme surgery I went through, I had been put on an exceptionally high amount of pain medications for a very prolonged period of time. These withdrawal experiences went on throughout several following nights. Sharon advised me to stop my efforts to quit the medications so abruptly. Over time, I adjusted the approach and learned to tackle cutting back on the meds in a more gradual way.

I informed my oncologist of my withdrawal crisis and over time, with the guidance of the pain management clinic, I eventually got off the morphine and cut back on the oxycodone, etc. I had been put on a very high dosage of oxycodone far beyond what might be a normal maximum dose for similar high levels of pain. That's how much pain my body was racked with that initial year following cancer surgery. But that experience gave me a new appreciation of how rough it must be for a seriously addicted drug addict. Though my addiction was due to my cancer event and my addiction was certainly not as serious as some of the hard-core addicts on the streets, it still gave me a minimal hint of the kind of anguish they may suffer as they struggle to come clean. The misuse of oxycodone is actually one of the popular drugs of choice on the street these days, and it is said to be in the same category as heroin in its effect when altered and used that way. For precautionary measures in view of all the news of an epidemic of thieves steeling this drug for either their own recreational drug abuse or for selling on the street, I found it advisable and necessary to hide my own prescription at times.

That episode with going through withdrawal was an unforgettable experience I wouldn't wish upon anyone. Sometimes without me realizing it, those drugs were dulling my mind. The longer I was on them, the worse the addiction became. My body and mind became seriously dependant on these drugs. My heart was beginning to be adversely affected as well as my breathing. Several times while in bed I experienced the feeling that my body was shutting down and that death was imminently possible. I had to take action. Eventually I got the determination and courage to tough it out, come what may, and take myself off of those particular drugs. As I have indicted already, I did need help from the pain management clinic. As a man of God and as a preacher of the gospel, I determined that I must beat these addictive drugs.

I think of the story of Johnny Cash where he locked himself in a room and with his wife June by his side he spent several days in anguish as he went through drug withdrawal. Some of his had to do with amphetamine's, barbiturate's, and tranquilizers. You might wonder how me, a minister of the gospel, could end up addicted to prescription medication. It was never a conscious choice to become drug-dependant. Modern-day healthcare offers a drug for everything and when you go through an extraordinary health crisis, it is easy to get hooked on the drugs your healthcare team puts you on. You don't see it coming. It sneaks up on you and before you know it, you're trapped in an addictive state with no clear understanding of how to get out of it. At some point, with God's help, I mustered up enough determination to make up my mind that I could not let this go on any longer. It was to the point where my life was hanging in the balance and sudden death could happen at any moment. Today I'm no longer dealing with their effects. I remain on many medications that are necessary but harmless to keep my body working right. My mind cleared up as I came through the period of withdrawal. Also my heart and breathing got better and I was ready to move forward in my recovery.

LOOKING BACK

When I look back at all my wife and I went through for the past few years, I am amazed at just how much did happen and mostly I see an amazing God who brought us this far. During much of that time period, I was too drugged to accurately balance our checkbook. I made several big mistakes with that, often off by hundreds of dollars. I could not drive for much of 2010. When I finally did get behind the wheel again, it felt like I was seventeen again and driving for the first time. Christmas Eve with our annual family gathering at our home in 2010 was so special too, as I appreciated still being here after such a close call with death that year. Somehow, even in the midst of all that went down in 2010, I still managed to get back behind the pulpit for a few preaching engagements later that year, even between treatments. I could barely stand at times, and so I sat on a stool to preach. But preach I did, as God gave me a message to share about all that He did and can do as we trust Him.

8. TIMES OF REFRESHING

"...times of refreshing may come from the Lord...."—(Acts 3:19)

Stanley M. Horton, a Bible scholar teaching the book of Acts, in one place spoke about miracles, revival and turning to God. He shared the truth that miracles and revival are not for only the past but for today as well. He went on to teach that we can experience such things if we will have repentant hearts and live for God.

I cannot recall the exact date in 2010, but it was months after my surgery and after quite some time of recuperation at home before that first time. I speak of my first time back to our home church on a Sunday morning. Finally the day had come where I decided to venture out to church. It would be an emotional time for me. I had been away for so long and missed my church family and the worship and preaching there. I remember that it felt so refreshing to be there after such an ordeal the past several months. I could not stand up for worship time. I was still too weak, so I sat and just took in the moment. I would preach there in October and bring my message that I intertwined with my testimony of how much God had done. Even though I was physically weak and sickly at this point, my home church as well as other churches I preached at during those days were all so gracious towards me.

I think of something the Apostle Paul said to the Galations believers. *"Even though my illness was a trial to you, you did not treat me with contempt or scorn. Instead, you welcomed me as if I were an angel of God, as if I were Christ Jesus himself."* (Galations

4:14). Then, and many times since that day, a lot of people have said that I was a walking miracle of God, and I am certain they are right. The year of 2010 would be a year of great highs and lows, but that day was an especially high moment in my journey. I have tried to recall some of the events and various things in this book that 2010 was about. There is much that I have not touched on and need not try to recall here, but so far, I have at least attempted to bring out some of the primary things my memory and my wife's journal has recorded from those days. I have never intended in this book to sound like I think I went through more than others have. Countless people have and do face many struggles, many of which are far worse than anything I have faced. What my own difficulties have done in my life is they have made me more keenly aware of a hurting humanity. I pray God is using it all to enable me to be more compassionate and understanding of what people go through.

"Praise be to the God and Father of our Lord Jesus Christ, the Father of compassion and the God of all comfort, who comforts us in all our troubles, so that we can comfort those in any trouble with the comfort we ourselves have received from God."
(2 Corinthians 1:3-4)

A NEW YEAR

I move on in my journey into the New Year of 2011. I cannot help but think of a New Year as a new opportunity to serve Christ and to enjoy my wife and family, and to take the message of the gospel to a few more thousand people as God opens doors to do so, and He has. One of those opportunities that God opened such a door to minister to others that year was when I was given the privilege by way of an unsolicited invitation, to write a column in our local newspaper that would reach tens of thousands of readers. I was asked by our local newspaper to write something on the subject of the 10th anniversary of 9/11 when our nation was attacked. I felt it to be an honor to write on this subject. I would never on my own initiative, have presumed myself to be the right person to attempt to write on the anniversary of that event, but I was appreciative of being asked to do so.

God guided me in writing that column and blessed it many times over. I have had the opportunity to submit several columns for publication in that newspaper over the past four decades and I count it a humbling privilege to be able to get God's Word out through that format. The year 2011 would take me to some forty preaching engagements. I was back on track and doing one of the things I love to do, and that is to preach. Only God could take a man who months earlier had been diagnosed with 3rd stage cancer and put him back on the road to preach all over central NY State the following year. I wish I could say that 2011 brought with it a total recovery and excellent health, but it did not. Neither has the years following. Some things you just learn to live with. I would likely, barring another miracle from God, continue to live with chronic pain and many other complications from the damage done by cancer, but that is a small price to pay to have the privilege to still be alive and still proclaiming the good news of Jesus Christ.

I would have more scans, more visits too numerous to recount to the hospital, and more hospitalization, to name just a portion of what 2011 brought. But I was still alive. I began to develop a fresh fondness for life. I was and am absolutely thrilled to live and proclaim what the Lord has done. One time that year I wrote and tried to explain and share how I was feeling in the summer of 2011 and I sent it out via email to family and friends. The following is what I said:

"Just up early this morning and listening to some of the old hymns on a CD, finding myself reflecting on things past and present and what I am feeling these days. I cannot put my finger on exactly why it is, but ever since surviving cancer that should have killed me by now, something has happened in my mind and spirit. That experience and the miracle of surviving will never leave me or become old news. I know all too well that God chose to let me still be here. I am very

fortunate, or I should rather say, very blessed. I awake each day with a sense of quiet, reserved thrill about life. Throughout the day, I experience that thrill and anticipation of good things happening. Very few bad days. I don't include chronic severe pain or other health issues. Those side effects do not matter, or maybe I should say it this way: they do not rule my day. I literally find myself treasuring every new breath I get to breath. As I am getting older, I also experience a certain sadness that death will come eventually and I will have to leave my family some day. I of course also look ahead to heaven. Without sounding like a mushy, gushy guy, I have come to treasure family and friends more than ever before, and I count myself so blessed by them all. Just the simple everyday stuff of life like having a hot cup of coffee in the morning and reading the newspaper or Bible has become a high event for me as I look forward to building something in my shop, or reading another book, or just taking in a deep breath and knowing every moment I still get to have left is something priceless and special. When I preach and sing for the old folks or preach in the churches, this spirit in me comes out and I find mutual love taking place between myself and them. I cannot adequately tell what I am feeling, but it is good and it leaves me a man so thankful to be given an extension on life that almost came to an end in the months going back into last year. I hear God saying in exchange for my added years, that much is expected of me in regard to my family, and in regard to ministry. Whatever I have left I am to give myself away to make others' days better. That is a big reason for writing this book. God gave me a peace ever since cancer. On the negative side of it all, he also has given me a heavy heart in the sense that He has given me a greater burden for lost souls. I cannot live a life of just ignoring lost people and people that are going through a hard time. I am compelled to expend my energy on trying to show others Jesus and His grace that is available to each one who will turn to him. Much of my efforts fall on deaf ears when it comes to the younger generation who think they will live forever and sadly many have no interest in God. I guess this is just how it will be for me in my final years. Life feels good and hurts at the same time. This past Sunday was one of our most special moments as we ministered at an Adult Care Community location in Norwich, NY and there was just something extraordinarily gentle and Spirit-filled about that meeting. God just keeps on doing something very special at these preaching-points in our travels. We are blessed beyond description, time and time again in these meetings. What God is doing just seems to get better and better with each passing year we do this."—Jim. (Summer of 2011)

PRAYER—PRAYER—PRAYER

At this point as I begin moving forward into 2011, I cannot help but keep reflecting back to the previous year and reminding myself why we were able to come through so much. I am a firm believer in the power of prayer. I ran across a copy of a plan Sharon and I put together after we found out I had cancer. I was determined to flood this crisis in our life with prayer, fasting, and God's Word. I typed out an outline to go by. I titled it: *'7-Day Prayer & Fasting Commitment'.* I cannot re-write the whole thing out in its details here, but I can give the general gist of what it entailed. It was a commitment we would carry out the week of April 29—May 6, 2010 before my May 7 surgery. It included partial fasting, communion every morning, reading the Bible three times per day, prayer three times per day, and worship of God three times per day.

Every time of prayer was to include claiming by the authority of Jesus Christ a miraculous healing. I also applied anointing oil from the land of Israel and laying on of hands for healing. I also put together a forty-two point list of specific details to pray for in regard to every facet of the surgery, recovery, all medical procedures, our family, each other, just anything we could think of that needed to be saturated with prayer. It was a disciplined, detailed exercise and commitment to God that we faithfully followed throughout that week. I have already mentioned in a previous section of this book how there were thousands of other people we know of who were praying for

115

me. I still run into people who tell me they are still praying for us regularly. I highly recommend that anyone that is reading this and you are facing cancer or any other difficulty, to saturate the situation with prayer and give it all over to God. No matter what your outcome may be, your prayers and commitment to Christ will be worth it, in life or in death.

ADJUSTING TO THINGS

2011 was a year that brought with it a continuation of much of what we were dealing with in the year that just came to a close. I would continue to adjust to new eating habits. For a long time I had to cut my food into baby-size bites. I enjoy a good steak and surprisingly, steak was not one of my bigger problems in swallowing and digesting. But I had to cut each bite down to about a quarter-inch piece. As the year moved forward, I had graduated to being able to take more substantial size bites of food. The gut aches would continue to be a frequent problem and still do, but I could get past those episodes and generally do OK. I would often have to avoid social events especially later in the day as my strength would diminish, and again even that I still must do to this day. Recovery from the immediate most severe effects of chemo and radiation would remain with me well into spring. Eventually those effects would subside although there is indication those treatments did some permanent damage of which I still deal with, but between the surgery and the treatments and the radical alteration of my insides, I would learn to have to live with several lasting complications, not the least of which is the abdominal pain and the right side pain.

Sometimes people will say disturbing things that they can be very wrong about and which can only cause more hurt than help. In the course of dealing with my chronic pain from the alterations that surgery did, I have on rare occasion been told by Godly people that if I truly had faith, the pain should be gone. Some have said I had faith to be healed of the cancer but that I somehow have failed to demonstrate enough faith for complete healing of all remaining symptoms such as the pain I live with every day. One time a person told my wife Sharon that as a man of faith and a minister of the gospel I should not have any pain anymore. Such a statement to my wife was very upsetting to her and nearly brought her to tears. She did not nearly come to tears because of any correctness in what was said but because of how incorrect such thinking was.

Such thinking is sadly all too often expressed and it is terribly way off base and misguided thinking. But again, I do not fault such people for their views. They really, albeit mistakenly, believe what they are saying to be true. I blame a lot of that false teaching on some unbiblical teaching from false prophets prevalent on TV these days.

REGARDLESS OF ALL THAT, LIFE IS STILL GOOD

My strength began to somewhat return. As spring and summer would be soon approaching, I looked forward with great enthusiasm to enjoying getting outside and living life. I did have a bit of a set-back when in March of 2011, I was diagnosed with double-hernia. It is almost humorous and laughable to me as I recount all these things. I must sound like *calamity Jim!* The hernias were a result of my abdominal and groin muscles becoming extremely weakened from the cancer surgery. I had been so ill and weakened by everything that I was unable for months to get adequate exercise. Through lack of physical activity, my muscles became soft and easily susceptible to being strained.

So it was back to the operating table to repair double-hernia. I could barely stand up as the pain had me bent over at times. Another hospitalization. Another time of recuperation. But through this latest ordeal I did come, and I found great relief from that repair job. By the way, as a wise friend once said, there is no such thing as minor surgery. It is only minor when it is done on someone else. A very true observation. I most definitely did not find double-hernia surgery to be a cake-walk, especially while still dealing with complications from the cancer surgery. Of course it was not remotely in the same ballpark as heart or cancer surgeries I'd had, but it was not the minor ordeal that I had previously thought it to be. Then again, maybe I was just weary of surgeries by then.

FISHING—PREACHING—WORKING

I recall fondly my childhood days of going fishing with my dad and brothers. Dad was the most patient of fishermen. I tend to give a fishing hole only minimal time and chance to prove fruitful or *fish-full* in my case. If I am not catching fish within a fifteen-minute to maybe half an hour span, I am on to another location. I do not know how many times I have heard someone say when they are not having any luck at catching fish, that it is just nice to get out in the great outdoors and enjoy nature. Yeah, right. I don't feel that way. If I go fishing, I want to catch fish, and if I do not catch them, I am not having a good time just breathing the outdoor air or taking in the sounds, sights and scents of nature. No, I am there to catch fish, and anything less will not suffice. I had given up fishing back in 2007. It had been four years. In 2011, with a fresh excitement and appreciation for life, I wanted to get back out there and fish. I also intended to resume a fuller preaching schedule. Not only that, but I had a desire to try and see if my health would be sufficiently up to undertaking some work projects around our home. I was no slouch in 2011.

Sharon and I went fishing a lot. That does not mean the same thing as catching a lot of fish. That did not happen. We sure gave it our best effort, going out to sixteen different locations in streams, rivers, lakes and ponds. Mostly we ended up after all just taking in the heat of the sun and nature. We did manage to catch a few fish plus probably the biggest catch was accidently firmly hooking my finger with a three-pronged hook. Ouch! I still squirm when thinking about it. I have seen others squirm when I re-tell it. It had a secondary backwards hook too, which went deep into the fat of my finger. I had no other choice but to grab hold of the needle-nose pliers in my tackle box and literally twist and pull to remove it. That kind of put a damper on that day's fishing outing and we went home.

My preaching itinerary increased dramatically and we spent the year traveling to many places to minister. The year 2012 was already filling up with more invitations to preach and it would prove to be a very active year. We decided to get a lot of home improvements done. Besides a lot of work that we hired contractors to do, I took on several heavy-duty projects. I found my efforts were bringing my body back into a stronger condition. My stamina temporarily increased. But the work would always inevitably land me flat on my back to recover every couple of hours or less. I would likely never get back to full strength. Too many alterations of my insides and too much trauma had taken a toll on my health. But I did regain some minimal strength. I could only work for about an hour at a time before needing to rest, and only two to three hours in a day. But it was an improvement. We got a lot done in 2011.

AN UNLIKELY AND WONDERFUL SURPISE

From what I have researched and heard, most cancer patients cannot expect to likely be declared cancer-free until about five years after the initial diagnosis if they are among those who even do get to beat their cancer. I was told at one point, after I had finished my treatments, that if I lived, I could expect to have to wait until about seven years with my type of cancer before having any realistic hope of being declared cancer-free. Even that was only a remote possibility. Going by the statistics for this cancer, there was no reason to hold out much hope that I would ever get to the point of being cancer-free. If that was God's plan, I was fully OK with whatever had to be. But meanwhile, I was earnestly asking God to over-ride the statistics and totally eliminate the cancer right away. Hey, why not give it a shot? You never know what God may choose to do.

Following one of many CAT scans, on July 21, 2011 at 4:23pm, my Oncologist called and talked to my wife. The latest CAT scan was normal. Upon my wife's inquiry, my Doctor was able to state right then and there, that yes, she could actually say I was cancer-free. This was five to seven years sooner than anticipated. Cancer-free. What a thrill to hear those words. Why me? Why no such news for so many others with cancer? Why did I get to live while some of my friends with the same kind of cancer did not? I cannot answer that. I cannot even dare to try. Was my healing strictly the result of good medical care or am I indeed the recipient of a miracle? What I am certain about is that any miracle is an unearned gift from God and I know God's ways are higher than ours.

Being declared cancer-free was of course the best news we could have hoped to ever hear. It did not necessarily mean that my body would now be free of all residual effects and complications that the cancer experience with the surgery and treatments caused. Not by a long shot. As I tell in this book, the cancer has left me with numerous complications which I deal with every day. But that does not take anything away from the wonderful words my Oncologist spoke that day when she said *"cancer-free!"*

"As the heavens are higher than the earth, so are my ways higher than your ways and my thoughts than your thoughts." Isaiah 55:9

I receive whatever additional time and breath God graciously chooses to allow me, with the determination that I will honor Him with my life, and make it my firm commitment to live for Him as He fulfills His purposes for keeping me here.

SOME THOUGHTS ON
SHOWING GENUINE CONCERN

People deal with many difficulties in life. There are times they just need someone to genuinely care about how they're doing. Those years of 2010 and beyond were ones in which countless times, I was asked by so many people, *"How are you feeling?"*, and I appreciated them showing their concern. I know they were being sincere in asking and that they really did care. Many of those times I wasn't doing well at all. In fact I was feeling absolutely awful from the cancer complications. I often still do today, years later. That's not me complaining. That's just the truth of the matter. I can't pretend that everything is always rosy. It isn't.

I have discovered over the course of my life that sometimes well-meaning people are not really prepared to hear an honest response to how a person is feeling. They may really care but they may not be expecting or be open to a response such as: *"I'm actually not doing too well."* I've also heard others of whom I find their understanding words of encouragement very supportive, those that give the reassurance that it's OK to tell the truth about how we feel. But indeed most of us admittedly prefer to hear people say they're doing great. The problem with that is none of us are always doing great. If we tell someone we're not having a very good day, it may tend to disappoint those who asked us how we're doing. I'm not being critical of how people respond to an honest answer. I'm just sharing some thoughts here in hopes that I can offer some helpful advice.

Due to the fact that well-meaning people would often be quick to tell me how good I was looking after they'd just asked me how I'm doing, I didn't think I could very well say I wasn't feeling well. Most of the time I would just put on my best smile, perk up, and assure them that I was at least doing *"OK"*. Sometimes my response is simply along the lines of saying my spirit is good even if my body may be weak or not doing so well. For a lot of us there seems to be some sort of built-in mechanism to counter any negative word, even if the negative word is simply an honest answer. We need to be willing to leave room for the possibility that for some people some days are just not always filled with positive good things. The fact is though, I'm just glad people care enough to ask.

On my part I hope that I'm cautious to really care how others are doing too. If we're not careful in how we allow people to respond when we ask them how they're doing, it may from their perspective seem like we don't really want to know. I have had occasions of asking someone how they are doing and when I've slowed down and given them enough time to answer honestly, sometimes they would say they were not doing too well. Then rather than just brushing their response off or telling them how well they look, I would dig a little deeper and show some concern. If I inquired more about what they were going through, they would tend to perk up and be glad someone actually wanted to know about their situation and really cared. I think we all just get too busy and in a hurry, and we inadvertently rush people or brush their complaints off when we need to be more careful to really care enough to listen.

It's OK for people to not always be chipper and smiling or whistling a happy tune. It's also OK to not always have an upbeat answer to people's problems. If we're going to initiate the conversation by asking how someone is doing, we need to expect and welcome their honest response, and for that matter allow them enough time to say how they are doing. If the response is that the person is having a hard time or doesn't feel on top of the world, we should allow for that and be OK with their honest answer.

I consider myself to be a very positive, optimistic, faith-filled person, but I also have my down times when I don't feel like being all cheery or feel like saying what a wonderful day it is. Cancer has severely tested me. Not every moment is wonderful. Even Jesus had some of those down moments. He wasn't exactly whistling a happy tune in the Garden of Gethsemane as He agonized over His imminent death on a cross, or when He heard that His friend Lazarus had died. I remember many years ago in a work place I was employed at. Every day, like many of us do, people came into work, and as they walked by their fellow employees, they would say the customary *"Good morning. How are you doing?"* and then too often, keep moving along not actually waiting for a reply. One of those times, I said to one man as we passed each other in a hallway, *"Hi. How are you doing?"* and I proceeded to walk on. Just as I was going, he turned around and with a rather serious look said: *"Do you really care?"* That moment and his response stuck with me all these years. Like a lot of people, I probably still all too often just say a quick *"Hi. How are you doing?"* when passing by someone and sometimes I don't take the time to hear a person's response.

Let's actually allow for people to say they're having a rough time. Be a listener and be patient, even with the so-called chronic complainer. Actually more often than not their seemingly chronic complaining may be based on legitimate onslaughts of difficulties. I know that can be the case. I've been there. Not the constantly complaining part as that is not what I do, but knowing what it is like to just seem to have multiple health issues piling on. I find it's best when I really show someone that I'm genuinely interested in what's going on in their life and not treat their difficulties with perky responses, but instead express my concern for them, and mean it. It's important that we not make it hard for them to talk about how they're really doing or what they're going through. Then they want to share what's going on in their life and it's a chance to offer a word of encouragement when that's what is needed. When someone is only pretending that they really care, people can sense their insincerity and such false concern hurts more than it helps.

May we all truly care enough to not just hear the good, positive reports, but also be open to hearing the hurting, not-so cheerful reports as well. As a Christian, I know that some fellow believers sometimes may think that one is failing to demonstrate faith in God or the joy of the Lord if that person says he or she is doing poorly. But that's a mistaken conclusion. I hope I have encouraged others to be more open to having a listening ear and an open heart to how their fellow man is really doing.

MORE CHALLENGES

I touch on a few more thoughts around the subject of my cancer and its complications that ensued. The year of 2011 brought with it a lot of challenges as I continued to fight for my life and tried to get through the more difficult days. December 27 of 2011, I had one of my most severe episodes of food getting stuck on the way down through my post-surgical shortened esophagus. If I eat too big of a bite of some things or too quickly, it can get lodged in there and then take some uncomfortable time to pass on down through my new tubular-shaped elongated partial stomach. From what I've been told, my surgically altered stomach is now for all intents and purposes, just a short extension of my remaining esophagus, and it is very closely situated right next to my right lung, even compressing my lung somewhat, instead of being where a stomach normally would be situated in the abdominal area. Since surgery my lung capacity and breathing is slightly diminished as a result.

On this particular day I mentioned, the food got hung up in there extra badly and it took Sharon about five minutes of gently hitting by back and chest to help cause it to move down. It's not the same as choking which has more to do with the windpipe. This problem is in the middle of my chest in the esophagus area. It was an especially scary episode. I have had countless additional similar episodes like this. As I moved forward I could not say for certain what the days ahead would bring in my ongoing journey of dealing with the complications from cancer.

AN *"ANXIOUS"* DETOUR

"Do not be anxious about anything, but in everything, by prayer and petition, with thanksgiving, present your requests to God. And the peace of God, which transcends all understanding, will guard your hearts and minds in Christ Jesus." (Philippians 4:6-7)

"An anxious heart weighs a man down, but a kind word cheers him up." (Proverbs 12:25)

As I continue to write this last chapter in part one of this book, I hope that I am cautious in how I share the substantial number of health complications that I experienced as a result of the cancer experience. I would not want the reader to come away with the thought that all this author does is *"complain, complain, complain"*. Nothing could be further from the truth or the intent of my story. It's not about complaining. It's about recalling the events that make up my journey through the disease of cancer and especially drawing attention to how God faithfully brought me as well as my wife Sharon through it all. If you come away with a greater appreciation of Almighty God and His concern for humanity, you will have gained the most important purpose of what I've written.

The following is about a cluster of some additional cancer-related experiences not previously mentioned which I became quite anxious about. I am not normally the anxious type. Maybe by discussing this *anxious detour* as I like to call it, I can bring out a few helpful thoughts for others in their times of unwelcome distractions and bumps in the road of life. It is a compound set of problems with the first aspect of it beginning in January, 2012 and has continued since then even at this writing more than a year later. These are the kind of times when one really does need to learn how to live one day at a time, especially if you are facing a possible permanent difficulty.

I will get around to explaining the details of these experiences shortly, but first I want to say some things here about detours and anxiety. Some may think anxiety is off limits for a man of faith. What are you anxious about? Whatever might be giving you anxiety, God can help you through it and bring you to where it is at the very least more manageable. I do not say that lightly. In our ministry travels we encounter many people dealing with anxiety and I try to share a helpful word to ease their concerns. I understand that people deal with real concerns that can at times be very difficult to handle calmly and anxiety-free.

LIFE'S INTERRUPTIONS

Detours interrupt the flow of things. With each new challenge that the cancer has brought me, I try not to just see it as a problem, but rather as an opportunity to encourage others in some small way.

I do think these assortments of difficulties probably result in me being a more compassionate minister to those who are hurting. When these complications have come up, I could very well say that it's like coming upon a detour that would briefly take me off my path of normal activity. Indeed, isn't life often about a lot of detours? As these new complications interrupted my preaching schedule as well as my flow of writing this book, I think of what we have experienced in our ministry travels. Many times, we have come upon road construction or other things going on that forced us to take alternative roads to get to our preaching-points. Sometimes it has been storms or illness that has altered our schedule.

Such detours sometimes have proven to be only minor inconveniences, while other times they can prove to be a bigger problem. Ideally we like things to go along smoothly and as planned, but it doesn't always work out that way. Such is life too. It could very well be said that the folks in the Adult Care Community whom we minister to have been detoured as well, from the life they used to know. Things for them have not gone as planned in their latter days. Instead of living their lives out in their home they have known for many years around familiar surroundings, having a sense of independence, now they live in a health-care facility, following someone else's pre-planned program of activity and being dependant on others for their care. There is a certain disappointment in seeing one's life come to where he or she must accept this detour of life and adjust to such a radically different setting. Eventually in life your plans get interrupted and altered. You find yourself having to deal with difficulties you never anticipated. There will be times it seems like these detours are too much to bare. Yet you will bare them moment by moment because you have to.

WHAT IS THAT NOISE?

It was January 5, 2012. A loud noise suddenly started up in my head that was soon followed with blurry vision, severe headache, pressure in my head, light-headedness and confusion. At first, my oncologist considered the possibility it might be a stroke or that cancer might have spread to my brain. That is enough to get anybody anxious. This new problem eventually was diagnosed as another complication from cancer. Initially it lasted for six weeks straight about eighteen hours a day. As time progressed its intensity lessened some to where it was intermittent but still at least several hours most every day. I think it was all the more upsetting for me because the past two years of cancer and all I went through with that had taken such a toll on me physically and emotionally and now this new event was just one too many things to deal with. I was running out of the capacity to handle more health problems very well.

All total, in an eleven-month span between January and November of 2012, I was checked over by seven different doctors and specialists, and had two brain scans and multiple additional procedures to diagnose this thing going on in my head. At one point doctors had to consider whether it might just be a simple common case of tinnitus whose primary symptom is a low-level ringing in the ears which many people have, but due to the intensity and scope of what was going on, they knew it had to be something more significant. I met a few people who told me they had tinnitus and that it was not big deal. Something wasn't *"ringing"* true about what I was hearing from them. Oh they were being truthful, but the level of noise in my head did not seem to be matching up with something a person could just easily live with. Especially with all the additional symptoms beside the noise, there had to be a different diagnosis. Something about this whole event did not add up to tinnitus, or at least not only tinnitus. Sure enough upon further tests they concluded that it is a delayed complication of cancer and chemotherapy, and they could not cure it. The chemo damaged some nerves, and the symptoms from that damage finally began surfacing.

I never was even the least bit anxious over my esophageal cancer diagnosis or any of the experiences I went through prior to this newest complication. I know my eternal destiny. When I die, I will be with Christ, so knowing I am saved and assured of eternal life in heaven takes away the fear and sting of death. However, I confess that this thing with my head did have me feeling some considerable anxiety. What bothered me the most about it was that I did not want to have to stop preaching. My body could fall apart, and it had been lately, but I did not want my mind or my intellect adversely affected. Three things I especially enjoy for mental exercise are preaching, writing, and reading. I believe in using my mind as fully as possible. This head problem was a real threat in that regard.

If this newest complication from cancer was not enough, in 2013 additional delayed complications from cancer surfaced. Again, all of it was a result of cancer surgery and treatments. My nerves had been seriously damaged from chemo, and additionally some nerves were disrupted quite substantially from the surgery. I began dealing with the onset of problems related to my mouth. There is a condition called *'primary or idiopathic burning mouth syndrome'*, related to problems with taste and sensory nerves of the peripheral or central nervous system. In my case it was caused by the side effects of cancer treatment and also comes under the heading of *'Endocrine disorders'*, such as *'underactive thyroid' (hypothyroidism)* which, yes, believe it or not, is yet another complication I have been diagnosed with from the cancer surgery alterations to my digestive system. My blood-sugar levels often suddenly with little warning drop into the forties, a critical level, and bring on confusion, shaking, sweating, weakness, etc. and I begin to black out. When that happens I have to quickly take up to four glucose tablets and drink orange juice. I have to prick my fingers and check my blood-sugar level when the symptoms start. I never was hypoglycemic until after the cancer surgery. My altered digestive system does not adequately absorb and distribute vital nutrients to my body, thus the low-blood sugar episodes. Since then it has become a significant health issue I deal with sometimes a couple times a day. While it is a challenge to live with this hypoglycemia, and at times can bring me to a critical point, it is not my biggest concern. Lots of people deal with it. If I am extremely careful, I can manage my blood-sugar levels through well-planned-out dietary habits.

Getting back to the nerve damage symptoms, by April of 2013 the delayed onslaught of multiple symptoms reached a critical point to where it all just became too much to bare and resulted in my having to cancel several preaching engagements. I saw three more doctors and was put through a number of tests. Changes were made in my medications including some new ones. I saw a second neurologist on May 24, 2013 and he was able to more precisely diagnose what was going on in my body. I had *'peripheral neuropathy'*, in laymen's term, *nerve damage*, directly resulting from chemotherapy. At the time of this writing, it affects approximately 15 million to 20 million patients in the United States, and among other primary causes such as diabetes, chemotherapy for cancer treatment is one of the leading causes of it, and symptoms can develop even a few years later after chemotherapy as it did with me.

I read in a book, *'Beating Neuropathy'* by a Dr. John Hayes Jr. where he talks about cancer patients living longer now, but that there is the potential of developing peripheral neuropathy as an effect of chemotherapy. My neurologist began me on a treatment plan. As one can quickly see, I ended up with an unbelievable number of cancer-related complications. Indeed, these latest complications with the head noise and now the mouth could easily rattle most anyone and be a cause for considerable anxiety. The lengthy list of real health issues I found myself now living with since the cancer diagnosis was just part of the package. I would have to learn how to live with these latest complications as long as they might persist and I would keep trusting God no matter what. For me, that is the easy part. My trust in God has never wavered, and with God's help it never will.

BELIEVER'S ANXIETY

Finding myself confronted with anxious concern, I can all the more empathize with others who are dealing with anxiety. The

Apostles Paul and Peter in the Bible encouraged believers to not be anxious, but they were anxious themselves at times. Even Jude in the Bible spoke in a positive and encouraging sense using the word *"anxiously"* as he talked about *"waiting anxiously for the mercy of our Lord Jesus Christ to eternal life"*. Jesus understands that we do get anxious. I was to say the least, very concerned over what was going on in my head. That is what some of us like to say when we are in fact *"anxious."* We like to say we are just *"concerned"*, as if to suggest that admitting to having anxiety would somehow reflect poorly on our faith.

The truth is we do get anxious sometimes. I believe that every experience in my life has the potential to somehow help someone else along the way that might be facing a difficulty. I believe even my weakest moments can encourage others as they see that a man of faith in God can still struggle and have anxiety. The difference for Christians is that in such times, they can turn to Christ and through His empowerment, handle the anxious moments better than others might.

WITH GOD'S HELP

I have been able with God's help to resume functioning sufficiently to study and occasionally preach. I accept that sometimes we must learn to live with inconveniences and difficulties. I still trust God. He is in control, and I hold onto the words of encouragement in God's Holy Word about anxiety. I look to God in prayer for His peace and as the Bible says, to *"guard my heart and mind"*. These present troubles are but a temporary detour. Either here or in eternity, *"this too, shall pass"*, as the saying goes. God willing, meanwhile I move forward on my journey. I leave it in God's hands. I have witnessed miracles of God. I have prayed for many people to be healed.

Why God sometimes has seen fit to do a miracle or give a divine healing and other times He does not do so is something only He knows. Even Elisha the prophet who was so faithful to God became sick unto death and God did not heal him. Just like the man Job in the Bible, I too cannot answer the question about why God allows certain difficulties in this life. What I am sure about is that whatever He does or does not do for us is His business and He never makes a mistake. He is not obligated to give us an explanation. I would like to say that these complications in my body are just an inconvenience. As a man of faith, I tend to want to just brush it all off as no big deal and only say something positive about it. However, that would not be truthful of me. These things remain very troublesome health issues as part of my cancer experience which I must wrestle with almost every waking hour. But I do not allow myself to become discouraged. Someone once told me that to be discouraged is to give up or quit. I am no quitter. No matter how determined an attitude we have, there is never any guarantee of success, but what is important is that we give our best effort in whatever we are facing.

There is a line from a movie with John Wayne. In that movie *'The Sea Chase'*, he says that he might fail but he can't quit. That says it so well. The grip of anxiety is diminished now as I adapt to these inconveniences. I will not try to play down the severity of it all just to sound more positive or spiritual. I just take it moment by moment and keep praying that God will see fit to give me a miraculous healing or at least enable me to live with these things if that is His choice. I accept the fact that due to these problems or any of the other cancer-related complications, I have to work a little harder now to concentrate, study, write and preach or for that matter to do anything else in my everyday life. I realize there are far worse things that many people deal with. It has all been a detour, but detours are not where we are intended to remain at. We must move on. God has put a song in my heart and no cancer or any other crisis that life can throw at me can ever take it away from me. The story of this part of my life that brought cancer into our lives is a story still being told by each additional breath that I take.

God has put a song in my heart. Has He yours? He loves to hear His people sing, and He will gently look down on you and with a smile only the Heavenly Father can give, He will listen. As long as God gives me breath, I will keep on singing. God tells me He is there for me. He has done the heavy lifting that otherwise would have been too much for me. I think of the song, *'Leaning on the everlasting arms'* and as I lean on God, the journey is not nearly so rough a trip as He absorbs the bumps and levels out the road ahead.

A NEW ROAD AHEAD

This book has largely been about journeys, especially Part-One. The year 2012 was especially trying on me as it involved a lot of challenges. I had dealt with those new delayed complications from the whole thing with cancer, one of which nearly engulfed my attention the whole year and was a cause of considerable stress. I had gone through a major change in my health care as I turned sixty-five and went on Medicare. I could no longer receive my health care through Sharon's coverage in the Veteran's Medical Center and I went through a complicated change to new doctors. That alone was quite the challenge having to meet all new doctors and set up new appointments and the transferring of a voluminous amount of medical records. I had spent myself emotionally as I undertook the project of writing this book which I worked on the entire year, and for that matter, on into 2013.

By December of 2012, I felt exhausted. The past three years since that initial diagnosis of cancer had finally caught up with me. I found myself tumbling down into the dumps. One evening, just a day after Christmas, as I contemplated where I was at, God showed me something. The challenges and experiences of the past few years were behind me now. That journey was over. I was now about to take off on a new journey as I entered 2013. Everything before then was the past. I would soon be sixty-six. It was time to go down a brand new road into the latter part of my life. Although the lingering complications from it remain a part of my everyday life, the worst of the cancer was a done deal, a part of the past.

The hectic schedule and emotional changes in connection with my health care was all behind me. Progress on the book was coming along well and I would hopefully finish it soon. As 2013 was only a few days ahead, that New Year took on an especially fresh sense of something new. I now could look in my rear-view mirror at everything from 2012 and before and see it all as fading out of sight. All of that is the old journey. I instead could look with eyes forward and look at what is in front of me. A brand new journey lay ahead, not a continuation of any of the past events, but now all new. Somehow as I thought this through that evening in my living room on December 26, 2012, it helped lift me back up and I was ready to move forward and do new things in new places. It was an epiphany, a fresh understanding of things that came to me. The words of the Apostle Paul in Philippians 3:13 *"Forgetting what lies behind and reaching forward to what lies ahead"* suddenly became more meaningful to me than they ever had before. Life is many journeys within a journey. I was now ready to take off again and soar the heights of a new phase of my life.

"Those who hope in the LORD will renew their strength. They will soar on wings like eagles; they will run and not grow weary, they will walk and not be faint." (Isaiah 40:30)

SO THANKFUL

Though I have for the most part, concluded this chapter and have said most of what I wished to say about the cancer, I add a note of thanks here. By this point in my book, I have already mentioned various times friends and family have been there for me, or helped me in numerous ways. My thanks go out to each one. I especially here, want to express how much my immediate family helped me. I am so glad my son Chris was there at the Fisher House with his mom the first night after the surgery. He and Heather kept her company at a time she needed someone to be close by and keep her strong. There were other times Chris has been available to help out when I have been too physically weakened to do things.

I am appreciative of those times we had to call on my son Jimmy such as when I was too weak and ill to even get from my car into our house and into bed, or when I was too weak to carry groceries into the house. Again, that is just a sampling of the many times he has been there to help. I think of my daughter Vickie who took the lead in joining the family together, both at our home when I told the family my diagnosis, as well as again in the waiting room before I went back for surgery. I think of my daughter Patty, who always made herself available if needed, and a time in particular when I was alone at home. I had a health crisis and was able to reach her by phone and she quickly came over to care for my health needs and to help me recover from a seriously low-blood sugar count *(hypoglycemia)* brought on by complications of my surgery. Others in the family encouraged me along the way. For these times and a thoughtful, caring family, I say *"thanks"* from my heart. I of course especially thank my wife Sharon so much for all the countless times and ways she has been there for me and continues to be. God has blessed me with a wonderful family.

AND SO THE JOURNEY CONTINUES

"Boldly and without hindrance he preached the kingdom of God and taught about the Lord Jesus Christ." (Acts 28:31)

So the book of Acts in the Bible just abruptly, unceremoniously ends. It has been said that Acts ends that way because the story of the Church and the work of the Holy Spirit has not ended, but continues to be written in the hearts of men and women. God is still doing His work, and ministry is a continuing process. As for my account of my journey through those initial days of dealing with the whole cancer experience, it is time to bring this portion of my book to a close.

From here forward I will share a little about our ministry and about the God of the miraculous. I have tried to give as accurate a picture as I could about my journey with cancer. By the time I am writing this, some years have passed since 2010 and my journey through the cancer experience and its resulting complications is still unfolding day by day. The past few years were some of the most difficult times we ever faced. In 2010, cancer took center stage in our lives. It was a time of ups and downs, of set-backs and progress. The final chapter on this experience has yet to be known. I hold onto the one sure thing that I do know, which is that God has never forsaken me and He never will.

PART II

GENERATIONS

DIVINE CALL OF GOD AND A VISION

"Remember the days of old; consider the generations long past. Ask your father and he will tell you, your elders, and they will explain to you." (Deuteronomy 32:7)

9. FACING AN ETERNITY WITHOUT CHRIST, A MAN GETS THE MESSAGE

"Come, follow me," Jesus said, "and I will make you fishers of men." (Matthew 4:19)

Anyone reading the next two parts of this book which deal with subject matter not directly or primarily related to the crisis of cancer I have been writing about might wonder how it all fits together. As I set out to write this book, the journey through the cancer crisis was the final motivation to write. It was something I wanted to tell. In writing it, my hope is that my own positive attitude and faith in God might prove to help others who may face their own crisis in life. But long before the cancer diagnosis, I had it in my heart to one day write about what God has been doing in my life as a minister of the gospel, as well as write about a miracle-working God who has shown me marvelous things over the years and has many times superseded the natural order of things with His supernatural divine power and presence.

GENERATIONS?

In titling part two of this book *'Generations'*, I was first motivated to use that word as I thought about the elderly generation that we have ministered to on a wide scale in the Adult Care Community. Tom Brokaw wrote the book *'The Greatest Generation'* which I read with great interest. I wrote a number of columns in our local newspaper about the younger and older generations in America, and what each generation has to offer the other. I also thought of that verse in 2 Timothy 1:5 that says: *"I am reminded of your sincere faith, which first lived in your grandmother Lois and in your mother Eunice and, I am persuaded, now lives in you also."* (2 Timothy 1:5) Paul reminded young Timothy, a convert to the Christian faith, that his grandmother and mother were women of faith too. So also in my case, I had Christian parents, as well as aunts and uncles who were people of great faith in God. Some were preachers. I count it a tremendous blessing to have come from such a background, and that the generation before me in my own family were people of faith. Then there is my own generation with several of my siblings and cousins who have a strong faith in God. In my family several of the next generation following me has that same faith, and now having had the opportunity to minister to our nation's senior population has just all been such a wonderful experience. And so I write this part of my book called *'Generations'* as I share my faith and the ministry God has called and privileged me to be a part of.

Whether it was going through cancer, or God opening doors of ministry, or God working a miracle, this book is about my wife Sharon's and my journey together in partnership with a loving, all-powerful God who has been there for us and with us through it all. Although at this point in my book I switch gears from my cancer experience to my ministry experience, I will at various points continue to weave my story of my cancer into my continuing ministry experience. There are times when some of the things I write about the ministry or about the God of the miraculous is impacted by the experience of the cancer that I went through. With that said, I hope I have adequately clarified how I feel that all this subject matter relates and fits into one writing. I have attempted to state my intentions and motivation for bringing this varied subject-matter of our God-given ministry and the miraculous into the same book along side of my account of the crisis of cancer. It is about a great God who has been there for us and who is there for anyone who is willing to invite Him to be with them in all aspects of their life's journey.

THANKFUL FOR FAITHFUL PEOPLE OF GOD

I thank God that He had a faithful servant who was one of those fishers of men Matthew 4:19 speaks of in the Bible. I thank God for that one man who in 1968, was willing to take a chance on visiting an inhospitable, hard-drinking, partying semi-hippie, or at least a hippie-wannabe of the sixties who desperately needed God. But before getting to that, allow me to first move further back in time. I was brought up in the fear of the Lord. For those who might not know it, that is a good thing, not a negative thing. The Bible says the fear of the Lord is the beginning of wisdom. It is at the very least about having a healthy reverential awe of an Almighty God, but that definition is not sufficient by its self. There is no need to try to soften up or make more palatable what fearing God is about. Quite honestly it is about more than just reverential awe and there needs to be more fear of God in this world today. It is to fear God who ultimately can and does have the final say about our eternal destiny.

My parents were such people. I still see in my mind my dad faithfully reading his Bible every evening or when his schedule allowed. I see him in that same corner of our living room, Bible open, often shortly after supper. My mom too, after Dad died, kept her Bible on the kitchen table where she read it from regularly. Seeing her Bible there whenever I dropped in for a visit was always a great testimony to her solid faith. My Dad did not talk much about what he was doing in that corner with his Bible. His greatest witness to me was his quiet but steady reading of his Bible. Today I have that Bible in my possession including the one he used in the earlier years as well as the one we his kids, presented to him in the sixties. I guess we thought his old one was showing too much ware and tare. Occasionally I pick up his old Bible and read from it just to get the *feel* of holding and reading the very Bible my Dad did. It is in quite rough, deteriorated condition now, but it is still the Word of God and still speaks volumes to me as to what a faithful man of God my dad was.

That Bible will be passed on down to my oldest son and hopefully on down to one of the grandkids. I pray it will continue to be a witness to the faith of my father who lived for Jesus. I think of how as we grow old, our bodies take a beating just like that old Bible, but just as that old tattered Bible that still has great value, so our aching, injured, beaten-up aging bodies still have value and purpose. I wish I'd had more time with Dad and that we had been closer. We did not have a poor relationship, but I always felt it would have been nice to have known him even better. Someone, one of his co-workers who knew him from his days of working in the shoe factories once told me that I was lucky to have known the man who was my dad. I would heartily agree. He went to heaven at sixty-three years of age when I was still in my early twenties. I often brag on what a great Dad he was to me.

A CLOSET, A MOM'S THUNDERING VOICE, AN EAR, AND A LESSON LEARNED

My mom was equally wonderful and a godly mother. She made it to ninety-two. I was able to get much closer to her because there were more years to do so. Sharon and I enjoyed her last Thanksgiving meal together at the nursing home she was in. We also had the pleasure of having her attend one of our church services we did at that nursing home. What blessed memories those are! My home life was ideal. I cannot imagine a better upbringing than what we all had. Church was a vital part of our lives. I do admit that I did not appreciate having to go to church as a kid.

I recall one Sunday as dad and mom were in the process of getting us all into the car to go to church. I was just a little boy at the time. At that age I did not think things through very well. I just decided I was not going. I hid in an upstairs bedroom closet. With seven kids, it was easy enough for my parents to not even notice that I was missing. Off to church they went. There I was, still hiding in the closet. As time went by it began to dawn on me that at some point they would discover I was not with them. As far as I know they got all the way to church before they realized I was missing. As I continued to now fearfully hide in the closet, I heard the car pull up and in came my mom. She called out my name in that thundering tone of voice that could set a young boy's heart to trembling. *"Jim!"* To make the story short, I ended up down stairs, into the car and off to the church.

Upon getting out of the car, I gave her a hard time about going any further. My mom grabbed hold of my ear and across the street we went and on into the church. I never again dared to pull such a stunt again. In later years my dear mom did not recall the part about the ear, but I never forgot. I like to joke about how my right ear lobe is longer than my left ear lobe as proof that it happened. Actually both ears are normal. Speaking of normal, some who know me might be tempted to say that's about the only thing about me that is normal. As I was going over this part of my book with my wife for my final editing, she chuckled when I suggested I add that last line for a little humor and she said: *"Yes, that's all that's normal about you."* So there it is. I threw that line in. When my wife was kidding me about my peculiarities, I further jokingly said: *"Maybe it's the mercury I used to play with when I was about a seven-year old kid!"* Seriously, I really did play with mercury that I got from a broken thermometer. Sharon in response to that revelation said: *"You've got be kidding right?"* When I said I was not kidding, she said: *"That explains a lot of things about you."* Well, we do have some fun with one-another like this. I admit it though. I'm probably one peculiar man, not an exceptional man, just peculiar. But then the Bible does mention God's peculiar people, so I'm OK with it if anyone finds me to be a little strange sometimes. For that matter, taking it one step further, the Bible refers to God's people as *"aliens and strangers in the world"*. (1 Peter 2:11). OK, I've had a little fun here with that spiel. Now getting back to the ear story and my mom.

Mom is in heaven now and perhaps God has shown her the video of that day. I do not fault her for any of that experience. As an adult now, I am thankful our parents took us to church. I'm even thankful I had a mom who if necessary would grab hold of a young boys ear if that's what it would take to get him in church. We could use a few more parents who are so determined to get their children into church. If we did, our nation might not be in the spiritually deficient condition that it is in today.

AWARE OF THE REALITY OF GOD
(...and a startling vision!)

There is so much I could include in this book about my upbringing and our church life, but for the purposes of this book, I must try to just touch on a few things. To make a long story short, we were brought up in the Church life and in the teachings of the Bible. From my earliest recollections, I have always been aware of the reality of God. Because I have just always known God is, it is hard for me to fully understand why so many find it difficult to believe God is. Though it would take until my adulthood to seriously give my life to Christ, still I knew the Lord was real and I was fully aware of His presence even from at least the age of five. At approximately only five years of age, God gave me two visions of end-time events. I had no previous understanding of these things. In both visions, I was in the atmosphere above the earth looking down. Christ was there with me, or perhaps I should say I was there with Christ. I sensed His presence to be one of assurance that I was secure with Him as the terrible scene below was taking place. I saw the earth engulfed in a cauldron of world-wide flames and billowing smoke. As time went by, I came to believe God was showing me in those two visions something concerning end times as the Bible tells us about. I have had that witness in my spirit all these years. The following passage of scripture comes to mind as I recall that vision / dream:

144

"Above all, you must understand that in the last days scoffers will come, scoffing and following their own evil desires. They will say, "Where is this 'coming' he promised? Ever since our ancestors died, everything goes on as it has since the beginning of creation." But they deliberately forget that long ago by God's word the heavens came into being and the earth was formed out of water and by water. By these waters also the world of that time was deluged and destroyed. By the same word the present heavens and earth are reserved for fire, being kept for the day of judgment and destruction of the ungodly. But do not forget this one thing, dear friends: With the Lord a day is like a thousand years, and a thousand years are like a day. The Lord is not slow in keeping his promise, as some understand slowness. Instead he is patient with you, not wanting anyone to perish, but everyone to come to repentance. But the day of the Lord will come like a thief. The heavens will disappear with a roar; the elements will be destroyed by fire, and the earth and everything in it will be laid bare. Since everything will be destroyed in this way, what kind of people ought you to be? You ought to live holy and godly lives as you look forward to the day of God and speed its coming. That day will bring about the destruction of the heavens by fire, and the elements will melt in the heat. But in keeping with his promise we are looking forward to a new heaven and a new earth, where righteousness dwells. So then, dear friends, since you are looking forward to this, make every effort to be found spotless, blameless and at peace with him." (2 Peter 3:3-14)

APPROPRIATENESS OF SHARING SUCH THINGS FROM THE LORD AND SOME BIBLICAL GUIDLINES

I think it is important that I share some thoughts here at the outset on whether it is acceptable in the sight of our Lord to speak in this book of a few dreams, visions and revelations *(and even some possible angelic visitations)* which I believe I have been the recipient of from God. I say that because I will be speaking of such things as

145

I proceed in this book. In the following I humbly attempt to offer some thoughts and guidance, and hopefully some wisdom on claims of hearing from the Lord.

First in regard to this vision about end times, some might have their doubts that God would give such a young boy these visions and that they might actually refer to the Biblical end-time events, or they may feel it is not appropriate of me to speak of them or any of the other visions / dreams I will mention in this book. With that in mind I take the time to go into a little detail about this subject. I do so to perhaps offer some wisdom and guidance to others who may have a tendency to want to tell others what they believe God has shown them or told them.

Certainly there are times when some may claim they have a Word or revelation from the Lord to share when in fact it may not be from God, or it may be something God did not intend them to share. They may share those things quite innocently but may be quite mistaken in declaring that what they are sharing is in fact from God. We should weigh these matters carefully. Most certainly God does speak to His people today through various ways including first and foremost His written Word, but also in dreams, visions, and the word gifts. With that said we must be aware that not everything that is attributed to God speaking is necessarily truly from God. As for when we really do receive something from God such as through dreams or visions, the Lord does want us to be careful not to get spiritually prideful as a result of Him showing us things this way. No worry of that being the case with me. It is simply not in my heart to think I am anything special for God having shown me such things as He has. If anything, I am more apt to tremble at experiencing such things from God because with it comes a sobering responsibility knowing I've been allowed to hear from God and to see such things.

Like the TV preacher and Messianic Jew Sid Roth who believes God is doing the supernatural every day and he has a program titled *"It's Supernatural!"*, I believe in the supernatural God and I do not want to hold back from sharing what God has said to share. I share such experiences in this book only after I have prayerfully sensed in my spirit that God wants me to do so, and I understand there is a responsibility on my part to share these things with the utmost care and humility. I measure very carefully anything that I believe to be from God. May all believers be ever so careful and diligent to do the same. The Bible for the Christian must be our ultimate rule of faith and authority. I dare not ever speak falsely or violate the principles of God's Holy Scriptures. It is always advisable to not say too much. Solomon said in Ecclesiastes *"Much dreaming and many words are meaningless. Therefore stand in awe of God."* (Ecclesiates 5:7) With that said I move on ever so cautiously in any of my accounts concerning dreams and visions from God.

Is it sometimes OK to speak of these things? Yes, sometimes it is OK to share a dream or vision from God if it truly is from God and if He has given it to you to be shared. In the Bible Jeremiah 23 talks about false prophets who say *"I had a dream, I had a dream!"* God also says: *"I am against those who prophesy false dreams."* That is a very sobering thought. This Word of the Lord that came to Jeremiah was a warning against false prophets and serves to remind God's people to be sure they are hearing from God when they make any claims about dreams and visions being from Him. While God gives this word of warning through Jeremiah, we also find that Jeremiah himself received a Word from God many times including through dreams and he shared what God told him in those dreams. Jeremiah of course was a great prophet of God and those things he shared are part of the inspired written word of God that we have in the Bible, and the things any of us might hear from God are not even remotely on the same level as Holy Scripture. Never-the-less, God does sometimes speak to His people through dreams and visions.

Job 33:14-16 comes to mind where it says: *"For God does speak—now one way, now another—though no one perceives it. In a dream, in a vision of the night, when deep sleep falls on people as they slumber in their beds, he may speak in their ears and terrify them with warnings."* One preacher in a Christian magazine said the church has largely ignored this aspect of how God speaks to us today. What I do share in this book I do so because I believe it brings glory to God and may minister to others as it draws attention to the reality of God and the fact that He does speak to people today.

Why God would show me such things as He has over the years is something only He can answer. I'm not at all unique in having heard from God. Actually I have met many people who have been given dreams and visions from the Lord. I suspect most just choose not to talk about their experiences, probably often because they don't feel God has given them the freedom to do so or maybe they are concerned that speaking of such things might not reflect humility. I was recently reading a book titled *'Spiritual Avalanche'* by Steve Hill, a well known Assemblies of God evangelist. He recently nearly died and following that crisis in his life he tells of a vivid, detailed vision God gave him. The book is based on what God showed him in that vision concerning the church. He too, takes great care in sharing the vision God gave him realizing some might question his decision to share the vision. He points out that some visions are meant only for the person who received it, while other visions are things God does want shared.

Over the years following that time in my life since seeing that vision of end times, God would show me many other things in dreams and visions. Again, it is not all that unusual for people to receive a vision from God as He chooses to reveal something to us. I spent a long time in prayerful consideration before I came to the place where I was confident that God was directing me by His Spirit to include these experiences in this book. He has His purposes. A survey a few years ago revealed that possibly as much as twenty percent of the American population has received some sort of revelation, be it in a dream, a vision, or some other manner that they believe came from God. Certainly the dreams and visions aspect of such revelations happening in our time is supported by the Bible:

"'In the last days, God says, I will pour out my Spirit on all people. Your sons and daughters will prophesy, your young men will see visions, your old men will dream dreams.'" (Acts 2:17)

For a five year old, such a vision could be upsetting, but God knew what He was doing. The only possible adverse effect it may have had on me temporarily was that as a child, I was especially uneasy around fire-works displays and severe lightning storms, probably because of the fiery vision I had. That uneasiness eventually passed of course, but I grew up always mindful of those two end-time dreams. No doubt very early on, even at five years of age, long before I was even saved there was evidence of a calling of God on my life and He was already preparing me to be a preacher with a prophet's heart, that is to say, not a heart to tell the future but a heart to boldly proclaim God's Word. In later years, as I answered the divine call of God into the ministry, I found that I could identify with what the early 1900's evangelist Billy Sunday expressed was his calling. He believed God called him to draw the lost to the message of the gospel and also to bring a message of revival to a sleepy church and preach a message of repentance. I am of course no Billy Sunday, but I share his heart that he expressed.

Of course first things first. I would later in my own life need a major heart-change and get right with the Lord myself before answering any call of God to preach to others. Somehow, God just made me aware from my earliest years that He exists. Sharing dreams and visions from the Lord, and other spiritual experiences? It is all about a great God and never about lifting one's self up or in any way boasting about what God has shown you. In the Bible, the Apostle Paul was shown things by the Lord in visions and revelations. He heard inexpressible words. He spoke of these visions as *"surpassingly great revelations"* and how God took actions to keep him humble at having seen these things.

I too, only cautiously speak of things I believe God has shown me. I know all too well that if need be, God can humble any one of us if He needs to. The Apostle Paul said *"I will go on to visions and revelations from the Lord."* (2 Corinthians 12:1b) He went on to emphasize that he had nothing to boast about in receiving these things from God. Many people have had God reveal things to them. I hope that sharing my own experiences might help motivate others to want to know Christ and to place their faith in Him. The bottom line however, is that for reasons known only to God, I have indeed been blessed of God to hear from Him frequently over my life-time in these ways.

MORE VISIONS AND DREAMS

If I may, allow me to continue with a little more on this subject of God showing us things. Through dreams and visions unmistakably from the Lord, I saw a lot of things in advance of their happening. Several were advance warnings of people who would soon die. I am not a morbid-thinking person, so I cannot fully explain why God has shown me in advance, the deaths of a number of people. My first wife Joan was one of them. I was told by the Lord in a dream that she would soon die. She immediately thereafter came down with heart trouble and went to be with the Lord less than a month later.

I recall one time when I and my older son were at a Full Gospel Businessmen's Fellowship International Breakfast in Oneonta, NY. The speaker was a well known preacher considered by some to be a modern day apostle and prophet. As he was speaking, I suddenly saw a very upsetting vision from the Lord. In the vision, God said my younger brother would soon be at risk of losing his life. It was such an overwhelming vision that I found myself quietly weeping right there in the meeting room. I told my older son that God had just told me that his Uncle, my younger brother, would possibly die soon. I knew it was from God beyond any doubt, but I also suspected my son might have found it to be a rather suspect vision. Maybe he didn't have any such doubts. I can't really say one way or the other, but I wouldn't be surprised if he did. Anyone with good sense is likely to always be cautious about how they react to testimonies of hearing from the Lord. I too, reserve the right to be a little skeptical about things people say they have seen or heard from God. We should be cautious and not be quick to automatically believe everything we hear when it comes to someone saying *thus saith the Lord.* At the same time we should also not be too quick to discount such testimonies. The Bible warns us to test the spirits when concluding whether something is really from God.

Much of the things I tell in this book will understandably be questionable in some people's minds, and that is a good thing. Being careful to examine what others tell us is from God keeps us all on our toes and careful to give wise and thoughtful consideration of what we hear as well as what we say. A couple weeks later after that vision about my brother, I told my mother about the vision. I made it a matter of prayer and she took what I said to heart and from what I understand, she made it a matter of prayer too. A few days later, I got a phone call telling me that a man had attempted to steal my brother's car and in the process deliberately tried to kill him by running into him with the car. My brother could have died from that event and was hospitalized and in critical condition for a while. Afterwards, I told him about the vision and I told him God had spared his life in response to prayer. I am so thankful that God let me know about this in advance and it gave me the opportunity through prayer to come against the forces of evil that desired to take his life.

Yes, prayer does indeed change things. I could go on and tell of things God showed me in dreams concerning some of my immediate family, but I will not take the time to do so in detail here. I am a proud father. My family has inspired me as I have faced obstacles in my own life. Each has had their own share of hurdles and I have been blessed with each one of them and inspired at times by how some of them have handled their own adversities.

I perhaps should mention another dream God gave me of something that was going to happen. I dreamed my mom took a bad fall and was hurt quite badly. The dream proved true as a little later she did fall. In fact she fell more than once and it really took a toll on her body. One of those times when she was hospitalized from an especially bad fall, I helped feed her as she was too injured to sit up and feed herself. That was another special moment where I was able to do something for my mom who had over the years been there so much for me. A few years earlier God gave me a dream about my sister Mary. In it I had a conversation with her about Christ, and further was given a Word from God that He would soon take her home to be with Him. Both aspects of this dream came to pass just as God had shown me.

MORE REVELATIONS FROM GOD
(... a very frightful and disturbing dream)

Going back even further, I recall a most disturbing pair of dreams from God in my early twenties. At the time, I was foolishly caught up in a life of alcohol and just generally living a life of sin. I could have caused the death of someone or myself on more than one occasion while driving drunk, and one of those times did result in a car accident. Thankfully, no one was hurt except a minor injury to myself. God on many occasions in my reckless youthful days, was surely watching over me and He kept me around. God knew I was well aware of what Christ did for me on the cross. As a matter of fact, in my teen years, I had made a profession of faith in Christ, but looking back, I was not sincere in that commitment.

Now in my twenties with a wife and a less than one-year old son, my life was heading straight for hell. Every night was a party with my gang of friends. My wife Joan was not a part of my wild way of living. She just did her best to be the responsible one in our marriage and hope that one day I would wise up. But there I was, living a life totally contrary to what I knew was right and what God wanted. He was not going to let me get away with ignoring Him. God is so full of love and mercy, and He was not willing that I should perish. I had been blessed by God with Joan, and now with a new son. I had been given every opportunity to know God and to be saved, yet I was like the prodigal son, squandering away my life and losing my very soul. The disturbing dreams? I dreamed of my own funeral. There in a room without walls, floor or ceiling, just total blackness and totally alone, I saw my body lying in a black casket. Then I had the same dream a second night. When I awoke, I instantly knew in my heart that it was a serious warning from God that if I did not leave my life of sin and get right with Him, I would soon die and go to hell. I wish God would be so blunt with every lost soul, but that way of getting my attention is apparently not His usual way of doing things. I told a friend about the dreams, and he said something that I believe was given to him by God, albeit I do not think he even realized that what he was saying was from God. I believe God was just using him to speak to me. He simply said, *"Jim, you better do something about it before you dream it a third time and it will be too late for you!"* We read the following in Genesis 41:32: *"The reason the dream was given to Pharaoh in two forms is that the matter has been firmly decided by God, and God will do it soon."* God definitely had my attention, and it would soon become apparent that He had a plan and was preparing me for what was coming.

ANOTHER ONE OF THOSE WARNINGS FROM GOD

Another one of the more startling dreams I received from God was in 1978. I had decided to pack up my family and go to Louisville, Kentucky, settle down there, and look into going to the seminary there to get my education for ministry. I was young and foolish in how I was going about it, but my heart was in the right place. However, God knew I was not going about things in the right order. Just before we left town to head out, I dreamed we were in Louisville, lost at night in a poor side of the city surrounded by apartment projects for the poor. It was a very detailed dream of what the street looked like, right down to the exact intersection. We went ahead anyhow.

Sure enough two nights later, there we were, in our car, sitting in that exact location with every detail of the surroundings exactly as I had seen in my dream. It was a scary part of the city. No doubt it was likely an area filled with drugs, crime, violence, all that stuff. I had never been there before, yet I had seen this exact location in a dream days earlier. The dream was a warning from God not to go to Louisville at that time in my life. I should have obeyed His clear warning. Such things as this should cause any doubters to rethink their views about the reality of God and whether He still shows us things in dreams and visions. He most assuredly does. We did not hang around any longer in Louisville, but headed back home. In later years, I would get my college education through an Assemblies of God college.

THE OMNISCIENT GOD IN ALL THIS

I could add a little thought to that whole Louisville thing. God did not want me to go to Louisville, but in another sense one perhaps could say that later in my life God brought Louisville to me in the person of my wife Sharon. Of course my family and I could never have known back then that in only a few short years later following that experience their mom and my first wife Joan would die. God however did know in advance all of that heartache we would face in losing her, and as much as we all wish she could have lived longer and stayed with us, God had other plans already lined up.

Those plans included my Sharon, who is my wife now, moving from Louisville, Kentucky to Oneonta, NY in 1983, just five years after we had made that trip to Louisville. Two years later in 1985 I moved my family from Johnson City, NY to Oneonta, NY. Following my wife's death in 1987, Sharon and I would providentially meet one-another and get married in 1988. I say all that to show how the omniscient God of all creation knows the end from the beginning, the future from the present. He knew Joan would go home to be with Him in 1987. Just days before she died she told me I would not go unmarried for more than a year or so if she died. I adamantly told her I would never marry another because I loved her so much. I was mistaken, not about my love for her, but about getting married again. She knew me that well and it was her way of saying it was *"OK"* for me to remarry. If anything, my getting remarried was a way of affirming how much I loved being married and how much I believed in God's sacred institution of marriage. Getting remarried was a complement to my first wife as it showed how much my marriage to her meant. She had made me a believer in marriage as our union was such a blessed experience. I find it disheartening these days to see so many couples forego marriage and just live together which is according to God, sexual immorality. By doing that, they are demonstrating a lack of love and commitment to each other and their children, and a disregard for God's plan.

Getting back to my story, God also knew Sharon would move from Louisville after being honorably discharged from three years of service in the Army, to Oneonta, NY when she did. He knew my family would move to Oneonta when we did. He knew I did not belong in Louisville in 1978 but that a woman from Louisville would end up in my life in 1988. None of this happened by chance or outside of God's perfect plan. Those of us who knew Joan cannot fully comprehend how her death at such a young age and which hurt our hearts so much could have been part of God's perfect plan. Nevertheless God was always in control and He had it all lined up to happen as it did. I can apply that same principle to the cancer I went through, or how our ministry has developed. He sees it all in advance and if we faithfully walk with Him and commit each day to Him, we can always take comfort that God is working out His plan for our lives even in those times we may not understand what is happening. As with the dream about Louisville, I could tell of countless other times God has clearly shown me things in dreams and visions and how those things came to pass just as God had shown they would, but enough is said on that for now and I move on. The point is, God does speak and we need to have ears to listen.

Jim Wheeler

THE MAN OF GOD

In a matter of weeks, maybe just days following those dreams of seeing myself dead in a coffin back in 1968, God sent a preacher to my door. I was not the nicest or easiest guy to witness to. I was smack dab in the middle of a battle for my very soul. The devil did not want to let me go, and the good Lord and this man of God did not give me up to the devil and a future in hell. To make another story short, I ended up giving my life to Christ that year of 1968. This time I meant it even if it did take years to really fully live out my new-found Christian life. At least I was now started on the right path. My wife soon did likewise and we were both baptized. In those troubled years away from God, I had even dabbled in the occult and it would take a while for me to let God deal with all the damage such a lifestyle had done to me, but in time, God would truly have my whole-hearted commitment to Him.

10. THE CALL

*"Then I heard the voice of the Lord saying, "Whom shall I send?
And who will go for us?" And I said, "Here am I. Send me!"*
(Isaiah 6:8)

*T*he year was 1975. I was at a Men's Retreat, a weekend gathering
of, if I remember correctly, about fifty Christian men including a few
pastors. The place was at a rural setting in a small town, Maryland
in upstate New York. The *"call"* was so clear in my spirit. During
one of the services in the small church building, as I listened to men
sharing their testimonies, something special was happening to me. I
was hearing the Spirit of the Lord speak to my heart.

Totally unexpectedly, I knew God was calling me right then and
there into the gospel ministry. During a time of fellowship later in
another room, I asked a pastor friend how he knew when God first
called him to preach. His response was simple and to the point: *"I
just knew."* Then he asked me: *"Why do you want to know? Has
God called you to be a preacher?"* I answered: *"Yes."* The next day
following the end of the retreat, I met with another pastor and friend,
the one who had led me to the Lord a few years earlier, to talk with
him about my calling. He gave me some guidance and advice and I
headed back home, thrilled over the divine calling of God upon my
life and the change that had been wrought in my life that weekend at
a Men's Retreat. That moment and event in my life set me on a new
course in my life such as I had never known before. It was not long
before I was officially licensed as a minister of the gospel in 1977.
Later on down the road, I would be ordained as well, and since that

first moment of God's call upon my life, the Lord has given me the privilege of preaching to thousands of people over parts of more than four decades of ministry, preaching in multiple venues in over sixty cities, in several states and Canada as of this writing so far.

9-11 AND A TEST

I take a brief break here from that account of my initial calling to preach. I want to give a little additional detail about what I think is rather significant regarding my ordination to the gospel ministry. As I have mentioned already, I was first licensed to the gospel ministry in 1977. That took place on the same property in Maryland, NY where I had first heard and answered the call of God on my life in 1975. Here I was less than two years later following that call of God, being officially licensed as a minister of the gospel on that same property at a business meeting. That was a major highlight of my life and one I will always treasure. I was with the Southern Baptists at that time in my life. I treasure my years with them and the friends I acquired.

Some years later while still with the Southern Baptists I was officially ordained during a special ceremony at Stamford Baptist Church, in Stamford, NY. That of course was another high point in my life of serving the Lord. Some of my family besides immediate family was there for that occasion including two of my brothers and their wives as well as my mom. What a blessed time that was, and what a privilege it was to be ordained by the same man of God, Waylen Bray, who had in 1969 played so big a part in leading me to Christ. I will forever be thankful to him for all he did in bringing me to that point in my life and the part he had in me becoming an ordained minister. Over the years his Christian walk, his character, his teaching and his influence on my life had discipled me and opened up to me a whole new life with Christ as my Savior and Lord. Continuing with how God brought me along as a minister, in 1996 the Lord led my wife and me to unite with the Assemblies of God.

Soon after beginning to attend Oneonta Assembly of God in Oneonta, NY the pastor there, John Grenier invited me to share a brief message from the pulpit one Sunday night. Although I had already been a credentialed minister since 1977, I felt that I should begin the process of becoming a credentialed minister with the Assemblies of God. I could have simply requested recognition of my ordained status that I already had through Southern Baptists, and it might very well have been accepted. I decided however, to forgo that and instead go the route of doing further ministerial studies through the Assemblies of God Berean Bible College. It seemed more prudent to go through their credentialing process from the ground up and thereby learn their history, polity and theological positions more thoroughly. Going through the further studies Assembly of God had to offer has proved to be a blessing. It would also be necessary that I complete some required courses of study beyond what I already had previously done before coming over to Assemblies of God. Thus I began my new studies and received my Assemblies of God license to preach a little while later. I continued my studies through the Berean Bible College the next couple of year working towards my ordination with Assemblies of God too. That was a tough process. I had to complete some twenty-eight courses of study towards graduating Berean Bible College, not the easiest thing to do so late in my life.

Having already been a minister for many years and previously ordained, I admit there were times I was beginning to wonder if I needed to put myself through such a challenge and if I should have just taken the easier route of seeking recognition of my previous ordination from years earlier. Assemblies of God does offers that route to ministers previously ordained who come into the Assemblies of God fellowship from a different denomination such as I had done. But here I was, taking this route to ordination with Assemblies of God. The course of studies and the many steps to take to be ordained with the AG fellowship was challenging, but somehow in my spirit I believed it was the way the Lord wanted me to do this. Thanks to some encouragement by our church pastor, I pressed forward with the process when it was sometimes tempting to give up.

This is where it got interesting. John Grenier in addition to being the pastor of Oneonta Assembly of God, was also serving as presbyter of our section. He had done much during the past couple years or so to assist me in the process of being credentialed with AG. In the year 2001, I had completed my AG ministerial studies. The date had arrived for my written ordination exam. September 11, 2001. It was going to be another challenge for me to take that test. Would I pass it, and if I did, how well would I do on it? I didn't want to embarrass myself. The date for taking it had been scheduled a while back. September 11, 2001, a date that would be remembered by an entire nation as well as the whole world. America would come under attack as terrorists hijacked four planes, and using three of them like missiles to attack the World Trade towers in New York City and the Pentagon in Washington DC and crashing another in Pennsylvania. Approximately three-thousand people would die that day in that attack. I was well aware of what was happening that day. How would I ever take my mind off of that and think only of the exam? Still, I had a test to take and so as the nation went through the horrifying crisis of that day, I spent several hours behind closed doors prayerfully and with single-mindedness answering questions as best I could. I had to block out of my mind to the best extent that I could, the events that were unfolding in our nation.

Somehow that day amidst the horror of the vicious attack upon our nation, God enabled me to stay the course and complete the task before me. The test completed, I submitted it to the presbyter. Done with the exam I focused my attention on what was happening in America. In the days and weeks ahead I would receive the news from the New York District Assemblies of God that I had passed the exam and was approved for ordination. On May 16, 2002 during the annual district council at an ordination service with hundreds of ministers and guests in attendance in Poughkeepsie, NY I was ordained along with several others.

I will always appreciate the privilege of being ordained to the gospel ministry, including my time as a Southern Baptist minister as well as this later ordination with Assemblies of God. That evening before a huge crowd of my peers in ministry when I was ordained, I recall what one of the ordination leaders said to me as he placed the ordination shawl around my shoulders. He looked at me and said: *"You are a miracle."* The district superintendant anointed my head with oil and spoke some words over me. Years later I can still hear those words *"You are a miracle."* As I think back to those days, it indeed was a time of miracles. In addition to all that was a miracle that day in my life, I think of September 11, 2001 and how in God's timing He had me sitting at a desk taking a test for His purposes and plans in my life while a few hundred miles away evil was temporarily having its way through those attacks of terrorists within our borders. While evil was rearing its ugly head, God was preparing another man to proclaim His gospel message. The Lord continues to call men and women to serve Him. The world may be under attack by evil forces but God is still at work and when all is said and done and the last trumpet has sounded, evil will give way to our soon coming King of Kings and Lord of Lords, Jesus Christ. I took a test during a dark hour in our history. Only by the grace of God was I able to stay the course while terrorists were attacking our nation. That is no accomplishment on my part. That my friend is a miracle of God.

NOT IN MY POWER

Getting back to what I was saying at the beginning of this chapter, only God could take a man who had no previous public speaking experience and prepare him to stand before groups of people and confidently proclaim the message of Christ. In my own power, this never could have happened. It did not happen smoothly over a short time. There were plenty of struggles, stumbles and failures along the way, but in time, God transformed me which he continues to do, and today I continue to answer that call of God that I first heard back in

1975 at a little church in upstate New York. I constantly thank God that He kept me around and was ever so patient with me and willing to use me for His Kingdom work. During the years since that initial call of God, I would have some experience in pastoral ministry which I found I could do a fair job at, but I did not sense that it was my primary calling, so I did not seriously pursue that direction in ministry. As God had to keep reminding me, it eventually become very clear to me that God was calling me to the ministry of an itinerant preaching evangelist, and not so much to pastor a church.

"So Christ himself gave the apostles, the prophets, the evangelists, the pastors and teachers, to equip his people for works of service, so that the body of Christ may be built up until we all reach unity in the faith and in the knowledge of the Son of God and become mature, attaining to the whole measure of the fullness of Christ." (Ephesians 4:11-13)

In studying what the work of the evangelist is and looking at that ministry from an historical and Biblical perspective, it is clear that the evangelist, while especially proclaiming the message of salvation, also over the centuries has been very much about building up the body of Christ, the Church. Over the years, God had increasingly been using me to preach a bolder message to His Church, to challenge God's people to be all that God intends His Church to be. I have felt the call of God to preach the Word of God in the power of His Holy Spirit and to preach the uncompromised, unapologetic message of the gospel to a lost world as well as to preach a message of revival to the Church. I can say with the Apostle Paul that my preaching may not be with *"eloquence or superior"* speech or *"persuasive words"*, but by God's grace it will be *"with a demonstration of the Spirit's power"*. (1 Corinthians 2:1;4) I don't imagine myself to be a great preacher by a long shot, but I do serve a great God who can take the preached Word and powerfully speak through it.

I have had the opportunity to do this not only in the pulpits of many local churches, but through the printed media including at this writing over twenty-five years of having several gospel preaching columns published in a local newspaper. I love writing, and so I really enjoy the opportunity to contribute to that column. God has and still does use me to preach in churches. But He also several years ago, opened up a wide door of ministry to our nation's Adult Care Community, otherwise known as the nursing homes. My first experience of preaching in one of these Adult Care Communities was in 1985. Soon, God used me in another one, and then in 1988, God began using me as well as my wife Sharon to minister regularly at another Adult Care Community in our current home town. Soon, more doors were opening in this mission field of our nation's Adult Care Community, and we were ministering in several more in nearby communities.

GOD'S AMAZING PROVISION

By the early 1990s, we were experiencing God opening the floodgates of ministry opportunity, in both churches and Adult Care Communities, taking us all over central New York and beyond, into places like Louisville, Kentucky, Indianapolis, Indiana, Valley Forge, Pennsylvania, and five cities in Ontario, Canada. In earlier years I had also stood before a huge crowd in a large Church in Danville, West Virginia to briefly speak. God enabled both Sharon and me to attend two Billy Graham Schools of Evangelism in Wheaton, Illinois and Toronto, Canada. On the trip to Toronto, we not only went to the school of evangelism, but we arranged to preach at several places while in Canada.

We calculated that we would need $1300. for this trip which had now evolved into a preaching mission trip, and we committed that need to God, believing He would provide it. We never solicited any support for this mission. The money came in as God supplied. Our home church surprised us with part of that amount which we needed and more came to us from other sources. The morning we were almost ready to go out the door to start on our trip, we had $1200. towards it, just $100. short of what we believed God would supply. A brother in the Lord knocked on our door and handed me an envelope. He said not to open it until we were on the road. Off we went and as we started down the highway, I opened the envelope. There in that envelope was a hundred dollar bill! A note was in the envelope. He had no knowledge of what we had or needed. This dear brother explained that God had told him to give us $100. toward our mission trip. He was not a man with a lot of money. He gave from his heart in obedience to the voice of God. We now had exactly the $1300. that God had shown us we would need for the trip.

That is amazing enough, but God did even more. Somehow even though our expenses were as we expected, we came home with money to spare. When God multiplies money, I do not analyze how He does the impossible. I just accept it and say *"thank you Jesus."* Years ago I discovered that when we give to God, He multiplies our giving back to us, whether it is the giving of our time, our talents or our financial resources. There are too many times for me to recount here where God has amply provided us with what we needed for ministry and everyday life. On a number of occasions, I can recall times when Sharon and I were eating out at local restaurants, just the two of us, and God spoke to some Christian brothers and sisters that were at another table to pay our bill for the meals. On those several occasions, we did not know this until it was time to pay, and the waitress would tell us who paid it after they had left. On another occasion, while we were still eating, a Christian brother walked up to us and shook my hand, leaving a generous check in my hand. There have been several other occasions when Christian brothers and sisters would send us money and tell us God told them to do so. While we have total faith in God to supply our every need, we also know that such faith does not mean we can do something stupid and expect God to provide.

FAITH AND EMPTY GAS TANKS
(...and a little "faith" humor)

One example I share here is from such a time back in 1978. I look back at it now with a sense of humor and I laugh at myself. At that time in my life, I had been very much into exercising faith. One night, as I was driving some friends of ours who were new in the Christian faith back to their home after a church service, I noticed that the needle on our gas gauge was pointing to empty. There we were, heading down a highway. Their home was just a couple miles away. Instead of finding the nearest gas station, I told our friends: *"No worry. I have faith in God. He will make our gas stretch and we will be fine."* I was young and still learning about living *"by faith"*. About a minute or so later, there we were, stalled out on the side of the highway with no gas left in the tank.

I learned a lesson about faith that evening, and while God could have kept our car going, He was not obligated to and I would not have wised up if He had stretched the gas. There are some times when situations do arise where all you have left is faith that God will multiply your resources supernaturally, but there are a lot more times when common sense is the order of the day and you can do what is needed. I needed gas and should have gotten some before heading any further along, but I misunderstood how faith works and I misapplied my faith. God expects us to be smart about what we do. Yes, for sure, there are times when we can do nothing else but exercise faith that God will provide and intervene. That night, all of us in the car actually had a good laugh and I never again ignored a gas gauge reading empty. As I recall that incident, I can still in my memory hear my friends especially having fun with the whole thing and long afterwards, in the days to come, frequently referring back to that night I told them not to worry about it. *We will just have faith in God to get them home. Who needs gas when you have faith?* Wrong conclusion. An empty tank is just that, and a gas station is the answer to such a dilemma.

Now I need to get back to what I was writing about before that story. After a long time of putting it off, God opened the door for me to earn my Ministerial Studies through Berean College *(now Global University)*. My reason for pointing all of this out here is to show what an amazing God we serve. Just look at what he can do with a man who once was headed for hell, but was saved by the grace of God and sent out to preach God's Word. It is all of God. Without Him, I truly could do nothing of any worthwhile significance. God can do wondrous things through any man or woman that will fully commit their life to Him. I am sincerely and always humbled at what God has blessed my life with and how He has chosen to allow me to serve Him.

"THEREFORE GO..."

I had been preaching the gospel since 1975, albeit with some occasional stretches over the years where I was not always fully active in that ministry, but a lot of the time I was. By this second year into the writing of this book in 2013, I will have been at it somewhere around thirty-eight years or so. I already have mentioned a little about my early experience of preaching in the Adult Care Communities. They are a community within our nation's communities. Jesus made it clear that the great commission involved His Church taking the gospel to all nations.

"Therefore go and make disciples of all nations..."
(Matthew 28:19)

Among other meanings, that word *"nations"* can be said to be a word for *"people groups"*. The Adult Care Community is one of those people groups. They are not all sitting around drooling, or in a semi-comatose state as some may think. They are not just living meaningless lives that do not count for anything anymore. They are not all just a sleepy bunch of people whose lives are over-with. They are for a large part, a surprisingly vibrant segment of our society made up of people who have dignity and great worth. They are a people with great potential and are a great resource of experience, faith, and wisdom. I have come to discover that many people, including some pastors, are uncomfortable with ministering to the Adult Care Community, and sometimes the Lord's Church relegates this segment of our community to only a minimal, low-priority field of ministry. The younger generations would do well to learn a great deal from this elderly segment of our population.

We have conducted many church services in the Adult Care Communities where the Spirit of God has been powerfully present and manifested, and where the residents have many times been livelier in their enthusiastic worship than we have seen in some churches. We have come into these places and watched as God has brought out an army of mostly but not all wheelchair-occupied saints of God to gather together for an old-fashion gospel meeting, singing the old camp meeting songs, clapping, shouting amen's and hallelujahs, and giving spontaneous testimonies. Are all the meetings like this? No, of course not, but many are. Are there some who are in semi-awareness states or showing various indications of being very sickly? Yes, there are, but even they are receiving the ministry of the Holy Spirit in these meetings.

We have many times witnessed some residents who we were told had not spoken in months or otherwise were normally unresponsive, coming out of their stupor during our meetings. We have seen Alzheimer's residents and semi-awake residents come out of their illness-related state of mind into near full mental awareness and entering into vibrant singing and praise. Such *"miracles"* are purely the work of God. I tell these people that as long as they still have breath, God is not finished with them on earth yet, and they are of great worth in the work of God's Kingdom. God gave me a calling within a calling. I have spoken of my general call of God upon my life into the ministry of the gospel, and more specifically as that of

an evangelist, but I want to especially speak of the calling of God
to the nursing homes that I was led into beyond preaching in local
churches.

AN ATTIC—A MAP—AND A SPIDER-LIKE WEB VISION

It was 1992. I had already been somewhat exposed to and involved
with ministry to churches since 1976 and to Adult Care Communities
since 1985. We had already seen an increase in doors opening to
ministry in the Adult Care Communities, doing several of these
preaching-points at a number of facilities in our own home town of
Oneonta, and some others in Hobart and Stamford, NY. But this one
summer day of 1992, I was in my office. I was looking at a NY State
map on our wall. I was seeking God about how I felt this desire in
my heart to be used of Him to preach the gospel all over NY State
and beyond. I could not see how it could happen. But I sensed it was
in God's plans that it would happen.

As I sat there, seeking God, and looking at that map, God gave me
a vision of a spider-like web of lines going out in all directions from
my home town of Oneonta to many cities all over central New York
and beyond. I just knew beyond any doubt that God had plans to make
this happen. At the time I could not imagine how it could happen,
but I knew I had received a vision for ministry from God. Without
recounting every detail, let me just say here that over the ensuing
next couple years, this vision began to become a reality. In 1993, God
began presenting us with many more Adult Care Communities to
minister at. We were beginning to travel to more cities, further and
further away, and the people in these places were expressing their
thrill and pleasure over the ministry we were bringing. For a while,
I played an omni-chord loaned to me. Later I purchased another
omni-chord and Sharon played the tambourine. For a while I used
a guitar and played that at our meetings. People in these meetings
were getting saved. In many cases, it seemed God was bringing
old-fashioned Spirit-filled revival right into these facilities. All of it

seemed miraculous. Countless times this ministry was confirmed as being from God and that we were right where He wanted us to be.

Many of our meetings were on Sunday mornings, as well as several during weekdays. We would hold anywhere from eight on up to as many as twelve to thirteen meetings in as many different cities each month. God was bringing the people out in numbers very unusual for a church service at an Adult Care Community. Attendance was sometimes in the 70s, 80s, even mid-nineties. Of course there were many meetings with much smaller attendance numbers, from as few as seven one time, on up to 20, 30, 40, etc. Average attendance has proven over the years to be somewhere in the 30-50 range. We have seen times when meetings would overflow out into hallways or into adjoining rooms. There were times residents would come near the entrance to the meeting rooms and upon seeing our meetings already packed, would either hang out in the hallway to take in the service or they would move on because there was no room for them to attend the meetings. One can only imagine the thrill Sharon and I have had at such a sight.

Today I have a map of NY State with lines drawn from Oneonta outward to all the cities we have ministered at, both in churches and in Adult Care Communities. There have been some sixty or so cities with several preaching locations in those cities, and on into other states and Canada as I previously have mentioned. That vision from God that at the time I could not see how it could ever happen, did indeed become a reality. Praise God who does such wondrous things. We have found over the years that the folks in the Adult Care Communities have time and again expressed how much they love the fact that we will bring them a church service on a Sunday morning. It is God who has led us to do it this way, so we just listen to Him and try to be faithful in following His lead. Also, my calling is that of an evangelist. The very nature of the ministry of an itinerant preaching evangelist necessitates that he be away most Sundays from his home church, to be preaching at other churches. We are careful to value and maintain a healthy relationship with our home church by attending as often as our schedule allows on Sunday mornings when we are not away for preaching engagements elsewhere. But most of our Sundays have had me preaching either at some church or some Adult Care Community.

I no longer solicit invitations to preach at churches. A wise fellow-evangelist who goes by the shortened name of Brother K once told me he never advertizes to get invitations to preach and that God keeps the preaching dates coming. He told me not to shake the trees to get preaching dates, but to just have faith in God to open up doors to preach. Now without me doing anything to get pastors to call me, I am getting increasingly more phone calls to preach at churches. When it happens this way, I can know all the more certain that it is of God's doing. Due to health-related issues of recent times, our schedule has been considerably cut back and I have been doing only a minimal number of preaching engagements on Sunday mornings. If He continues to open the doors, He most assuredly will strengthen me to do it.

As I have been saying, a lot of our ministry is in the Adult Care Community. In the broadest sense of the word, the church is the church wherever God's people gather together to worship Him. The Church in the Bible is not restricted to only referring to the organized local church, but is also the assembling of God's people. In that latter and broadest sense of the word church, our meetings at the Adult Care Communities is church, as it is an assembling together of God's people for the purposes of fellowship, worship, prayer, scripture reading and preaching. When we conduct church services at the Adult Care Communities, one could say we are in fact in or at church, and so all of our Sunday mornings, unless one of us is ill or otherwise occupied, are Sundays that we are at church, whether we are at our home church, ministering at another local church, or at church in an Adult Care Community. I can say with full confidence that God is the One who has sent us to do what we are doing and in the way we are doing it. With that said, the truth is, that over the years most anyone we know in Christian circles and among fellow ministers, have come to be very encouraging and supportive and approving of this ministry and how we do it. It is God who has trained and equipped us to do this ministry. At this writing as we began the New Year of 2013, God had taken us to approximately 800 meetings in the Adult Care Communities plus countless meetings in local churches. Whenever we think about all that God has done, we are totally humbled. It is not about us, but it is all about Him. He has done it all. Every time we arrive in a parking lot before going into a place to minister, I pray the same type of prayer which goes very much like this:

"Lord, thank you for bringing us here safely, and for the privilege of ministering to these people. May all our sound equipment and our voices work perfectly. May every aspect of our meeting go smoothly, be it the scripture reading, the praying, the singing, the sound equipment, the preaching, or the conversation. We ask your anointing upon this meeting, upon the people gathering together for it, and upon us. May we minister in demonstration of your Holy Spirit's power, and in the love, compassion, gentleness and joy of Jesus Christ. May what you do through us make an eternally significant difference in the lives of those we minister to today. May what we do today matter. Now Lord Jesus, give us confidence and boldness and lead the way. It is your ministry. May we follow you and go with you into this meeting. Have your way and do what you want done. In Jesus' Name we pray. Amen."

ON THE *"MISSION FIELD"*

For much of our years in ministry, especially once we really got into going full-throttle in the ministry to churches and also the Adult Care Communities, and had committed ourselves to a full-time ministry, we started putting out a ministry newsletter on a regular basis. It proved to be one way of sharing what God is doing and giving people the opportunity to keep us in prayer as we minister. I remember when I first made it known to friends and family that I had resigned from my full-time secular job to be full-time in ministry. I knew the time had come. We had sought direction from God about this for a long time. We knew we needed to be at a certain point financially to where it would be clear God was saying it was time. We knew it would involve both faith in God that He would provide and also some evidence that He was opening the way to do so. We needed a specific minimal level of financial resources to live on. Faith in God does not require that we forego good common sense. We would go full-time when it was clear that God had opened the way. God provided exactly that minimum amount of financial income we calculated we needed before taking this step. When the time was clearly right, I resigned my full-time secular job and we hit the road running, dramatically increasing our ministry itinerary, and having the time of our lives enjoying the blessings of God and the joy of being free to give full attention to ministry. Someone once said in jest to me that I was *"having too much fun"* doing our ministry. Soon, the Lord was increasing His financial blessings upon us, and I was earning my living from preaching the gospel, as the Bible says it should be, and I never had to solicit financial support. I just had to give my full attention to the gospel and God made it clear I was to have adequate provision to do so.

"... the Lord has commanded that those who preach the gospel should receive their living from the gospel. ...when I preach the gospel, I cannot boast, since I am compelled to preach. Woe to me if I do not preach the gospel!" (1 Corinthians 9:14; 16)

'ON THE ROAD AGAIN'

I remember one day right after we had gone full-time in ministry, and as we were hitting the interstate highway to go to a preaching-point, we were so excited to move forward on this great venture in a full-time way. We thought of the song by Willie Nelson, *'On the*

Road Again', and half-jesting, that became our little theme as we took to the road in ministry. Sometimes it seems like God was just giving us additional confirmation as while going on the road to a preaching engagement, that song would often inevitably be playing on the radio right as we started out. And we have certainly many times over, been on the road again probably at least a thousand times, to carry the message of the gospel to many places. What a ride it has been. God's plans are so much bigger and greater than we could ever have done on our own. The longer we continued in this ministry, especially to the nursing homes, the more God was opening our hearts to minister to hurting humanity. My cancer that intruded upon my life in 2010 only expanded my heart for others. If I could use one primary word to define what God has laid on my heart as a minister, it is to be an encourager.

A *"MISSIONARY"*?

When I first answered God's call to the ministry, I never really thought in terms of being a missionary. I still do not, and I am not officially designated or appointed as such. But of course the great commission of our Lord to preach the gospel is all about a mission and every Christian in the broadest sense of the word is called to be a missionary via his or her being a living witness to Christ's love and saving power. With that said, God does also give specific calls to some to officially be missionaries in a specific mission field. Along the way over the years, my wife and I began to find ourselves being introduced by some churches and pastors, by their initiative, not ours, as missionaries to our nation's Adult Care Community. I was used to frequently being introduced as an evangelist, but not as often as a missionary. This caught us by surprise and this was of course none of our doing. We have never identified ourselves as missionaries. I was never formally commissioned by any religious body as a missionary, and I do not seek to be. My primary calling which I was officially ordained as is that of evangelist. But even that title is something I really do not seek or desire. It's just useful in that it helps people to know what my place as a minister is in the body of Christ. Jesus encouraged his followers to be careful not to desire to be addressed by titles.

One time in the gospels, someone was heard to say to one of Christ's disciples something along the line of, Sir, we would see Jesus. I recall that statement being on a pulpit in a church I had preached at, and it was a good reminder that it is all about Jesus and nothing about me. That is really what this is about that I am discussing here. I think it is important. I especially am drawn to talk about this as I recall having been introduced as a missionary or an evangelist or even Reverend. I can graciously accept such introductions if someone chooses to do so, but my personal preference is to simply be addressed as *"Jim"*. I do feel strongly that the Lord's Church would do well to be careful about elevating its ministers to greater heights than God intended and be more careful to draw our attention to Jesus rather than emphasize ministerial titles so much. When I first became an ordained minister, a few people asked me how they should address me. Some said, *"Should I call you Reverend?"* Others asked if they should address me as *"Pastor"*. I simply responded that *"My name is Jim. Call me Jim"*. Likewise I generally address my fellow-minister friends in ministry by their first name or sometimes prefaced with *"Brother" or "Sister"* just as they address me these same ways. I just find that in the camaraderie that I share with fellow ministers, it's more common for ministers to address one-another by name, so without much thinking about it I tend to do that.

I guess I've said all this because I am just especially concerned that we be careful to not put anyone on a pedestal. When all is said and done the bottom line is that only Jesus should be exalted. With that said I do also recognize that the Bible tells us His Pastors are worthy of double honor. *"The elders who direct the affairs of the church well are worthy of double honor, especially those whose work is preaching and teaching."* (1 Timothy 5:17) Fellow ministers do have my utmost respect. Personally I am probably being overly cautious here in this discussion to say that I encourage people to avoid using titles when referring to me. I'm *"Jim"*. That's good enough for me.

Yes, Sharon and I do minister in a very real mission field, that of one of our nation's greatest generations as the author Tom Brokaw called them in one of his books that I read. However, when all is said and done in regard to titles, we are still just Jim and Sharon, and we are humbled and so grateful to God who would allow us to serve in this special mission field that is made up of some of America's finest and most faithful saints of God as well as to many churches.

GOD'S PROVISION

Another important thing I would mention here is that long ago I determined that I would never charge a certain amount of money to preach. I do receive generous financial remuneration from preaching engagements at churches, and that is God's plan. The Lord has provided us very well in the financial support we have received from ministering in churches. I however have never required a certain minimal amount of money to preach. Churches just normally do give financial gifts to God's ministers who preach the Word of God.

INTEGRITY

"May integrity and uprightness protect me, because my hope is in You." … *"In my integrity you uphold me, and set me in your presence forever." Psalm 25:21; 41:12*

I would emphasize that anyone aspiring to be in the gospel ministry make it one of their highest goals to be a person of integrity in every aspect of both their personal life and their public ministry. Character needs to be a high priority in the list of a minister's qualifications. It is a basic quality to build everything else on as success depends on it. Financial and moral integrity is especially important. Integrity also involves consistency. Keeping one's commitments is a very important matter, and to the best of my ability I am confident that I have demonstrated such commitment and consistency. There are times when either unforeseen or unpreventable situations arise which temporarily can interfere with things we commit to. It has happened to me a few times since 2010, especially due to my cancer-related health events when I have had to cancel preaching engagements.

Integrity is at times sorely missing among some ministers. I voice here my dismay with what I too often see and hear on some of the Christian TV networks. I have often while surfing TV channels, found myself stopping as I come across some preacher who gets my attention with a powerful message he is in the midst of. I have at such times often been enthralled with what sounded like great preaching by some big-name evangelist on TV, only to be disappointed as the preacher would inevitably wind up his message with a request for an inordinate amount of money from his listeners. Such behavior brings Christian TV ministry into disrepute and turns multitudes away from Christ, and also dupes many others out of their money as they get fooled and fleeced by these misleading ministers. I have also seen this happen on a lesser scale in smaller venues when occasionally a pre-packaged gospel presentation of music and preaching by some visiting itinerant ministers in local churches ended up being more about selling their music CDs, and other articles. A great message in song and the preached word ends up being spoiled by turning the event into a sales pitch and setting up tables to sell their wares. There are times and places where selling books, etc. are appropriate, but that should be the rare exception.

As for evangelists having a minimal financial remuneration requirement before accepting a preaching invitation by a church, I feel strongly that there should never be such a requirement. The Lord has led me to always make it my practice to avail myself as an evangelist to churches without requiring a certain guaranteed amount of money to come. God always ends up meeting all of our financial needs without me requiring anything. Sometimes I have thought churches were almost too generous in what they have given me, but mind you I never turn it down. It is their opportunity to bless God's servants and to be blessed in giving, and also they are following the guidelines of God's Word in giving financial support to the preacher. As for our ministry to the Adult Care Communities, we go out of our way to let them know we do not expect to be paid to bring our ministry to them. We stress that what we do is purely a volunteer-type ministry at no cost. Even with that said, many of the Adult Care Communities' administrators and residents insist on and delight in giving us financial remuneration. When that happens, we accept their generosity and we know it blesses them to give, so we do not refuse their gift. God from the very outset of His calling upon my life, made it clear that He would meet our every need, and He has and continues to do so.

"If I preach voluntarily, I have a reward; if not voluntarily, I am simply discharging the trust committed to me. What then is my reward? Just this: that in preaching the gospel I may offer it free of charge, and so not make full use of my rights as a preacher of the gospel." (1 Corinthians 9:17-18)

"Not that I desire your gifts; what I desire is that more be credited to your account. I have received full payment and have more than enough. I am amply supplied,..... And my God will meet all your needs according to the riches of his glory in Christ Jesus." (Philippians 4:17-19)

FURTHER MOTIVATION TO CARE

As I write about our ministry to the Adult Care Community, I have tried to and continue to insert where appropriate, a few bits of advice on how to conduct such a ministry, or to share some helpful ideas we have learned along the way. Perhaps there may be someone who might find the thoughts I share to be helpful in their own ministry to the Adult Care Community. Ministering to these precious saints of God and senior members of our population has helped in opening my heart up to hurting people. When my cancer intruded upon my life and I went through all the pain and difficulties of that crisis, it just all the more gave me a greater heart to reach out to the nursing home residents and try to lift their spirits through ministry. So sharing the story of this ministry has become very much a part of my own experience with cancer. I've probably said this before in previous chapters but I say it again. It has given me a greater level of compassion and motivation to serve in this mission field. That is a large part of why I have included the story of our ministry in this book along side of my story of my cancer experience. It is all about the one theme of a great God who has been involved in our lives, whether being there with us in our journey through cancer or with us in ministering to others who are hurting in places like the nursing homes.

FROM VISION TO MESSAGE

I have written some on visions and dreams from God. Before moving into more detail about the Adult Care Communities ministry, I want to just touch a little more on some things the Lord showed me over the years. I remember one such time back in 1976. I had only recently begun to preach. I was working on a sermon and had been trying to find a certain verse in the Bible that I had vaguely remembered which I wanted to use in my sermon, but I could not remember where it was. I went to sleep that night, not yet having that verse in my notes. I had a dream. In the dream, the very exact verse was brought to my attention, book, chapter, and verse. A very precise direction to where it was. I sensed that God was speaking to me and telling me exactly where it was. I woke up and immediately opened my Bible to that location. It was the very verse of scripture I had been seeking. That night, I did not need a Bible concordance. God was literally my Concordance as He showed me the verse location.

JESUS IS WORTHY

I have had several similar revealings, if I can call them that, from God in dreams and visions since then. But one in particular really got my attention and I want to share it here. This happened a few years ago. I had just barely gotten to bed. It seemed like I had only been in bed a few minutes. The room was totally dark and Sharon was sound asleep. As best I can surmise, I was on the edge of sleep, somewhere between fully asleep and yet not quite there. I really to this day cannot say for certain whether I was asleep or awake. Suddenly I was seeing before me the cross of Christ outside Jerusalem, Israel. I felt as though I had been transported back in time and to that very place. There on the cross was a vision of Jesus nailed to it. I will call this a *vision* as that is the best that I can determine it to have been. Obviously Jesus has never gone back on the cross again. The scene seemed so real. A darkness was upon the scene. The sky was blackened with clouds. I could sense commotion and activity all around the area where the cross stood.

In the vision, I found myself on my knees at the foot of the cross, only a couple feet away. I was looking up into the face of Jesus who was looking down towards me. His eyes were piercing, seemingly into my very soul. I saw in those eyes a warmth, a love, a heart of amazing compassion. Jesus was beaten and bleeding and His eyes were wet with tears. He had the appearance of a rugged but hurting Man. In the vision I began to tremble and weep uncontrollably at this sight of my Savior who hung there for my sins. He looked straight into my eyes and simply said these five words: *"Jim, I am worth it."* I then found myself fully awake. I felt like I had seen this as a vision as I lay on my side near the edge of my bed. It did not seem like it had been a dream. Rather, I had the sense that it had been a vision and that I had been seemingly transported back in time and space to the foot of Calvary. Whether a dream or a vision, it was absolutely, unquestionably from the Lord. While of course Jesus was not on the cross again and I was not literally transported back in time and to the

179

location of the crucifixion, it was most definitely a scene that God saw fit to give me a picture of and to actually speak to me. He said: *"Jim, I am worth it."*

When I fully awoke, I was still trembling and weeping. This vision had profoundly affected me and shaken me. I thought for a while as I lay there, about what had just happened. I eventually went to sleep for the night, but I knew I'd had a very special visitation of the Lord. Morning came and my mind immediately turned to the previous night's startling vision. From the moment I awoke that morning, I began thinking about what the vision and those five words from Jesus meant. Right away, in rapid order, God began telling me the meaning. I hurried to my office, sat down at my computer, and began typing what God was giving me. It was all coming so clearly and so quickly, that I had all I could do to just keep up with it. In very short order, God had given me a message to preach. I was on schedule to preach that very evening at our home church. I will not attempt to detail the whole message that God gave me from that vision, but the basic outline was as follows: *"I am worth": The Cost / The Love / The Worship / The Living or Dying for / The Waiting for."* Jesus was saying of Himself that He is worth whatever it costs us to follow Him; He is worth our love for Him; He is worth our worship of Him; He is worth our living or dying for Him; He is worth our waiting for Him … He is coming back! And the other side of this message is that Jesus says to us, we are worth to Him the price He paid for our sins to save us. Of course God gave me more detail for my complete sermon outline, but that is the general idea of the message God gave me through a vision, and is simply titled: *"I Am Worth It."* Of course I would not preach a message only based on a vision. It would be a Bible-based message and God gave me for a text, the following passage of scripture:

"But whatever were gains to me I now consider loss for the sake of Christ. What is more, I consider everything a loss because of the surpassing worth of knowing Christ Jesus my Lord, for whose

sake I have lost all things. I consider them garbage, that I may gain Christ..." (Philippians 3:7-8)

That evening, I changed my planned sermon and I preached this message that only the night before, God had given me through a heaven-sent vision of our wonderful Savior who is worth our total commitment. I recall that it was an especially moving evening as God spoke to the hearts of those few that were gathered that evening to hear the message. I would in the following months and years, have opportunity to take this message to many more places and people as God opened the door to preach it. I am also reminded through that vision, that Christ suffered the cruelty of that cross for me and for all of humanity. It helps put my own suffering from cancer into perspective as I realize my Savior went through vastly more than I or any of us ever will. He is able to understand what we go through. That vision from God has especially stayed with me and left an unforgettable experience in my mind and heart. I felt like I had seen Jesus face to face, yet I know in actuality, He is in Heaven at the right hand of the Father, and one day, when my life is finished here, I will leave the confines of earth and truly meet my Savior face to face.

'What a day that will be when my Jesus I shall see, and I look upon His face, the One who saved me by His grace; when He takes me by the hand, and leads me through the promised land, what a day, glorious day that will be.' (*'What a Day That Will Be' Used by permission*)

BE READY IN SEASON AND OUT OF SEASON

I think this is also a good place to share another remarkable experience of God doing something extraordinary several years ago. Such an experience as I recount here ought to help convince doubters that God's people still *hear* from the Lord. My wife and I were on our way to a church. While in the car sitting on the passenger's side, I had a sudden inspiration to jot down some brief, rough notes. I grabbed a small note pad and pen from the glove department and started writing as I sensed the Holy Spirit speaking to me. I had no idea why at that particular moment God would give me these thoughts to jot down, but in obedience to His leading I did it. By the time I got to the church parking lot, all I had was a very few quickly written notes. We did not say anything about this to anyone at church. During the worship time, the pastor came up behind me and asked if I had a message to bring to the people. I said something to the effect that yes I did, and he invited me to preach that morning. A few minutes later I was behind the pulpit preaching what God had given me only moments ago. This was nothing short of the divine hand of God at work. God gave me a message to preach and then spoke to the pastor, impressing upon his spirit that he was to go to me and ask if I had a word from God. God had spoken to him that I indeed had that message. It was a moment to fully trust God's leading. The Lord gave me the words to speak and it went very well. Afterwards, a leader in the church came up to me and told me he now knew for certain that I had a divine calling upon my life to preach. That whole experience was truly a *wow* moment as God clearly spoke and moved that day in a wonderful way through not only me but through the pastor who was prepared and sensitive to hearing and responding to the prodding of the Holy Spirit.

PLACING A CALL TO GOD

While still in the process of preparing this book for final steps before submitting it to a publisher, Sharon happened to come across a journal from a few years ago. In it we had kept a written record of a prayer plan we had committed ourselves to. For lack of a better wording, we titled it *'Storming the Church Doors'*. That might at first sound kind of like something negative or as though we were launching an attack of some sort against the Lord's Church. Of course that was not even remotely the intent of that wording. We had sensed that the

Lord wanted us to begin a special season of intense prayer for God to open more doors for me to preach. He had always opened many doors up to that point and I wasn't lacking for preaching invitations. But at that particular period of time we just felt that God was especially impressing upon us the idea that He wanted us to seek Him in this way. Our calling this prayer exercise *'Storming the Church Doors'* had the meaning of coming against any demonic or any other kind of forces or obstacles that might be trying to hinder God's calling upon my life as an itinerant preacher. It wasn't aimed at Churches or Pastors. We probably could have come up with better wording than those four words, but that is what came to mind as we prepared to begin that special time of prayer. I guess it runs along similar lines of when we hear someone say they are storming heaven in prayer. It's all about calling upon God to hear and answer our prayers. It's about getting serious with our praying.

This was 2005 that we recorded this in that journal. I cannot tell how many times we have seen God open doors to preach following praying for pastors to hear the heart of God and be moved to give me a call if God is speaking to them about that. He has done it too many times to recall here, but I mention just a couple examples. In the journal we wrote down different churches and the names of the pastors to lift up in prayer on certain days. One was September 15, 2005. Without me naming the specific church or pastor here in this book, we asked God to remove any obstacles that might be standing in the way of His will and for the pastor to call me and invite me to be on his calendar to preach. In my spirit I had sensed God saying to me that He wanted me to preach there.

This is where it gets amazing and wonderful. Only thirty minutes after we finished praying, that pastor called me and I had a preaching date. Another example happened in that same week. It was September 18, 2005, only three days later. Following praying for another pastor of another church to invite me to preach, I got a phone call the very next day from him to invite me to preach. To make it all the more amazing, he needed a preacher to preach for him within twenty-four hours due to a personal emergency in his life that had suddenly come up. God knew in advance way before we began this special season of prayer, that He wanted me to be in these very places at these exact times to preach. That is just a small sampling of how God brought His plans together during that season of prayer. He has done this sort of thing time and again over the years. We never cease to be amazed at what God does. I share all this to bring glory to our God and to encourage others to believe in the power and importance of prayer. We placed a call to God and He answered. That's a large part of what prayer is about. He doesn't put us on hold or take our messages on an automated answering machine. We get Him, not a machine. It's a direct line to Almighty God. *"Let us then approach God's throne of grace with confidence."* (Hebrews 4:16*)*. His line is never too busy to take our calls and He never refers our calls to another party. *"Hear my prayer, O Lord."* (Psalm 39:12)

I could tell of many other instances where God has orchestrated situations and caused a chain of events to fall perfectly into place, leaving no doubt whatsoever that the Holy Spirit's activity was clearly evidenced, right down to the minutest details, even seconds where the timing had to be of divine design. I will just share one more of those instances here. For reasons I need not go into detail about here, I needed to see two particular people in my circle of fellow Christian brethren about a very important matter. It kept on my mind for several days. One day my wife and I were driving down Main Street in our home town. I sensed a very strong prodding from the Holy Spirit to drive to our home church. I prayed as we drove, that God would arrange it such that the perfect setting would come about for this situation. We arrived there and in perfect timing right down to seconds, things turned out exactly as I had prayed for and even better. These very two people showed up there. No one else. Just those two. It turns out that one of them had only moments ago considered going somewhere else but something in his spirit told him to forego that plan and come to the church property at that time. Many detailed things had to happen for this to come together so precisely. It worked out to perfection and we knew it was totally brought about by the divine hand of God. If any of us involved had altered out plans by mere seconds, we would not have met and things would not have transpired as they did. Now that is undeniably all God.

11. A JOURNAL FOR A JOURNEY

"But you, LORD, sit enthroned forever;
your renown endures through all generations." (Psalm 102:12)

"I thought, 'Age should speak;
advanced years should teach wisdom.'" (Job 32:7)

VISIBLE RESULTS

*A*s I begin to write this chapter, I am nearing the completion of the latest journal of six journals so far, that I use for the purpose of keeping a record of my preaching engagements. As much as anything, this chapter might very well be seen as a chapter on *"How to Minister to the Hurting"*. Having experienced what I have most recently gone through with cancer since 2010, as well as some other difficult events in my own life in previous years, I believe God has enabled me to have a heart for others who suffer or face any number of the myriad of challenges life can throw at us. That being said, I write this chapter not only to share the ministry God has called us to, but out of a sense of wanting to encourage others who need encouragement. Although in my earlier years I had been preaching on and off going back to 1975, I did not begin keeping a journal of my preaching-points until twenty-two years later into ministry in 1997.

Those six journals I have thus far compiled add up to several hundred entries of preaching dates since that year of 1997 when I first began keeping track of where we have ministered. When we began doing a full schedule of Adult Care Communities in addition to the churches I had been preaching at, I felt like it would be wise to keep track of where we had been, and when and what I preached. It is also a way of sharing what God has done in these meetings and how He has touched lives. Perhaps it may even prove somehow to help show others some practical hints on how to minister to the elderly population in our nation's Adult Care Community or for that matter, to show concern for anyone that is hurting in any way and in any walk of life. I will attempt here in this chapter to glean from our journals and summarize some of our experiences and high points that we have seen in our travels, as well as offer insights on doing this kind of ministry which we have gained along the way. In this chapter, out of the approximately eight-hundred meetings we did in Adult Care Communities as of 2013, I will briefly mention just a few highlights from a few of them.

In my experiences in ministry, both in the Adult Care Communities as well as in the general population, I have seen anxiety, fear, loneliness, depression, hopelessness, and many other emotions in abundance. Hopefully and prayerfully, it is a book that can inspire others and reveal the greatness of the one true God who cares and is able to do great things in lives that are willing to be surrendered to Him. This book is the account of where God has taken my wife and me in recent years, whether it was me in an intensive care unit facing very possible, even likely death from advanced cancer, or the thrill of standing before a crowd in a church or of a congregation in an Adult Care Community for an old-fashioned gospel meeting, or witnessing Almighty God manifesting His power and presence through miraculous acts. Wherever God has taken us on our journey, the one constant in the entire journey has been that we have never traveled the journey alone. God has been with us every step of the way.

"Never will I leave you; never will I forsake you." (Hebrews 13:5)

The two scripture passages I have at the beginning of this chapter are texts I used in a couple of my columns that were published in our local newspaper in the religion section. Those particular columns dealt with subjects related to our ministry to the older generation. The column using the text from Job 32:7 was titled: *'Generations must begin to listen to, and respect each other'*. The column using the text from Psalm 102:12 was titled with the heading: *'Adult Care Community has much to offer'*. In the one, I spoke of the mutual respect generations, both the young and the elderly, need to have for one-another, and of the wisdom, experience and faith the younger generation can glean from listening to the older generation. In the other column, I wrote of some additional thoughts on our nation's older generation and of their value to society. In that column I included some thoughts from a couple of America's great citizens. I refer to one here. Robert Browning spoke of the invitation to join him in the process of growing older. He really believed the best was still ahead and our later years are what our earlier part of our life was preparing us for.

SOME DETAILS ABOUT WHAT AND HOW WE DO OUR MEETINGS
*(The * symbol is placed next to the samplings of ministry points I will share in this chapter)*

"Amen": It was at the University Heights adult care facility in Loudenville, NY. Forty-eight people and one dog in attendance. The dog's name was Bandit. We would many times over in our travels, have cats, dogs, fish, parakeets and other assorted birds at our meetings. They try to make these places as comfortable and home-like as possible. Animals are said to be very therapeutic for the residents. At one place, a parakeet said *"Amen"* while I was preaching! I am not and would not make this stuff up. On one occasion, Sharon had a severe allergic attack from a resident cat that got too close to her and she had to leave the meeting to get treatment and some air. Still, the animals are a nice touch and usually no problem. When I give

attention to the cats or dogs by petting them, etc., it seems to please the residents that I take the time to do that.

When we come into one of these places, we do not come with any formality or put on any overly pious appearance. We come in and from the start, we keep a very down-to-earth, friendly and personal approach. Even how we dress matters. I usually do not wear a tie or suit coat. Semi-casual is best. We make the people feel comfortable and at ease right away. Small talk, a sincere smile, words of encouragement, a touch on a hand or a shoulder, an interest in what they want to talk about and in what is going on in their lives. We are always careful to try and show genuine concern for what they are going through. If someone specifically asks for prayer, we usually offer right on the spot to quietly pray for them, and in a way that does not disrupt things or draw other resident's attention. When we first arrive, we set up our sound and other equipment which includes an amplifier, two mics, a CD player and CDs, tambourine, extension cords, my Bible, song programs, bottled water for us *(those little things matter)*, a stool, etc. We bring everything we need neatly organized on one wheeled luggage cart. We bring an extra CD player kept in our trunk of our car just in case the one we bring in happens to not work. That has on occasion happened. In the winter, we cover our sound equipment up in the trunk with a sleeping bag to help insure the cold will not affect the equipment.

Being prepared for every possible situation is our plan. I am just sharing some very practical steps we take to do this ministry. These things may be helpful information for someone who may sense God is calling them into a similar ministry. We even have an attractive custom-made slip-over cover that fits neatly over our entire luggage cart so that it does two things: One it keeps our equipment dry if the weather is bad, and two it looks neater as we enter into an Adult Care Community facility. We think every little thing we can do to enhance the appearance of what we do matters. Along the way, we have also learned not to refer to the people in the Adult Care Communities as *"patients"* or *"wheelchair-bound"*. Of course in some respects some of them are patients at times, but much more than that, they are residents of a community within a community, and most of them while using a wheelchair for convenience are not actually wheelchair-bound. Little things like these bits of information matter if you are going to enter these Adult Care facilities and minister to people. All we need from the activity director is a small table and an outlet. I do not require that they supply a speaker's podium or any of their own sound system.

The activity workers turn the meeting completely over to us and they usually sit in on the meeting. It helps a lot in that when we come into an Adult Care Community, we come in with total confidence that we know what to do without having to ask any staff to instruct us as to what to do. That confidence is evident to them and they know they don't have to do anything except bring the residents in. Occasionally a resident may have a sudden need and the activity worker is available to tend to their need. Sometimes alarms go off or other things happen that could potentially be disruptive in the meeting room, but we never let any disruption, resident's comments or other activity interrupt what we are doing, unless of course there arises a real emergency. We maintain a smooth flow of the service. I preach free-standing, very seldom using a podium that some places have set up. That way, I am able to move around more and get closer to the people. It contributes toward making the residents feel more casual and closer to the preacher. It is almost like casually hanging out in their living room for a visit.

Sometimes while visiting with the residents before the meeting gets started, I might sit in a chair next to the people that are gathered and just make small talk. It is another way of getting close to the residents and making them feel comfortable with us. We arrive in the parking lot with enough time to pray before going in. It takes about fifteen minutes to hand out music programs to the people and to set up our equipment. We never behave as though we are on a schedule to be someplace else. When the activity worker indicates it is OK to begin the meeting, we go ahead, and while the staff is bringing in the residents we always let them know we are not in any hurry and that we can start whenever they want us to. A lot of times they will tell us to go ahead as they continue to bring in a few more residents during the meeting. If more come in, we often have taken the time when possible, to hold up the service long enough to take a song program to them. We do not want to leave anyone out of what's going on and each resident deserves personal attention.

OUR PROGRAM

We put together a four-page folded song program in large print to give the people before the service begins. Our program is titled on the front page: *'In the Spirit of the Old-time Gospel Camp Meeting'*. We came upon that phrase after several times of hearing residents remark that our meetings reminded them of days gone by such as when they went to old-fashioned tent-revival meetings or camp meetings to sing and hear the gospel preached. Our printed program includes a photo of Sharon and me, the scripture verse John 3:16 next to a picture of the Bible, our names, home and email address. Also along with these things on the front page we have these words: *'On the road with the Gospel to one of our Nation's Greatest Generations in the Adult Care Community'*. Our back page includes the song title of our special, my sermon title and scripture text, the closing song, the license number for using the songs, and at the bottom, our final closing words to the people which says: *'Thanks for having us today. May God bless you as you continue on life's journey and as you serve and praise our Lord Jesus Christ.'* We do not collect the programs back from the residents. We let them know they can keep them. One, it would not be healthy to hand out used programs in another meeting somewhere else, and two, the residents often express their pleasure in being able to keep the program.

Along that line of thinking about what is healthy or unhealthy, another very important thing we do is in most cases we barely touch the resident's hands and we wash our hands before and after the meetings. It is not just about protecting our selves from transmittable illness, but about protecting the residents' health too. Of course we also trust God to put a divine hedge of protection around us and the residents when we are ministering in the Adult Care Communities. This is especially important considering how often we bring meetings to these places and there are always a lot of potentially contagious illnesses there. As for touching the residents, sometimes there will be some who just do want to give a hardy handshake. But whenever we can, we try to keep physical contact to a minimum. A light touch on a hand or a shoulder can mean a lot to a resident. We give our attention to all the residents that are at the meetings. Most of them are alert, but a few will be only semi-aware of what is going on or unable to respond vocally or physically. But we still touch their hand or shoulder and speak a few brief words of encouragement to them. Even just eye contact and a smile goes a long way for them.

Including the forty-minute program plus our set-up time and take-down time of equipment and shaking hands and talking with the people afterwards, we are usually inside for about one hour. We have a basic forty-minute program which includes introducing ourselves and greeting the people with some light-hearted small talk, then I read an opening scripture, usually from a Psalm about worship, then Sharon brings an opening prayer. From there we enter into a time of worship, singing along with music CDs. We do four or five songs with them plus a special that we sing for them. Then I preach a brief message from the Bible. We sing a closing song. Sharon shares for a brief couple minutes something from her heart and I close with prayer. I have discovered that these folks do not necessarily always want a soft, weak sermon, and they enjoy something that is more than just a short devotional. They enjoy a strong, uncompromised message being preached. For many of them, it is what they grew up around and they want the gospel preached in all its power. Music is important to them, and they love to sing.

Enthusiastic Crowd: At this meeting in Loudenville, NY that I mentioned, the room was overflowing from the turnout. They flowed out into the hallway. Very enthusiastic crowd. Very attentive as well. Many were clapping their hands and stomping their feet to the music. At these meetings we have had residents raising their arms in worship, shouting glory to God, even some bursting into exuberant praise and some even speaking in unknown tongues as the Holy Spirit gives the utterance that the Bible refers to. Also we allow time for spontaneous testimonies which sometimes happens. Time and again, without exaggeration probably hundreds of times, we've had residents tell us to *"keep doing what we are doing, and that we are doing what God wants"* or similar words along those lines. These encouraging words serve as countless confirmations to the fact that we are right where God wants us in this mission field. We come to be a blessing to the people but they bless us back so much.

JOURNALS

I have laid out in front of me the journals we have kept of our travels since 1997 when I began to keep a record. I wish I had kept journals further back when I first started preaching in 1975. I find it a challenge to know where to begin or what to share in this part of the book. It is simply too much to include all the high points. I will attempt to just mention a few excerpts and information. One resident at one meeting said this to me following the message: *"It is good that you brought a strong message. We really needed one that was forceful."* I have heard similar sentiments many times. I just simply preach. If they receive the message as powerful, that is just something God's Spirit does as He anoints His Word. Ministry in a nursing home is not just preaching a five-minute devotional to the residents, bringing two hymns, spending ten to fifteen minutes maximum and considering that to be a church service. I say that only as a word of encouragement to those who would aspire to minister to these dear people.

DIVINE HAND OF GOD

In 1992, my wife Sharon took a job at an Adult Care Community near our home. The activity director got wind of the fact that her husband was a minister. One thing led to another and that nursing home was asking us to bring our gospel meetings to their residents. We ministered there for several years as a result of that invitation. Seeing the divine hand of God in the calling to this mission field has been evident throughout the years in so many ways. In the case of this particular nursing home that Sharon worked at, it became clear to us that God had His hand in it from the beginning. He no doubt brought it to pass that she would be employed there primarily for His purpose of bringing us into a situation that would lead us to minister there. She was employed there for only three months and was trained as a nurse's aide, one more accomplishment I can add in this book to her impressive resume'. She soon came to the realization however, that due to her ongoing difficulties from her service-connected disabilities from her Army years, she could not lift residents or do other strenuous activity so she quit that job. When all was said and done, we realized God never did have her get hired there for employment so much, but rather to bring about our preaching ministry there.

WHATEVER PLACE GOD SAYS TO GO

My wife and I have felt it is a privilege from God to minister to the Adult Care Community and we thank God that He has given us this opportunity. If God had instead called me to Pastor a church, I would not have thought such a calling to be of greater or lesser significance. I treat my two-fold calling to the Adult Care Community and my calling as an evangelist to the churches as each of equal significance. Every avenue of ministry that God calls His church to is significant. Whether it is a jail ministry, Adult Care Communities, itinerant evangelists, being a pastor of a church, missionaries, ministry to the homeless, etc., all of it is vital in the work of God's Kingdom. Much of Jesus' ministry was to individuals in one-on-one encounters.

I had several opportunities to pastor churches, but I resisted those open doors because God consistently reminded me that He has called me to minister in a field of ministry that takes me and requires me to go to many places rather than to one local church, so that is what I do. Thus far God has not put it in me to be ministering in one place to one fellowship of believers, and at my age I am not expecting Him to call upon me to change course in ministry. While my ministry is an exciting one in that it has taken me to many places and to thousands of people, still there are times I have thought about being a pastor where I could serve in one place. It would provide the benefit of getting close to one local group of believers and not having the stresses of so much travel. Yet God instead puts it into my heart to be on the road ministering in many different places. I am thrilled about the place God has called me to.

As I think about the ministry in the Adult Care Communities, I have found that there is a false idea out there that residents in Adult Care Communities have to be treated like they are somehow no longer mentally mature adults, and people visiting them end up all too often talking to them like they are children. They are adults and for the majority of them, they are not as delicate as we might think, and most have their full or at least substantial mental faculties. I never treat them like helpless babies. For the few that truly are for the most part helpless due to their illness, I of course use sensitivity in ministering to them in whatever way is appropriate. For the most part, these folks in these places want the truth spoken in an uncompromised, strong way. As a matter of fact, they often hope that someone will come in and lead an exciting, bold church service with enthusiastic worship and Holy Spirit-empowered preaching. They have said as much to me many times. I have seen such Holy Spirit-empowered preaching in not just preachers who are loud and animated in their gestures and movements, but also in messages brought calmly, quietly and reservedly which as I get older is becoming more my style. God does not need the preacher to put on a show. He does however, want preachers who will be submitted to Him and open to being used of God in demonstration of the Holy Spirit's power along with the compassion, joy, love, and gentleness of Christ.

"When I came to you, I did not come with eloquence or human wisdom as I proclaimed to you the testimony about God. For I resolved to know nothing while I was with you except Jesus Christ and him crucified. I came to you in weakness with great fear and trembling. My message and my preaching were not with wise and persuasive words, but with a demonstration of the Spirit's power, so that your faith might not rest on human wisdom, but on God's power." (1 Corinthians 2:1-5)

Of course everything needs balance, and we make every effort to know when to be low-key and reserved and when to be more aggressive in what we bring to them. Many of these people have fond memories of powerful revival times in their younger years where the gospel was preached strong and the presence of God was powerfully manifested in times of worship.

*"*Hang onto your hat!*": Such were my words I wrote in my first journal in 1997 following one of our meetings at an Adult Care Community. I guess I was just excited over how we were seeing God do great things. Sixty-four in attendance at Barnwell Nursing Home in Valatie, NY. When I had first been exposed to the ministry in Adult Care Communities, it was normal to see maybe as few as ten or twelve in attendance on up to maybe on a rare occasion, fifteen or even twenty or so in attendance. Little did I know what God had in store for us in the years ahead as He began to bring out the large crowds to these meetings. I would never have imagined that God would ever bring out sixty-four residents for a church service in a nursing home. As time would tell, such numbers and even well beyond became quite frequently the norm. Over ninety in one service.

From the start, it was becoming crystal clear that we were engaged in something that was much bigger than us. God was doing something amazing and special. At a church, such a number might be expected, but at a nursing home such numbers seemed truly amazing. I look at my journal for October 19, 1997 and read my first words: *"64 people! Hang onto your hat! We had 64 in attendance, largest amount yet. They came from all 5 or 6 floors."* I went on to say: *"The people were as lively a group as I have seen, with their enthusiastic spirit. Lots of response. Such an encouragement. Contrary to anyone's pre-conceived impressions of nursing homes, this people group is vibrant and they express great need of a strong evangelistic meeting."* My last paragraph in this entry of the journal for this meeting said this: *"This ministry is simply becoming phenomenal in what God is doing. We have been getting blessed beyond belief."*

I try to just include a few of these types of entries from our journals to give some idea to the reader of what God has done. This type of entry I have shared here is typical of hundreds of the meetings. Why do I share these results of this ministry? It is most definitely not for the purpose of drawing attention to our selves or anything we have accomplished. It is first and foremost, as I have tried to emphasize many times in this book, to draw the reader's attention to a great God whom all the glory is due. But secondly, it is for the purpose of being an encouragement to others who might sense God's calling to this type of ministry.

God gave me this word from Him: *"If God is in it, the results will confirm it".* It is my hope that others can get a glimpse of the magnitude of what God is ready to do with those who are willing to serve in this ministry field, and certainly in any other ministry field. The opportunities to minister to our nation's older generation in the Adult Care Community are immense and the need is great. It is not a ministry that will be noticed by a lot of people and there is not a lot of financial gain from it, nor should there be. But God notices and the people are blessed. It is, as someone once told me, *"Pure ministry".* It is not something you enter into for monetary gain or recognition, and if your heart is for the people and to please God, those things will not matter.

Getting the Message?: The place is Hill Haven Nursing Home in Syracuse, NY. There was a bird in a birdcage next to where I was preaching. He raised his body up whenever I spoke a particularly strong word and looked at me a lot. I wonder if he was getting the message? Two people there were blind. I had preached on how Jesus came to open the eyes of the spiritually blind. One lady in a front row seat sang with great vigor and spirit. She said later: *"it was good that you brought a strong message. We really needed it."* *A Lot of Prayer: Folt's Nursing Home in Herkimer, NY. I wrote the following words in my journal: *"By now I probably sound unbelievable, so often giving these glowing accounts, but I just have to say it—this meeting was a taste of heaven! What a joy, what a sense of God's presence!"* One entry I made in my journal that day reads like this: *"This past week Sharon and I had a disciplined plan of praying for this meeting and it sure paid off. God was there in power and in gentleness."*

That brings to mind an important aspect of this or any ministry. Prayer and more prayer. It is absolutely a crucial element necessary in ministry. We always make sure we are prayed up and have committed everything to God in preparation for these meetings. We are certain that prayer has played a huge part in the awesome evidence of God's presence and blessing in these meetings. It is about total reliance upon God. This meeting began our fall schedule. What a spiritual high it was. I wrote in the journal near the end of my entry for this meeting that *"now it is time to come back to earth and get prayed up and prepared for our next meeting."*

'MISSION: CANADA'

I could not write of our ministry experiences without talking about Ontario, Canada and the journey God took us on there. We had sensed in our spirit that God was leading us to go on a preaching mission trip into Canada. We were all set to attend a Billy Graham

School of Evangelism in Toronto, Canada. We decided to make a mission trip out of it while there. The mission trip would cover eight days, July 19-26, 1998. We preached in five cities at five Adult Care Communities, including in the cities of St. Catherines, Kitchener, Toronto, Ajax, and Kingston, all in Ontario, Canada. We visited Niagara Falls on the way. We attended the two-day Evangelism School which was a tremendous experience with probably a thousand or so people I would guess. It all went great.

Thrilling Meeting: At Conestoto Lodge Retirement Residence, we had a small crowd, but one of our most thrilling meetings. The people loved it and were disappointed that the news of our coming had not been adequately announced by activity workers and that so many more would have loved what we brought. One lady was overflowing with the Holy Spirit. She was Catholic and she could not stop talking about our meeting and how thankful she was for it. She followed us out to our car and kept waving at us as we drove away. This meeting there and also meeting this woman, made our entire mission trip worth it all. She said our *"ministry made her heart and soul jump for joy and that (her) heart was filled big!"* I have noted that she was Catholic.

In our meetings over the years, we have had a wide assortment of Christians representing many denominations, plus many Catholics. What we have found in most cases is that by the time these dear people have reached this point in their lives, they simply do not make a big issue out of what their denominational affiliation is, whether they are Catholic or Protestant, evangelical, Pentecostal, etc. That stuff just does not seem to matter so much to most of them anymore. At these meetings in these settings, we really do see Christ's Church approaching that unity that Jesus prayed for. I guess when your life is nearing its end, some things such as denominational barriers come tumbling down and you get your priorities right. Herein perhaps lies some lessons for God's Church to learn from this older generation.

Without Compromising God's Word: At Lansing Retirement Residence in Toronto, we were setting up for our meeting when the administrator of the place came in and told me to come with him to his office. There he informed me that twenty-five percent of the residents were of the Jewish faith. I was therefore to be very careful not to offend any Jewish resident that might possibly be at the meeting. I was not to proselytize or mention the name *"Jesus"*. God helped me with that situation. I just used the word *"Lord"* instead of *"Jesus"*. I preached my message without compromising God's Word. One woman just before the meeting started, asked me if we were bringing a *"religious"* service. When I told her what we were doing, she angrily got up, said a few unpleasant words, and left. It was sad to watch one more soul reject Christ. It was sad to see a person who was so close to eternity still rejecting Christ and soon it could be too late. I was deeply burdened for her. We prayed for her that following evening. I counseled one man who cried over his wife being gone whom he had been with for over forty-nine years. I was able to understand a little about his grief as I shared with him that I too, had such grief in common with him, having lost my first wife who died in 1987. Other than these couple of bumps with the administrator and with this angry woman, the meeting went great.

*"From across the border.": At Balley Cliff Retirement Center in Ajax, one woman asked if we were *"from across the border."* I answered yes, and she said *"That's OK. You're pretty good anyhow!"* A man told Sharon: *"You're pretty cute."* I heard one lady whisper to a lady next to her about me, saying *"I think the preacher is going to sing too."*

"ANGEL" SENT BY GOD

Also in Kingston, while at a motel, Sharon got to talking to the receptionist at the front desk. She was recently born again as a Christian and she wanted our ministry newsletter. Sharon and her both shared their testimonies with one-another. It was another one of those many times God gave us opportunities to minister to people along the way. She shared with Sharon that she had personal needs she needed prayer for. Sharon prayed for her right there in the Lobby with another customer present. She hugged Sharon and told us she had goose bumps from meeting us and experiencing God in this experience. She was filled to overflow with God at this point and praised God. She called Sharon an *"angel sent by God"* to her and said we *"brought joy back into (her) spirit"*. She hoped we would return and bring evangelistic meetings in her area soon. She said that all her life, no one had told her that Jesus loves her. She thought that Jesus only condemned her. We had the words *"Jesus loves you"* stamped on our ministry gift packs which we gave to her. Such ministry opportunities can spring up anywhere at any time, and serves to be a reminder that God's people should always be ready to share the gospel. Our mission trip in Canada was one of many opportunities to pray for people who were hurting, or needed healing or a word of encouragement.

THE MAIN THING

"...now is the time of God's favor, now is the day of salvation." (2 Corinthians 6:2)

*Precious Elderly Souls: Praise God, the main thing that it is mostly about happened at University Heights Nursing Home in Loudenville, NY. Thirty-seven in attendance. Enthusiastic crowd. Following my message, three residents gave their hearts to Jesus. Salvation of three precious elderly souls. What could be better? I recall such times with especially great joy. Then there is Groton, NY at Groton Nursing Facility. An elderly woman gave her life to Jesus and wept for joy over getting saved. These are just a few examples of those special times in our meetings where the main thing took place, the salvation of souls, securing their eternity with Christ, even late in their life when time was running out.

AWAKENINGS

Close Encounters: Scotia, NY. We held our church service in the Alzheimer's unit. Thirty Alzheimer's residents. One stood about six inches in front of me face to face as I preached. Over the years, we many times ministered in Alzheimer's units. We have time and again witnessed residents coming out of a lack of mental awareness or alertness and for a brief forty-minute meeting, become almost miraculously fully alert and aware of what is going on. Many times staff have informed us that some who were singing and praising God had not, previous to our meetings, been vocal or alert for months. God for a few precious moments, through the power of His Spirit during worship and His preached Word has touched these lives and reached past their physical limitations and stirred their spirit and soul.

Churches: As I have looked through my journals, I have also come upon many entries about ministry dates in churches. Except for right here, I have not stopped to write about my experiences in the churches. I have chosen to speak of our meetings in the Adult Care Communities in this chapter and not get much into the preaching-points at the churches where I have preached. There have been many wonderful experiences at the preaching engagements in churches around central NY. Many people at these meetings have experienced salvation, the miraculous, physical healings, baptism with the Holy Spirit, falling under the power of the Holy Spirit, deliverance from oppressive spirits, a special Word from God, and so many things that God has done following the message and during alter ministry.

Truly the days of God manifesting His presence and power through *"signs, wonders, and miracles"* has not passed but are still active today. Such has often followed the preaching of God's Word in our travels and ministry. I have been in awe of what God has done. Again and again I emphasize that in my power, none of these things could ever happen. May no man or woman ever draw attention to themselves in their ministry. But when God does do something special, may they draw attention to the great things God does. It is really God's ministry and we only get the privilege to be used by Him in His work. It is God who does these wonderful things and only God who is able to do these things, and our attention should be on Him. It seems throughout church history, but especially in recent years, people have made celebrities out of big-name preachers and TV evangelists, and it can bring disrepute and harm to the Church when men and women are overly exalted like that. But with this brief note about the ministry in the churches, I move on and continue with what God has done in the Adult Care Communities.

HATS—BEARDS—KISSES—BLESSINGS—ETC.

In one Adult Care Community we went to, a woman was unhappy with me for not removing my hat soon enough. I had only barely entered the room where we were going to hold our meeting, and I had not yet taken my hat off. She let me know in a very firm tone of voice that I was to *"remove (my) hat in church!"* I just gave her a smile and removed my hat. Never argue with or be confrontational with these dear people. I cannot remember how many times residents told me I needed to get rid of my beard. Most however, do not feel that way, but there have been some. I have had a few who actually would reach out and touch my beard. Then there are those times when residents told Sharon they were going to *"keep"* me.

I have seen it the other way around as well, when someone would comment that my wife was cute and they were keeping her. And then there are the kisses. I cannot recount how many of the elderly ladies have planted a kiss on my cheek. Another thing I get a lot of is being called *"Father"* by the Catholics and being asked to bless them or visa-versa, they pronouncing a blessing on me. Though I do not want to be addressed as *"Father"*, I understand that some just prefer to do so, and I just go along with them. There are many light-hearted moments in this ministry. One of the most enjoyable things that God gives us opportunity to do is pray for people. But not just residents that are at the meetings. We have had occasions to pray for individual staff members, or at bedsides of the dying. The meetings often include not only residents, but staff workers, visitors, other ministers, and sometimes children. It is a ministry that often brings with it a lot of emotions. People's hearts are stirred. Tears flow at times. Fear, loneliness, depression all are a part of their lives, but so too is joy, humor, and hope. A few times I have listened as a resident expresses the desire to go home to be with the Lord or to be re-united with a loved one that has gone on before them. I have been asked to pray for a person to die. God without fail always gives us the appropriate response and direction on how to handle what the residents ask for. Most Adult Care Communities have a good, upbeat spirit. But we have also been in those that just seem to have a presence of more sadness than others. Usually in those ones, by the time we are done with our meetings, people are talking about how they sense a lifting of that depressed spirit or otherwise express that our ministry was very much needed and helped them.

One thing we get told a lot is that residents have not had enough upbeat church services and they find what we do to be very different from what they are used to. Somehow beyond our understanding, God has tremendously blessed these meetings and the format that we bring. I do believe bringing in a quality sound system, using mics, singing up-tempo music, etc. makes for a good effect that the people especially get enjoyment from. We sing both hymns as well as contemporary choruses. They especially love the old hymns. We are always looking for ways to improve the services and to keep a certain dynamic to the sound and to how we speak. They need life and a genuine church atmosphere at the meetings. If we come across as formal or dull, they will just wish they were doing something else somewhere, like playing bingo or some other fun activity the activity department offers. Our program moves along at a crisp pace, yet not hurried. God over the years equipped us, and taught us things that work in these meetings. When we are at our home church just taking in the service on a Sunday and not ministering, we find ourselves yearning to be out there on the road ministering. But we also need those occasional Sundays when we are at home being ministered to.

IT IS ALL ABOUT PEOPLE AND JESUS

It is often said that numbers are not important, and that churches should not emphasize how many people attend a service. In our ministry, we do in fact keep track of attendance figures. One, it is useful as we look back in our journals to see how the response was to our meetings. We get a sense of how many song programs to bring, and whether an Adult Care Community showed much interest in coming out for the meetings. Most importantly, those numbers represent people. We are told numbers of people gathered together for various events in scripture. The 5000 or the 4000 men plus women and children when Jesus fed the multitudes; the 120 in the upper room on Pentecost Sunday, and many other instances of the Bible recording crowds or numbers of people. So when we record how many were in attendance at a meeting, we are rejoicing over how many souls came together to worship God and be ministered to.

At one of our Billy Graham Schools of Evangelism in Wheaton, Illinois, I remember one speaker talking about the tendency of evangelists to use *"evang-elastic"* numbers when declaring how many attended a meeting or got saved. Such stretching of numbers is of course very wrong, and we are very careful to never exaggerate numbers or responses to the message. Jesus came to minister to people. Those numbers reflect *"visible results"* as I remember one pastor referring to them as, and indeed numbers tell us that people have met with Jesus at these meetings. Whether few or many, it is about people and Jesus.

"Whew!": That is the word in one of my journal entries as I looked at all that God had done. I have listed only a tiny fraction of some meetings and attendance figures to give the reader a hint of the turnout God has brought about in these meetings. Throughout the ensuing years in this ministry God has continued to do great

things and bring out significant attendance such as I have already mentioned. I must pick up the pace now as I flip through pages of the journals and pull out just a few more of the high-lights from the meetings. It would take way more pages than I want this book to be, to detail everything in our journals or even to speak of one-tenth of the experiences.

I will say this: The best way to learn how to minister in this mission field to our elderly is to just *"launch out into the deep"* as Jesus once told some fisherman, and use what God has given you. As you do that, God will trust you with more and more, and expand and improve your ministry. Someone said you cannot get to the other side of the lake unless you take the first step of leaving the shoreline. Another thing I would recommend to anyone wanting to do this kind of ministry is for them to go along with someone who is experienced in this field of ministry and watch firsthand how it is done. Someone did that for us and it helped immensely. If God has called you to a ministry, he will equip you and send you. He will open doors and He will bring the results. You must step out in faith and trust God to work out all the details.

*"Already in heaven"!: Sometimes it is just not all joy and hallelujahs. I talk up the wonderful moments, but then there are times like at an Adult Care Community in Sidney, NY. A lady heard me talk about heaven and responded angrily saying to me that she was *"already in heaven"!* Another angry lady at the same meeting threw a bookmark we had given her, back at Sharon. Only God and those ladies know what kind of a day it must have been for them. We still love them, and we know they were having a difficult time in some way or another. I know. As I reflect back on my own past, I remember that I have been loved when I was not always easy to love.

IT IS A GOOD THING WE DON'T
HAVE TO DEPEND ON HOW WE *"FEEL"*

Going through my journals, I discover that there were many times I just did not feel so well or all that enthused about what we were doing. You do not have to always *"feel"* all tingly and excited over ministry or even in your everyday daily walk with God. Feelings are not dependable. Faith is. Someone has said that *"feeling will follow faith."* I have experienced that statement being fairly accurate many times. We walk by faith, not by feeling or sight. I have spoken in this book about visions, dreams, angels, and hearing from God in various ways. I have mentioned signs, wonders, and miracles. But I do not depend on those manifestations and revelations. I walk my walk with God first and foremost by faith. There have been times when I felt too weary to keep preaching. I have thought I would have to quit. In my particular case, a lot of this has to do with my health issues. I am not at full strength for what might be normal for a man my age, so yes, there are a lot of times when I am not sure my stamina is enough to continue. But God always strengthens me in those times and hopefully I can keep preaching for a long time. God has set my heart ablaze to preach.

"...his word is in my heart like a fire, a fire shut up in my bones. I am weary of holding it in; indeed I cannot." (Jeremiah 20:9)

*Overflow Crowd out the Door!: Pearle and Gilmore Nursing Home. Norwich, NY. Journal entry reads as follows: *'Overflow crowd out the door! Wonderful meeting.'* A lady told Sharon how *"good we worked together."* We have heard that statement many times. I make it a point to always tell people we are *"partners in ministry"*. A long time ago I learned that when God calls a married person to ministry, He calls that person's spouse to it as well. I could not do it without her. She makes the phone calls. She schedules our

nursing home dates and we do our program together all the way, from set-up to tear-down.

I am so thankful for her. God has given her the gifts of coordinating events, organizing, planning, communication skills, and so much more. She truly is a people-person. Not perfect. Whoops! I hope I do not get in trouble when she reads that part about not being perfect. But seriously, she is one good gal and a vital, equal partner in ministry and in every way. None of this is easy for her as she is a disabled American veteran and cannot work. Her primary part of our setting up is to plug in some cords or mics and handle the music CDs. She also does all the phone work of contacting activity directors and arranging our ministry schedule.

A FEW ADDITIONAL SAMPLINGS FROM
OUR MINISTRY JOURNALS

Spiritual Awakening: Vestal-Johnson Nursing Home, Vestal, NY. 68 people in attendance. *"It was like a spiritual awakening. People just kept coming. Over-flowed into another room. Glorious meeting."*
Veterans: NY State Veteran's Home, Oxford NY. 72 people. One man asked me after my message: *"How do you know God is here?"*
Mom: Willow Point Nursing Home, Vestal, NY. 78 people. My mom was a resident here. She attended our service. That made it very special for me. Mom said afterwards to me: *"I did not know that you could sing."* Anyone of course can sing, but I guess she was recalling how back when I was a little boy, you could not get a single note out of me to sing a song. Amazing what God can do as He changes our attitudes. Powerful anointing of God's power today. This ministry continues to manifest as a supernatural phenomenon. Received lots of confirmation from residents upon this ministry again.

Speaking of moms, I want to mention here Sharon's mom. August of 2000, Sharon and I went to a special celebration of the Assemblies of God in Indianapolis, Indiana. I think there must have been tens of thousands at that event which was held at the RCA Dome, home of the Indianapolis Colts NFL football team. While on that trip I preached at two Adult Care Communities, one in Indianapolis, Indiana and one in Louisville, Kentucky where Sharon's mom was a resident. Her mom sat right up front next to us as we brought the church service. That was a very special moment and one I know my wife cherishes in her heart. *Another Confirmation:* Vestal-Johnson Nursing Home, Vestal, NY. 80 people. Received from residents further spoken confirmation that this is God's calling for us. These confirmations amount to speaking a Word of the Lord over us. One employee would not go to work because she wanted so much to stay in the meeting. Glorious time.

REFLECTIONS ON MOM

Record-breaking Attendance: Willow Point, Vestal, NY. Over 90 people. What a phenomenal number for an Adult Care Community meeting. Outstanding meeting with record-breaking attendance. It has been about three weeks since mom died here. Her friends there express how much they miss her. A worker spoke highly of mom. She said: *"She got us ready for eternity".* What a great testimony of mom's faith and serving the Lord right down to her final days. What a thrill to see such a huge sea of residents, visitors, and staff gathered together in this meeting. It was so great to get back again to the nursing home where my mom had been a resident. I look back with fondness to November of 2003. Sharon and I had spent our time there with mom for Thanksgiving dinner with her and another resident at the table. I thought back to my childhood and recalled all those wonderful years that mom prepared a great Thanksgiving dinner, and often the whole family would get together with seating and tables stretching almost out of the dining room on into the living room.

Now here we were in 2003 with mom for her final Thanksgiving dinner at Willow Point Nursing Home. Mom around that time asked me if I would sing *'This World is not my Home'* at her funeral service. Mom stepped over from this earthly life onto heaven's shores on

February 22, 2004. Sharon and I just happened to be there that day standing around her bedside with other family members as she breathed her final breath. If I remember the scene correctly, she seemed to slightly lean forward a couple of times and with her arms, reach forward or upward as though she saw something, perhaps someone. I do not want to make more of it than what it was, but that day in my spirit I just sensed a presence of God and to me it seemed likely that just as she was on the edge of eternity she was very possibly seeing loved ones on the other side. She was gone from us. She had lived a full and wonderful life. She went home to rejoin loved ones who had gone on before her and to meet her Savior face to face. My voice at her celebration of life service was not very smooth or in tune that day at the service, but I sang that song that she so loved. Never has there been a better mom.

MORE SAMPLINGS FROM OUR MINISTRY JOURNALS

At another bedside: Countryside Care Center, Delhi, NY. 52 people. Ministered to dying woman at her bedside. One woman asked me to pray for her *"dirty mouth"*. Prayer ministry for 3 residents. One man had not been in a church service in 75 years. He was glad he came. We have had a number of times where residents have decided to renew their commitment to Christ and to start going to church services after God inspired them in our meetings. *Tent Meeting:* Summit, NY. 33 people. I have come across a meeting I preached at in a tent meeting revival service. This would be the second time I had ministered in tent revivals in recent years. I had been invited to preach at one of their summer meetings. Following the message, I did some alter ministry, praying for those who responded to the message. The leader of the service told the people there was *"an anointing of the Holy Spirit"*. Thank you Lord for your power. I am so glad for what only God can do, and that He has allowed me to be used by Him.

I wish I could include in this book the countless times God has taken me to churches around central NY and could tell of the great things He has done at those times and meetings, but I will in this book, primarily try to stay on track with writing about the ministry to the Adult Care Communities. *Just as Important:* Pines of Utica, Utica, NY. 14 people. One of our very small turnouts, but just as important as the larger turnouts. God is not impressed with big numbers. He is just about the work of touching and saving lives. Pleasant meeting. Gentle time. Helped a man on the street who needed a meal. Many times God has placed in our path in our travels, someone who needs a meal and we try to listen and consider carefully when God says to help. That is as much a part of our ministry as anything else God uses us for.

Twenty-Five Cents: Folts Home, Herkimer, NY. 43 people. A resident was insistent on giving an offering to our ministry. She gave me twenty-five cents. Makes me think of the widow's mite in the Bible who gave what she had. What matters is where her heart is, God bless her. *"Take me home":* Golden Living Center, Phoenixville, PA. After attending an Assemblies of God National Evangelist's Conference at Valley Forge College, we brought a meeting to this facility. One resident asked Sharon to *"take me home with you".*

Preaching after surgery: Barnwell Nursing Home, Valatie, NY. Besides two churches, this is my first nursing home meeting since finding out I have cancer. I am determined to preach right up until my cancer surgery, and then God willing, resume preaching after months of recovery and treatments, maybe even preaching during the months of treatment if physically possible. I received a Word from God through one resident who said in regard to my cancer, *"God will not take your life or ministry away from you at this time."* *Stool:* Valatie, NY. First time back to preaching since my cancer surgery in May. Been five months laid up unable to preach. I use a stool now to sit on when I preach. Cannot stand up long due to poor health and lack of strength.

Determined to Press on: Owego, NY. 29 people. Great to be back to holding meetings in Adult Care Communities. I have been unable to preach for four months due to chemotherapy and radiation treatments. Did do a few churches during that time though. Very extremely weak and debilitated from all I have gone through, but determined to press on. One resident was shocked to see how gaunt I had become, losing 60 pounds. *"Still alive."* FOX Nursing home, Oneonta, NY. 51 people. Great meeting! Included doctors, chaplain, activity director, several staff, visitors, residents. Counseled one lady. Another woman said *"message encouraged" her and she was so glad I was "still alive" and we could be there to minister.*

Powerful Anointing: Vestal-Johnson Nursing Home, Vestal, NY. Spectacular meeting, sensed a great move of God and powerful anointing. Overflow crowd into three rooms! *"Bring a calmness to them.":* Wilkinson Center, Amsterdam, NY. 31 people. Prayed for 105 year old woman at her bedside, laying hands on her chest as her son requested, to pray for her heart disease. Also prayed for her son, a Native American, and he also prayed for us. Residents said we *"bring a calmness to them."*

Residents said they appreciate so much that we bring them a church service on a Sunday morning. They expressed that they wish other ministers would do that. I understand it presents some difficulty for churches to send out their pastors to minister at nursing homes on Sunday mornings, but I just thought I should mention that many of the residents desire this if at all possible. Maybe some churches could consider appointing some of their pastoral staff to do this on a rotation basis. Just a thought. *"Best thing she had ever done":* Susquehanna Nursing Home, Johnson City, NY. Wonderful meeting. Some residents did not want us to leave. One said *"it was the best thing she had ever done on a Sunday morning."*

Obviously I have only mentioned a very small handful of the over eight-hundred meetings God used us in over the years. But hopefully the few I have shared give some idea about what God has done in this ministry.

RETIREMENT? ...NO CAN DO!
...NOT YET ANYHOW ...NOT BY A LONG SHOT!

I think I heard the word *"retirement"*, only it didn't sound quite that nice. It sounded more like *"quit!"* or *"give up!"* And I think I know who it is that is only too anxious to whisper those kind of words to me and even try to convince me that I've done enough and that I deserve the luxury of sitting on my butt and just watch the sunset each day. That old devil would love for me to shut up now and leave the preaching to the younger generation. He wants me to desert my fellow comrades in the work of God's kingdom, and leave the battle field where God's army fights for souls.

Well, on more than one occasion I almost made the mistake of thinking I was justified in retiring from any further preaching of the gospel. After all, my body had gone through horrendous painful crisis after crisis the past few years, and now I was tired. Surely God was saying *"Jim, it's OK. You've been faithful. You've pushed yourself beyond any reasonable limits. Go ahead and relax."* Hold it right there! Put the brakes on any such thinking. That's not God. I've been around long enough to recognize when it is God speaking and when it is that old devil called Satan. Let me take a few moments here to address this close call with calling it quits.

It was late September of 2012. Chronic pain and a multitude of other complications from my cancer experience continued to plague me, by this time going deep into the third year since the big surgery, and it would still be a part of my life on into 2013 and probably beyond. On a scale of one to ten with ten being the worst pain, I was living every day up around a level seven and sometimes an eight or nine. Many times due to the intensity of the pain, I had all I could do to move just a few feet to make it to my bed and lay flat on my back. Actually I still have to do that a couple times a day for half an hour or so. For some reason that doctors have not been able to totally figure out, my cancer surgery left my right side in continuous high-level pain. They believe it has to do with nerve damage that cannot

213

be corrected. Not all patients who have this particular surgery end up with this type of lasting nerve damage and pain, but some do.

A series of heart attacks in previous years left me well acquainted with what severe pain is about. I think I am a fairly rugged individual and I can take my fair share of pain. However there were times I prayed God would give me more toughness to handle it all. Maybe I should have included a chapter titled: *"Lord Make Me Tough"*. That may be a good way to pray sometimes. But anyhow, it was getting to *seemingly* be too much. As I say that, I can almost hear someone good-heartedly saying *"God never gives us too much to bear"*, but I stand by it. There definitely have been times it *seemed* it was too much. Clearly many people in life are confronted with situations that are too much at times. I felt like I needed to come to peace with the idea that it was just too much to deal with and still be able to continue in ministry. I seriously considered retiring completely from any further efforts to preach. Hey, the Pope did in March 2013. Shortly after he announced he would be retiring, lighting struck the Vatican twice. Coincidence? God trying to say something? Probably not, but it made for an interesting bit of news and a few chuckles.

Anyhow, here I was, trying to convince myself that God was OK with me making such a decision to retire. It's amazing how much we can convince ourselves that it is God speaking when sometimes it isn't Him at all. As much as my pain was severely limiting my activity and I thought it had finally pushed me beyond my limits, I still had the overwhelming desire to keep preaching. Would God really continue to keep giving me that desire if He wanted me to now retire? One morning while I was reading my Bible in my quiet time with the Lord, I read a verse from Joshua 13:1. Joshua was by that time an old man, *"advanced in years"* as the Bible puts it, and he had already faithfully served God for many years. I have to wonder if he had by that point in his life ever considered that maybe it was time to retire and take it easy. If ever a man had earned the right to relax and just enjoy his senior years in retirement, Joshua certainly had.

God acknowledged that yes, Joshua was old. God spoke to Joshua about his advanced years.

With that said, the Lord pointed out to Joshua that there was still *"very much"* to do. Following that word from the Lord Joshua did continue in his calling to lead the people. When I read that verse in Joshua 13:1, it jumped off the page and spoke to me. With all that I was dealing with every day, I was feeling like I had done just about all that I could do in ministry, and I was ready to retire from any further preaching. I thought to myself that surely no one would have faulted me for calling it quits. Some even encouraged me to feel free to do so. They understood how much I was going through and under most circumstances, most anyone would stop working if they were experiencing this level of physical disability. If I was still engaged in secular work, I would have no hesitation in concluding that it is reasonable and even advisable to go ahead and retire. If I was a pastor of a church I no doubt would have had to retire because the level of health challenges I deal with would simply be more than a pastor or anyone else with such a substantial set of responsibilities would never be able to keep up with. Being that my calling is limited to preaching and singing, I can push myself to handle that much.

The divine calling to ministry carries with it something different from secular employment. There is just something about the call of God to preach that drives a person to keep going a little more and to even push one's self beyond normal limits. Now as I read this verse in Joshua, I was hearing the Lord tell me, that yes He was well aware that I am hurting, and yes, I am in my senior years and they are very rough years, but just as He said to Joshua, so He was saying to me too, that He still has *"very much"* more that He intends to use me to do. Any ideas of imminent retirement were put aside that day. I realized I could not and I must not stop yet, even if it means expending my life to try. Even as I thought I had settled this matter in my mind, I took another hit when on January 15, 2013 I had a very hard fall in my kitchen which left me badly beaten up physically. This would be my seventh fall since my diagnosis of cancer, and all of the falls were direct results of my weakened body from complications related to the cancer. With that added stress and pain on my body from this latest fall, it just made it all the harder to not give up. But with God's help and encouragement, I determined that even this latest injury would not win the day. I would as far as is possible, go forward with my preaching schedule which had recently filled up my calendar again. It especially seemed clear that I should go forward regardless of the possibility I could very well collapse if I pushed myself to keep preaching.

The week that I fell this seventh time was one in which I had been working on a message to preach at a church in a few weeks. One of the primary points in my message had been that *'Christ is worth our living or if necessary, even dying for'*. Now here I was, severely injured on top of my ongoing health issues and I had that message prepared to preach. How could I now decide to not preach? If I really believed Christ is worth whatever the consequences might be in faithfully continuing forward, I sure could not now back away in the face of my own health situation. Live or die trying, I must go ahead and give it my best effort. I am not being overly dramatic or exaggerating the situation. My body was totally racked with debilitating pain. An hour or two on my feet took everything out of me and I was frequently ending up having all I could do to get flat on my back in bed to recover several times a day. The latest injury had left me short of breath and at times unable to stand up. It was likely comparable to a fractured rib type of pain.

On outward appearance when people would see me out in the public, they would comment on how well I look, but little could they know that inside I was often having all I could do to keep standing or keep my face from grimacing. After that latest fall I at times felt as though my body might not be able to handle this latest beating that I had sustained and I knew pushing too hard could have severe consequences. But, I realized I needed to trust God with whatever happens and be willing to even give my last breath if necessary, to preach. I know. That kind of talk must sound overly dramatic but that really is how I feel about it, and yes it really could come down to that. Maybe there would yet come a time when regardless of my determined spirit, I might not be able to do it anymore. For now, it was my decision to keep trying. I agree with the Apostle Paul's statement in the Bible where he said for him to live was Christ and to die was gain. I do not have any death wish, but I do understand that my life is to be lived out for Christ and when I die, I will be with Him for eternity.

God had spared my life these past few years. He had given me the privilege to still be alive and it was not just so I could retire and sit in a rocking chair. He did not promise it would be easy. He did reassure me that my calling is still there. It was still time to preach the gospel, and I still loved doing it. That hasn't changed as of this writing. I find great joy in preaching. My salvation was of course not dependant on doing any good works, but my obedience to and the leading of the Lord did compel me to keep at it. I never *"had"* to preach. Rather, I *"get"* to preach. Someone at one of the Billy Graham Schools of Evangelism that my wife and me attended years ago brought out that point to us who were attending the seminars. He reminded us ministers that it is never about having to preach. Rather it is that we get to preach. It is both a joy and a privilege given by God.

Ever since the first time in 1975 when I first heard the call of God to preach the gospel, it became my dream to answer that calling. The Lord brought me through all of the steps of my ministerial college education and ordination to see that dream realized. With God's help I would continue to preach as long as He gives me the strength and I would not retire before God's time. When and if God decides it is time, then and only then will it be right and He will give me peace about it. By the time this book is published and into the hands of any potential readers, I may or may not still be preaching. Time will tell. But my best guess is that I'll still be going at it, even more intensely than ever before.

April of 2013 brought yet another threat to my continuing in ministry as an avalanche of health issues reached a critical point. I really do believe that the devil has tried throwing many things at me to discourage me and drive me to quit on God. No doubt he goes after many a minister in similar ways. Better men than me have been so tested and with faith in God, they have prevailed against our enemy Satan. I must too. I mentioned a little about these new set of health issues back in a previous chapter. Among other things it involved a new cancer-related complication / symptom with my mouth brought on by delayed effects of chemotherapy and radiation treatments. The one thing a preacher needs to be in good working order is his mouth and now I was dealing with a symptom that severely interfered with my being able to preach. I had to wonder if the devil may have been involved in this latest symptom. Certainly he would like to shut up a preacher. Well, if that was even remotely the case, he would lose that battle in fairly quick order.

I did temporarily retreat from a preaching schedule again, and waited to see if God would strengthen me sufficiently once again to resume preaching. Admittedly this time around almost got the best of me and I was again confronted with the very real possibility that my preaching days might be over. Too many health issues were just getting me worn down. Through a series of signs that proved to unquestionably be from God, the Lord showed me that He would revitalize me and renew my strength to preach again. He sent a brother in the Lord to me with a Word from God. In due course of time, I was able to return to a preaching schedule. God is so very good.

One preacher said the last sound he wants to hear when he leaves this earth to meet his Savior is the sound of his head hitting the pulpit. He wants to go out preaching the Word. I too can identify with what he said. If I let my challenges drive me to totally quit on my calling before God says it is time, I would be a man not only forsaking God's calling but also my dream and that would leave me empty and aimless. If we give up on ourselves, we have no place to go. I like what one person said to me about the cost of following Christ.

She basically said that it is up to the Heavenly Father how much it costs, not up to you. Someone has said something to the effect, Lord grant that my last hour will be my finest hour. I share that sentiment and I pray that God will let my final days on this earth be my finest days in His service. I like the attitude of Martin Luther King Jr. about pressing on with all you've got when the going gets tough. He encouraged people to run if flying is not possible, and if running won't work for you then try walking. He took this thought yet further by telling us to even crawl if walking is not possible, but when all is said and done, we must be sure to do all we can do to stay on the move and go forward.

I thank the Lord for this glorious privilege of proclaiming His gospel. I will keep at it as long as He enables me to do so, and when or if I can no longer do so, I will try to step aside as graciously as possible and accept whatever He wants. It will all be on God's terms, not the devil's or mine. I like Billy Graham's advice to Gary Player, a frequent winner in professional golf. He encouraged him to thank God even for a bad hole, and then have a determined attitude and mind-set that says you will do better next time and show what kind of person you are by that demonstration of what you're really made of. I too, am determined by the grace of God, to move past the bad moments in my life and show what I'm made of and how I'll come back. When it is possible, no matter how many times life knocks me down, I want to get back up and show what I am made of, and finish well. More importantly, I want to show what God is made of. He never quits on us. I cannot quit on Him. God willing, it is the onward and upward call of God for me.

After a three-month hiatus from preaching due to that latest challenge with my health events in the Spring of 2013, God began to speak to my heart and I began to experience a reviving of my spirit as God was re-energizing me. I was hearing a very clear call from God to quickly get back in the saddle again as the saying goes, and go preach again. At that particular point in my life I was sixty-six. I was in the latter part of my life. There could not likely be many years left for me in this brief time we get to spend here in this life. I don't say that as a depressing or negative thought. That's just the truth. Life is brief, and there comes a point in your life as you get older when you begin to think more about how quickly your time is running out and how important it is to get moving on what you want to accomplish. A precautionary note should be added here about considering one's time growing short. Solomon said these words about life as he had been talking about the *"few days of life God has given"* man: *"He seldom reflects on the days of his life, because God keeps him occupied with gladness of heart."* (Ecclesiastes 5:18; 20). So, yes there is a point to be made for recognizing life is brief and the time for action is now, especially being sure to be actively carrying out what God has given you to do in your life. But we also should avoid giving more attention than is due regarding our days of life, and instead be glad in the Lord.

God was prodding me and telling me to immediately go full-throttle back out the door, into our car and head down the roads to many preaching-points. He told me the latter portion of my life that I now was facing would be the best years of ministry and that rather than slow down or cut back on preaching, He would now take me to new places and would give me a fresh anointing to preach the gospel beyond anything I'd done thus far. God was about to enlarge the calling He had on my life. My spirit was awakening again and regardless of any challenges, I was about to launch out into the deep with new vigor, holy zeal and a fervent heart as God gives me a fresh message to take to thousands of people even at this stage of my life. Through that Word which God had delivered to me by the man of God just a couple months earlier from the Biblical story of King Hezekiah, I knew God was now restoring me to finish the course He had sent me out on years ago. Just like King Hezekiah, God was bringing me to a place of recovery from the multitude of new health symptoms which had temporarily kept me from doing ministry. Also like with King Hezekiah, God was having me *"return to the house of the Lord"*, in my case meaning He was placing me back behind the pulpits to preach the gospel which I had temporarily been held back from doing.

With all this said I confidently assert that I believe God is now going to take the latter part of my life and use me to preach in a greater capacity to more people than in all my previous thirty-eight years of serving the Lord. Hopefully this book will prove to be one of those ways God will enlarge the ministry He has called me to as this book gets into the hands and hearts of many people. Retirement? Not so fast. God has very different plans.

Oh by the way, that Word from God that the brother in the Lord came to me and shared? I not only had received the assurance that God would return me to the pulpits to preach. God also told me I would recover from some of the physical problems that had played a primary part in holding me back from ministry. I began to experience healing following that visit by the man of God and over a few weeks time I indeed did recover. God still heals.

"Yet when I preach the gospel, I cannot boast, for I am compelled to preach. Woe to me if I do not preach the gospel!"
(1 Corinthians 9:16)

...And so the mission continues...

PART III

GOD OF THE MIRACULOUS

A CONVERSATION ABOUT BELIEVING GOD FOR THE OTHERWISE IMPOSSIBLE

Get outside every day. Miracles are waiting everywhere.

12. CRACKED EGGS

"EGGS OVER MEDIUM-LIGHT, THANK YOU"

A light-hearted look at the God of all the universe who cares even about the small things and who can smile with us and have some fun with us as we look to Him for comfort and encouragement

There's the well known nursery rhyme about Humpty Dumpty who couldn't be put back together again after his great fall off of a wall. He had been sitting there on that precarious location and following the fall, we are told the king's horses and his men couldn't restore him to wholeness.

As I come to this part of my book, it is time to have a little fun. That's how I approach it anyhow. This book thus far has had a fairly serious tone to it as I have written about my cancer and about the call of God. Along the way, I have tried to insert an occasional bit of humor and light-hearted thoughts. Now I want to especially concentrate on the lighter side. Allow this somewhat old guy to share something he experienced that not even he fully understands. I just know what I saw, and I want to use that particular event as a vehicle to talk about a more important subject, that of the God of the miraculous.

I know I must qualify as an *"older"* guy *(not "old")* because recently following a brain scan related to some post-cancer complications, my doctor's diagnosis was put in the simplest of terms when he said I have an *"old-age"* brain. I also was told the scan revealed that I had *"minimally-diminished brain volume"*, in

225

my particular case due to chemotherapy. They know that because the miniscule difference was detectable between a brain scan before my chemo treatments and a post-chemo treatment brain scan a few months later. I have not lost any of my intellect or mental capacity, at least not as of this writing. But then that favorable assessment of my mental status is no doubt biased as it comes from me. To be sure, with the doctor's diagnosis, my wife has had some fun with it as she humorously refers to my *"small brain"* whenever I have one of those moments I might seem confused or forgetful.

LETS JOURNEY TOGETHER FOR A FEW MINUTES

So anyhow, I invite you to come along with this young *"old man"* as I talk about the God of the miraculous and as I only incidentally mention some cracked eggs. I say *"incidentally"* because I stress that if you read this chapter and come away primarily thinking about the egg story, you will have missed the real substance of this chapter. The egg account, as wonderful as it is, is for me most importantly only a tool to direct your attention to the God of the miraculous. Also in the title of this chapter, I refer to having eggs *"over medium-light"*. I approach this subject the same way. Some things need to be kept light, or should I say, medium-light.

Included in this chapter I write my account of an experience with some eggs from that light-hearted approach, yet with a medium amount of seriousness to what I am really wanting to say here. Again, my real goal is not at all to make a big deal about some poultry products, but rather to draw your attention to an amazing God who can and sometimes does do the miraculous. If I can bring out a few spiritual truths while having a little fun using what happened with some otherwise ordinary eggs, I feel I will have accomplished the greater point of this part of the book. I do so along a similar approach as Jesus' use of objects in parables to teach something greater. Assembly of God Evangelist Steve Hill whom I previously mentioned in an earlier chapter used the sport of skiing and avalanches as a tool or parable to share spiritual truths in one of his books.

Per chance there be some who might not be willing or able to believe my account of what happened with the eggs, that is OK because it is not necessary to do so and the egg event is not the main thing. If nothing else, perhaps the reader can just let it be a good story to bring out the more important thoughts that I share about what God does. Personally, what happened with the eggs is quite an amazing thing for me. For me it reminds me of an amazing God who chose to bless me in a very special way. Most important in this chapter however are the insights into what God can do for you in your everyday life. The reader would do well to already be smiling as you proceed to hear my story. Keep in mind that God smiles too. That is one of those aforementioned spiritual truths. We do not often think of God in that way, but I am confident that He does both laugh and smile. We are made in His image and we laugh and smile. He must too. As you keep this in mind, you can keep a light-hearted mind-set in advance as you continue to read what follows.

BLESSED ARE THE CRACKED...

I like what I received in an email sometime back from one of my sister-in-laws. I thought it would fit nicely here in my book. It reads: Blessed are the cracked, for they are the ones who let in the light! Some, after reading this chapter, might diagnose this author as *"cracked"*. I will take that risk with a smile *(not "egg")* on my face.

NOW GETTING BACK TO THE EGG BUSINESS...

Recently, out of the recesses of my memory I recalled something from when I was a little boy growing up in Johnson City, NY. A man used to deliver eggs to our home. I remember him sometimes being referred to by the neighborhood kids as simply the *"egg-man"*. Besides his primary means of employment, he was also shall I say, in the egg business. I love those old memories from the past. I have a story to tell and it is no nursery rhyme like Humpty Dumpty. By the way, just for the record, I have never appreciated the idea that Humpty Dumpty was left like that, … a broken egg with no hope for restoration to wholeness. With that thought in mind, here is another one of those spiritual truths I mentioned could come from this story: *One of the great things about God is that no life is hopelessly broken if you will turn your life over to Him.* Unlike the King's men and horses that could not put Humpty-Dumpty back together, God can make you whole again, no matter how much damage has been done.

BROKEN

This author I might say, has been physically broken and is in the process of restoration to wholeness of health and certainly I have plenty of well-founded hope. God let my body take a beating in recent years, but today, thanks primarily to Him, I am still here and living life quite fully. When I say *"God let"* me go through a physical beating, that is not said in an accusatory tone. Nothing can touch our lives unless God allows it, and if He allows it, He has His purposes. I accept that truth even when I don't like what comes my way. I know God does not make any mistakes. Admittedly, I have sometimes during my crisis of cancer, felt like what one writer from a Christian magazine wrote in his column. I don't have his exact words so I am not quoting him, but the gist of what he said was that life sometimes can feel like a great heavy boulder is clobbering you repeatedly.

I suppose Humpty Dumpty had to be left broken to teach our young minds early on that not everything can turn out the way we plan. Or maybe the lesson was simply to avoid sitting on precarious walls. But, guess what? If God wants even a cracked egg to be whole again, He can pull off that feat. He literally did such a thing right in my kitchen. Are you still with me? With making that statement about un-cracking cracked eggs, I suppose it is possible I might have already just lost some credibility with a few readers. I hope not. Please, I encourage you to continue with me and read on. Keep smiling. It helps. When I light-heartedly shared this miracle with others, and it truly was a miracle, I heard some light-hearted responses back such as *"Egg-ceptional!"; "Egg-citing!"; etc.* You get the picture.

Of course there also no doubt were those who were a *"doubting Thomas"*, but that is OK too. What I do know is that God is sovereign and we cannot do anything to cause Him to do a miracle. He will do miracles when He chooses to. There are a lot of times and situations when we may wish and pray He would intervene miraculously and He does not do so. Other times He does. It is all up to God. Here is something to ponder: Is it any harder for God to un-crack a cracked egg than it is to feed thousands of people on a few loaves of bread and a few fish, or for Jesus to walk on water? God even caused a donkey in the story of Balaam in the Bible to talk. If that can be believed, and Bible-believing Christians do believe it, then surely it is not much of a stretch to believe God can do anything He chooses to do, yes even with a few little seemingly insignificant eggs. I think of the account of Elisha the prophet of the Lord in 2 Kings 3:18. Three kings were on their way to do battle against an enemy and they ran out of water. Upon seeking out Elisha, he told them to make the valley full of trenches and that without any rain or wind, the trenches would be miraculously filled with the water they needed. He then told them that doing this miracle would be but *"a slight thing"* in God's sight. Indeed just as it was no big hard challenge for God to do that miracle, likewise it is no hard thing for Him to un-crack those eggs in our kitchen, or for that matter to do anything else He wants to do.

I've personally been blessed with miraculous healing from God and as wonderful as such an experience is, I was equally blessed when God spoke to my heart in our kitchen via what He did with the eggs. I cannot stress it enough times in this chapter, that the thrust of this chapter is not really about some eggs, but rather about a great God of the miraculous. There may be some who would be tempted to say that God would not waste His time doing such a miracle with eggs. They might say *"What's the point in Him doing such a seemingly insignificant thing?"* Some might not feel it is important or necessary for Him to do that. It is however of course, not up to us to decide what is or isn't a significant thing for God to do. Neither is there any sound basis to say as some mistakenly suppose, that God no longer does the miraculous. Such a conclusion is unbiblical. Of course He still does miracles. The preponderance of evidence that is available by countless recipients of miracles down through the centuries and into our day attests to that. God put my broken life back together when He saved me. Now there's a miracle if ever there was one!

The bottom line? Anything God does is remarkable. So aside from the story of the eggs, let me continue to talk a little about miracles throughout this chapter. Many Christians strangely enough, will accept miracles in the Bible, or even so-called *"big"* miracles in the present like healing someone of a brain tumor, but tell them God healed a cracked egg to make some point or started an engine after anointing a car with oil *(I have done such things and seen engines start)*, and some precious believers may not be able to wrap their head or their heart around God doing what they might consider to be insignificant miracles. The truth is, any miracle from God is significant, whether it be the parting of the Red Sea or healing a cracked egg. It's significant because all of it requires the supernatural power of God. Whatever He does, He has good reasons in doing it, and He doesn't have to explain to us what His reasons are although I sometimes have wished He would.

We may not fully grasp the significance or level of importance in some miracles, but again, God has His purposes and if it's something He does by His miraculous powers, it's significant. Most importantly, it is always first and foremost to bring glory to God. If you receive the spiritual truths I share in this chapter, you will have grasped the most important things that are being said here. Don't worry about my egg story. I'm just enjoying telling it and sharing what God gave me from it. Still smiling? You see, while you're smiling it is hard to think any negative or questionable thoughts about this author or whether this guy with a fantastic egg story is out of his tree.

THAT'S MY STORY AND I'M STICKING TO IT

And so the familiar saying goes. If I remember correctly, it was sometime around mid-2011. I cannot now recall more exactly when it happened. But happen it did. I was in the kitchen. I had some eggs on the stove. I was boiling them. About mid-way through their boiling time, I looked at them and discovered they very clearly had multiple cracks. I just figured I would have to have my cracked eggs and so I let them continue to boil the remaining time. I turned around to our sink to rinse something off that I had been washing. Between our stove and our sink, there is only five feet. It is a very narrow kitchen. At this particular time in my life, I had been having an especially difficult time with my recovery from everything I had gone through with the cancer. I was dealing with its effects in every facet, including physically, emotionally, and spiritually. Cancer has a way of doing that to you. It can affect everything about you. I needed or at least desired a fresh encounter with God. I often feel the desire for such fresh encounters. I think it is OK with God if we have such a desire as long as our faith does not depend on those special manifestations of an encounter with God. For me it is just part of the way God has allowed me to enjoy our relationship. The simplest and best way I can put it is that God and I have fun together. One TV preacher hesitantly said it was fun to have a relationship with God and he said it almost apologetically because he wasn't sure it was appropriate to say that. I have no problem with saying God and I have fun together.

SURE YOU NEED GOD … WHETHER YOU WANT TO ADMIT IT OR NOT

I just talked a little about needing God and desiring fresh encounters with Him. God is the source of our very life and it is He that can sufficiently strengthen us to face the hurdles of life. To admit we need God is not a sign of being an overly-needy, weak person. God is not a crutch as some people like to suggest. I like the old bumper sticker that says *"Real Men Love Jesus"*. That is a good and true saying. Men and women, young and old need the Lord whether they admit it or not. Sooner or later we all get to some crisis point where we realize we cannot always go it alone in the face of adversity, and in such times, many of us are likely to call out to God for help and assurance that He is there for us. Only a fool would say there is no God and leave Him out of the equation. Discovering we do in fact need God is actually a great place to be. In that moment, we are in the position to experience the heart of God Almighty who can lift us up and lighten our load.

SURPRISE, SURPRISE, SURPRISE

That three-peat phrase reminds me of one of the Gomer Pyle character's phrases he said in one of his lines on the old Andy Griffith TV series. Likewise I was in for a surprise. There I was in my kitchen, prayerfully desiring that God would give me a fresh sign that He is still there for me even though I always know He is, or even just a gentle whisper from that quiet voice of His Spirit. I knew He was there for me, but sometimes we just want to have Him confirm it again. Somehow, it helps. It was only a minute or so before I turned back around to check on the eggs. My mind was already set to look at some cracked eggs boiling. I expected the cracks to have worsened. It would be time now to remove the eggs and let them cool. I looked, and to my initial surprise, not one egg had even the slightest hint of a crack. How could this be? Those eggs that only moments ago were clearly cracked were now one-hundred percent perfectly whole. The cracks were just gone. I am only telling what I saw. The eggs had definitely been cracked and were inexplicably now whole. Only for a brief moment was I truly surprised at seeing this event. Then just as quickly, I became aware that for reasons beyond my immediate understanding, and from all that I could deduce from my observation, it was clear that God had just then done something special in our kitchen. In that moment I sensed God was saying with a smile: *"Jim,*

I am here." What else could I call it? What else could I conclude? It was not a big flashy, noisy miracle. Just a quiet, very special moment alone with God doing the otherwise impossible.

EXPECTING THE MIRACULOUS

I offer a few more thoughts on the miraculous. It has never been all that surprising to me that God would do the miraculous. For whatever reason, I have always found it easy to expect miracles. I guess that is just something God put in me from the moment He had given me life. Maybe God determined I would need such an expectant heart as it certainly comes in handy for a man who would be called by God to be a preacher of the gospel. Something that could not possibly happen in the natural realm had happened and as far as I am concerned, it could only be explained by the divine hand and heart of Almighty God. I immediately knew something bigger than what happened to those eggs was going on. God was directing my attention to Him and His presence, not to the eggs. When I proceeded to write this chapter, I knew God did not want the reader to concentrate on the miracle with the eggs, but rather to give thought to the spiritual truths He was leading me to write about. That's why I stressed early on in this chapter to not get hung up on the egg story and miss the main emphasis about the miraculous.

Over the years in my journey through life, divine activity of God has become the norm for me, not often in big showy ways, but rather in the small everyday routine of life. I live in expectancy of the miraculous, or at the very least, frequent divine intervention and activity. I have experienced divine activity enough times to know God still does miracles or otherwise intervenes in our everyday life, even the small stuff. There literally are too many times to recall here when I have experienced God obviously being involved in my everyday life in countless ways. Sharon and I regularly pray about every little thing as the need arises and then watch as God lines things up to turn out the way we need them to. I know many others who can testify to the miraculous power of God or in some way have experienced evidence of His actions in their lives. I can also say I know of many who flat out do not believe God still does the miraculous or even cares about our everyday needs. In a few cases it may be that perhaps because of their doubtful minds, they end up missing out on so much more that God wants to show them and how much He wants to be involved in their daily routine.

In saying that last statement I want to be quick to say that I understand the frustration that some may feel over never seeming to hear from God or experiencing such divine activity in their lives as I write about having had. I surely do not want to cause anyone to feel it is their fault for not hearing a Word from God or otherwise experiencing Him in miraculous ways. Actually in some instances, not all, but some have probably received a special Word from God and just haven't recognized it when it happened. I have heard others say they never hear from God in the ways I speak of, and sometimes I get the sense that they think it must be something they are failing to do in their walk with the Lord. Some have said they wish they too would receive a special Word from God. The fact is, there is nothing I can do to cause God to give me a special Word from Him or to bless me with a miracle. What I can do is I can have an expectant heart and be open to the possibility God will bless me in these ways. Jesus talked about having ears to hear and eyes to see. This indicates we need to not only hear and see with our physical senses but also be spiritually attuned to what God is saying and doing. I tend to make it a point to be just as spiritually receptive to what God saying and doing as I am physically receptive to what is going on around me.

Some quite frankly, and for my thinking, inexplicably actually do not want to experience God and I can well imagine that God is perfectly fine with obliging their wish to not hear from Him or receive a miracle if that's what they really prefer. But it remains in His hands as to what He will or will not do. If you are one of those who have not experienced God in the realm of the miraculous or in being given a special Word from Him, you have lots of company and all I can encourage you to do is keep an expectant heart, and try not to close your mind or your spirit to the limitless possibilities of what God might choose to do. He may surprise you one day. If not, you still have the written Word of God, the Bible, which is far more dependable and wonderful, and you walk by faith, not by sight or experience. That is enough. His written Word is more than sufficient and we do not really need more beyond that.

I think of the accounts some people have given of near-death experiences where they lived to tell of their glimpses of heaven and yes, sometimes hell. The stories seem unbelievable to a lot of folks, and some indeed may be tall tales or a result of chemically-induced reactions in their brain while many others may very well be true. I read a book from one of those people, an elderly and credible Christian man, that believed he had such an experience. As he told his own story, he realized that there would likely be doubters as to the validity of his story. He mentioned how there were others with similar stories and the fact that they had many skeptics. He had some thoughts about their experiences. He expressed his feelings that people don't necessarily make up the journeys they believe they've had to heaven, and he states that his is not made up either. Rather, he goes on to share that God sometimes may give us such previews of the after-life or whatever it is God has chosen to let us get a glimpse of. Similarly, I could say that I was simply given a brief divine experience with some eggs based on what God wanted me to see.

MIRACULOUS EXPECTATION

David Ben-Gurion believed that those who don't believe in miracles are not realists. In some cases but not all, many who doubt the miraculous or who never experience the miraculous tend to be ones who close their minds and their hearts to the possibility of the miraculous or they tend to be very locked into viewing life only from the perspective of their physical senses. Life however is not limited to only the physical sphere but also there is the spiritual dimension.

A lot of cessationists *(those who believe the days of miracles are over)* have actually become ex-cessationists after they experienced a miracle of their own. Ralph Waldo Emerson expressed that people tend to just see that which they're prepared to see.

Could it be that some folks never experience the miraculous because they have chosen to not believe it can happen? I cannot be the judge of anyone, so I dare not say. What I do see evidence of a lot is that those who are open to the idea that God still does miracles are often the ones who experience it. It is said by some that Christianity is the community of miraculous expectation. If I am open to experiencing the miraculous in my life, my heart is then prepared to receive and God manifests the miraculous all the more. That is just a blessing from the Lord, and I am humbled that He does this. There is nothing any of us can *"do"* to get God to do a miracle. We can believe God for a miracle and we can be open to the possibility of a miracle, but it is still up to God. I do not think God generally forces anyone to enjoy His miraculous powers if they do not want to.

For me, and from my point of view, the supernatural including miracles or hearing from God, is what God intends to be the norm rather than the exception in the Christian life. I like what one preacher was preaching on TV when he was speaking about people living by faith and believing God for the miraculous. He was saying that Jesus taught the principle of believing and claiming the Word of God for their needs. The preacher said that if you've got the guts to say it, God's got the power to do it! Of course God does have the power regardless whether we have the *"guts to say it"*. I should add here that I am not into the extreme thinking that sometimes is connected with the popular *"name it and claim it"* theology. However, I do believe in claiming the promises of God's Word, and that includes believing He will meet my needs and if He so chooses, He can and will do the miraculous. I will take the kind of Christian life where excitement and the thrill of knowing Christ is the norm. I will take the Christian life where one experiences the manifestation of our miracle-working God as complimentary to his faith, and where I am awed and amazed on a frequent basis at the power of God. No, I cannot live on a spiritual mountain-top experience all of the time, but I can enjoy a Christian life that is anything but boring and just limited to only the experiences of the natural realm.

Just recently I was reading an article in a Christian magazine about a woman named Heidi Baker, known worldwide for her healing miracles. She was doing Christian ministry in Mozambigue. She believes in the possibility of experiencing God and expects miracles as a normal part of the Christian life. This is how I too, live out my Christian faith. I live expectantly of what miraculous thing God will do next, and I anticipate experiencing God. Now I should add here, that I did not *need* a visual experience like those eggs to give me the reassurance that God was there for me during a particularly difficult moment. I walk by faith, not by sight, but as I walk by faith, I have also enjoyed experiencing God in many ways and times. I am glad to read of this woman's story and hearing how she too experiences God and considers the miraculous to be the normal part of the Christian life.

"SEEING IS BELIEVING"?

I think I would like to add another thought here about the miraculous that I recently heard from one of my fellow-minister friends who pastors our home church. I hope he will not mind me sharing his thoughts here. It just seems to fit so well with what I talk about here. He was preaching on the resurrection of our Lord on Easter Sunday, March 31, 2013. I am fairly certain he will not mind me borrowing his thoughts here. He will no doubt be glad to know I am paying attention to his sermon. He recalled how some of Jesus' disciples did not at first believe Mary's report of the risen Lord. He talked about the well known saying that seeing is believing. I thought of how in fact quite often even seeing does not always result in believing. That was one of his points. It is certainly often like that even with some of the undeniable, irrefutable miraculous things I have testified to having experienced or other divine activity that God has brought about in my life. Some have witnessed the fulfillment of things God did in my life along those lines which I shared, yet even in the face of clear evidence of the supernatural activity of God, they still do not believe. So indeed, *"seeing"* does not necessarily always result in *"believing"*.

NOW ABOUT THOSE EGGS...

In that moment of time in our kitchen that day, the undeniable fact that God had just showed up in this amazing way began to hit home. What just happened? And why? They were just eggs. Did God just heal cracked eggs? Really? If He did, I could say *"Wow"!* I could also ask *"Why"?* But my reaction was not so much a *"wow"* or a *"why"* as it was a subdued awe of what a great God I serve and know. I even recall that at that moment I quietly said under my breath: *"God just did something. Thank you Lord."* This event once again reminded me that He cared enough to manifest His power and presence, even right there in my kitchen and He did so through the quiet restoration of some otherwise insignificant eggs. He is the God of all the universe, the One who created all things, and here He is, un-cracking some cracked eggs? I could almost visualize Him with a smile in that moment, almost a mischievous *(in the sense of "playfully")* smile as He gave me this quiet, mysterious light moment.

I had been through some great ordeals the last couple years by then, having looked into the very face of death it's self. No exaggeration there. Maybe close encounters with one's mortality has something to do with being more receptive to the miraculous? Just a thought. I know that it is only by the grace of God that death had not yet claimed my life. As the saying goes, apparently God was not finished with me yet. It was surely by the hand of God that I was even alive and had come through third-stage esophageal cancer that frequently results in death. Yet to me, the undeniable miracle of healing these common, everyday eggs somehow in that moment seemed a bigger miracle than all of that. I say that because it was a very special moment with God. It felt in that moment like He was letting me know in a quiet, gentle way that He was present there in the kitchen with me. I think too, that He was trying to get me to laugh, something I hadn't done much of during those difficult days. And laugh I did. Obviously He did not *"heal"* cracked eggs for the sake of any eggs needing to be *"healed"* per se. God did not want me to concentrate on the eggs but rather to remind me of His presence and some glorious truths about His activity in my life and what He can do in other's lives. I am fully confident and convinced that He also wanted me to write about it in this book.

Something about God being involved in even the smallest details of my life spoke volumes to me of God's heart, and I knew given time, God would begin to reveal to me some of what this was about. To some reading this, they might think it is just plain silly and would question why God would bother with healing cracked eggs or why a grown man mature in years and experience would tell about this experience, or for that matter even dare to tell it! Believe me when I say that I have gone back and forth many times as to whether I should include this experience in this book. Every time I began to consider not including it, I sensed very strongly God's Spirit telling me He wanted me to tell of it here. Apparently it is a significant thing to God, so I included it and in the best way I can, I am telling what I received from the Lord through this event. The thing is, it simply did actually happen. There is no getting around it, so hey, I might as well tell it and leave people's reaction to it in God's hands.

The Apostle Paul in 2 Corinthians 11:16 spoke about the fact there were likely some folks who considered some of his writing to be *"foolish"*. He said that if they do think he is foolish for what he was telling them, receive him as foolish, so that he *"may boast a little about what the Lord has done"*. I too, only want to share what the Lord has done. Since what I am telling here is the truth and is something special that God has done, I share this account of the cracked eggs and trust that God will speak to someone's heart through the telling of it. God chose to do this unlikely thing and through it, He spoke to my heart. I wrestled with what it meant and what God wanted me to get from it. As I gave it a lot of thought, the Lord began to open up my understanding about various truths concerning His miraculous nature, and He has led me to share those truths here. Here is another one of those truths: Some might think God is too *"big"* to do such a *"little"* thing. I prefer to look at this way: God is *"big enough"*, that He is willing to take the time to do the little things. The one thing I can say is that it absolutely happened. Empirical evidence includes in its definition, as originating in or based on observation or experience. By that definition, what I saw did truly happen and God did something supernatural in our kitchen. Again as Sid Roth would say, it's supernatural!

"INCREDIBLE"

Again I realize a lot of folks just cannot bring themselves to believe God would do a miracle of any sort. The Bible says these words: *"Why should any of you consider it incredible that God raises the dead?"* (Acts 26:8) Who is to say what God can and cannot do or what God will or will not do as long as it does not contradict scripture? Obviously the context of that scripture was in reference to Christ's resurrection, but the principle can still be applicable. I would love for someone else to have witnessed this miracle of the eggs with me, but that is not how God arranged it to be. That would be too easy, and besides that, it could be a distraction from what is more important here. Maybe God wanted to see if I would have the courage and faith in Him to tell others about this experience even when I have no one else to back up my story. I guess it was first and foremost intended for me personally, but being only human I cannot resist telling others.

If the only thing I got out of this miracle was amazement over what happened to the eggs, I would have missed the bigger picture that God wanted to show me through it. I could have just written a couple sentences about that miracle if that was all this chapter was about, but that event is secondary to what I am discussing here. No, God did not want me to just see what He could do with those eggs. God is not in the entertainment business or into putting on a show to excite our senses. He is into bringing glory to His Name and to teaching us truths about Himself. This event and the things God taught me through it is part of the story of my cancer journey and the overall journey of my life. It's almost as though after all the wondrous ways God had been with me through the cancer ordeal, He then put an exclamation point on it all through the simple, quiet thing He did with a few otherwise unimportant eggs. To omit it would be to leave out an important part of my journey and an opportunity to bring out some spiritual principles for others to live by.

HOLY MOMENT, YES … BUT NOT HOLY EGGS

I removed the eggs from the boiling water and looked them over carefully, trying to see if there was any observable crack remaining, even in the faintest detectable degree that might reveal the cracks had somehow become faint *(if that is even possible)*, but there was no such indication. The eggs were perfect. I was still hungry though, and they tasted mighty fine. I wonder how many people would have gone ahead and eaten those eggs that had just moments earlier been touched by the hand of God? But my taste for my eggs prevailed. I did not need to preserve those eggs and put them on display like a trophy or something especially Holy, or as some no doubt might have done, put them on ebay. It was certainly a Holy moment, but those eggs were still just eggs.

Sometimes I think we might have a tendency to do this with great moves of God from the past. We recall those historical times of great revivals or of something God did in the past in our own lives and if we are not careful, we park there too long when it is time to move on. If we are not careful, we may find ourselves holding onto past events like trophies when in fact those special events or moves of God were

241

for that moment in time. God wants us to live in the present and enjoy what He does today, and be prepared for tomorrow. The eggs were not sacred or something to preserve and put on display on a pedestal or in our china closet. They were briefly in a specific moment in time a tool for God's use and part of a special visitation or maybe I should say, a special manifestation of the presence and power of God. I can say here with a light heart and a smile that personally for me it does not matter whether or not anyone takes me seriously concerning my story about the eggs being cracked and then becoming whole again. What matters to me here is that I was able to draw some spiritual truths out of what happened and share it in this book. God definitely was showing me something that day, and He gave me a fresh look and some insights into His goodness and miraculous nature.

GOD CAN USE MANY WAYS TO SPEAK TO US

When writing this book, I have been amazed at how many times a thought or a quote would come across my path in a wide variety of ways and I would make a note of it to include in my book. I receive those things as gifts from God. I love to watch the old TV shows, especially the westerns. One of my favorites is the old Bonanza series. In one of my favorite episodes, Little Joe, the youngest of the family in the story, ends up knocked out by a bad guy and left in the desert to die. He manages to make it to an old town long since vacated and known as a ghost town as it was called in those days. Anyhow, to keep my story short here, Little Joe wakes up later in the town to discover it is filled with people. They recruit him to rid the town of a gang of outlaws. Later he is found by his father and brothers just on the outskirts of town. Only now he looks and the town is back to being a vacated town with nothing but dilapidated buildings and tumble weed. No people! He tries his best to convince his family that there had been people there and how it had been a bustling, busy town full of life. Finally dad tells Little Joe that when a person knows something in his own heart, there's no need to explain it or prove it.

Knowing what he experienced is enough. Imagine that. I got material for this book while leisurely watching an old western.

I JUST KNOW IN MY HEART...

I have just talked about some cracked eggs becoming miraculously healed, un-cracked whole eggs again. Like the line in the western, I know in my heart what I saw. It may seem preposterous to some. I cannot do a better job of explaining it or proving it. Just knowing it is enough. One man said it well when he talked about sharing something God puts in a person's heart that he knows people may find hard to believe. His thoughts on this ran along the line of those times when you believe God has put something in you and because of how greatly it has touched your own life, there is an overwhelming desire to share it with someone else regardless how it may be received. I know what happened that day in my kitchen, and it is too wonderful to keep to myself even if others may not accept it. The only difference in my story about the eggs from the story in the western is that the western was fictional and my account of what I saw is true.

Can you imagine what the Holy Bible would look like or consist of if the forty different writers that God used to compile its sixty-six books had refrained from telling the accounts of God doing the miraculous for fear they would be thought insane? Our Bible would look a lot thinner and we would not have much to go on to believe we serve the God of the miraculous. But thanks to God, men inspired and moved along by the Holy Spirit dared to tell in writing of the amazing miracles God did. Like the line from the western, they knew in their heart what they saw and they just told it as God did it. They did not have to do a better job of explaining it or proving it. Just knowing what they saw God do was enough. No doubt, there may very well have been times when some of those writers of the Bible were thought to be out of their minds with their accounts of the miraculous.

In the Bible Jesus' own brothers thought he was out of His mind with the things He was saying and they tried to take Him home.

The Apostle Paul was testifying to the gospel of Christ before King Agrippa. A man named Festus spoke up and told Paul his *"learning was driving (him) mad"* and that he was out of his mind. Knowing Jesus and Paul were thought to be insane in their thinking and in what they were saying about the miraculous power of God, I am OK with the possibility my story of the eggs may seem too much for some to believe. To those who hesitate to believe God for the miraculous, may I say, go ahead and believe and have some enjoyment in embracing an all-powerful God of the miraculous who might just surprise you with a miracle of your own. He might even do something to put a smile on your face and make you laugh. God and I have fun together. The egg event was at the very least, God having fun with me. He is like that. But by now if you've heard my heart, you surely know this chapter is not so much about those eggs as it is and has been all along about the God of the miraculous and some insights I believe God has given me to share here about believing Him for a miracle.

DON'T SWEAT THE SMALL STUFF

There are a few more things I have sensed God was telling me in all this besides some thoughts I have already shared from it. One, He cares about every detail of my life. Nothing is insignificant. Often in life, people have a tendency to get all concerned about every little thing and it turns into worrying. These small, seemingly insignificant eggs remind me not to *"sweat the small stuff"* as someone has said. But on the other hand, to think that God took the time to do something special using some plain old eggs tells me He does not see things as being small or large, more significant or less significant. God is very detailed. We see the very clear evidence of that in creation. Nothing in my life or yours is insignificant to God. The Lord planted the following thought in my spirit and I share it here: *"If it matters to you, it matters to God too. And if it does not matter to you, it still does matter to God."*

CONTEMPLATING *"A GENTLE WHISPER"* FROM GOD

As I contemplated what God might be trying to show me in this, God was also reminding me that He has a sense of humor. It was as though He was giving me a look at His light-hearted side. As I have said, He was having a little fun with me. That really was my first thought and still remains the primary thing I personally got out of this experience. I find that to be, shall I say, very *"comfortable"* for lack of a better word. I mean, come on ... un-cracking cracked eggs? That day in the kitchen, God and I had a good laugh together. That is the truth. I found myself chuckling over it, and quietly with a smile, saying *"Thanks God."* We look for the spectacular show that God can put on, but sometimes He just does some quiet, unexpected calm thing like He did that day. The effect is the same as or maybe even better than the noisier, showy stuff.

The older I get, the more I look forward to and appreciate the quieter things of life. For example give me a good old-time reverent hymn over any of the contemporary loud and fast praise songs of the Church today and I get far greater sense of God's presence and power from that great hymn. A whole new generation is missing out on the wonderful worship experience the old hymns afford, and I fear they have no idea what they are missing out on. I guess that partly says something about my age. The younger generation, and some of the older generation, still prefer the newer stuff and that is OK. I will take the calmer, quieter songs of worship contained in the old favorites.

I am awed by an awesome God who controls a universe from hundreds of billions of galaxies right down to a few eggs and further down to the sub-atomic level. If God could put Humpty Dumpty together again, in this case some cracked eggs in our kitchen, surely He could handle the tiniest details of anything I was facing or the biggest of hurdles that lay ahead. At the very least, God was reminding me that He was right there with me. One thing about it is that after such a long, difficult road through the cancer and feeling like I had been beaten up in a dark alley, this special time in the kitchen with

245

God that day was a welcome, refreshing light moment that I needed and appreciated. It brought a smile to my face.

It was such a simple, low-key experience that somehow quieted my soul and seemed so far removed from the hectic hard-hitting battle of the past couple years with cancer. Here were some eggs in a pot of boiling water. It was not the typical setting for a major event; no big religious conference with big-name dynamic speakers; no lightening; no thunder; no earthquake; no big show; no getting slain in the Holy Spirit or prophetic word. It was just God and I and some eggs. It was more like a gentle whisper from the Lord. I do not think I can totally conclude all of what this miracle was about. Someday, God will perhaps make it clearer, but for now, I just accept it as a gift from God. It is a part of my journey and it is a part that matters to me because God did it.

"YOU MIGHT FEEL LIKE THOSE CRACKED EGGS IF…"

As I right those words, I can't help but think of comedian Jeff Foxworthy with his famous line where he says *"You might be a redneck if…"* and fills in the blank with funny lines about a way of life. As I have written this chapter on the God of the miraculous, and how the Lord is there for us as we look to Him, I could not help but think of the various ways that sometimes we may feel a little like those cracked eggs I mentioned. Life sometimes seems like things are breaking apart and you are not sure how or if you can feel whole again. Like a cracked egg, the situation looks hopeless. There are those times when unless God intervenes on your behalf, nothing short of a divine act of God will put things back together again.

When I received the diagnosis of third-stage esophageal cancer, and knowing its survivability rate was not very high, I could say that my wife and I felt like those cracked eggs. Our world was threatening to be shattered at this ominous news that had unexpectedly intruded upon our lives, and it might have been shattered if we were not people of faith. Anything short of God's intervention to preserve my life would likely bring my life to an imminent end. But just as those cracked eggs in our kitchen miraculously became whole again, so I could say God restored my life to wholeness and healed my cracked and nearly shaken hopes for the immediate future together with my wife and family.

My line of thinking here is that no matter how fractured or damaged your life may be, or no matter what seemingly impossible situation you may be facing, God is able to put your life back together again, or to do the otherwise impossible in whatever you are facing.

"YOUR LIFE ... IF ..."

Here I want to borrow a little phrase or at least similar to that line of the comedian who says *"You might be a redneck if...".* I want to put my thoughts a little differently.

Let me put it this way: *Your life or your situation might feel like those cracked eggs if:* you are facing a financial crisis, and your only hope is a miracle of Divine provision from God who desires to meet all your needs. *Your life or your situation might feel like those cracked eggs if:* your marriage is falling apart, and your only hope is a miracle of intervention by the Divine Councilor, the Holy Spirit. *Your life or your situation might feel like those cracked eggs if:* your family is going through a crisis too great for you to handle, and your only hope is the love of the Heavenly Father.

Your life or your situation might feel like those cracked eggs if: you are dealing with a new health crisis beyond what you feel you can endure, and your only hope is the God that heals. *Your life or your situation might feel like those cracked eggs if:* you have recently suffered grief over the death of a loved one, and your only hope is the God of all comfort. *Your life or your situation might feel like those cracked eggs if:* you have fallen into a pit of drugs, alcohol, or sexual addiction, or a life of crime, and your only hope is the God who rescues and sets the captive free. *Your life or your situation might feel like those cracked eggs if:* you have found yourself overwhelmed with a

247

sense of loneliness, depression, fear, hopelessness, or heartache, and your only hope is the God who will never leave you or forsake you.

Your life or your situation might feel like those cracked eggs if: you are facing your own mortality, and your only hope is the God who will walk with you through the valley of the shadow of death. *Your life or your situation might feel like those cracked eggs if:* you are questioning your purpose and eternal destiny, and your only hope is faith in Jesus Christ who saves. You could go on and on along this theme and fill in the blanks that fit your situation or need.

BROKEN LIVES?

The world is filled to overflow with broken humanity. Lives are cracked and seemingly facing hopeless futures. Who can put lives back together again? Who can restore broken relationships and lost opportunities and dreams that have been dashed against the rocks of adversity? Who can offer hope where there is no hope, or who can do the miraculous where it otherwise seems impossible? Jesus, the One who can *"heal the broken-hearted"*, is the One who can restore wholeness to the broken life that will look to Him in faith and let Him be Lord and Savior. *"Cracked eggs"? ... "Broken lives"?* God can handle it all.

A REITERATION AGAIN: *"IT IS NOT ABOUT THE EGGS."*

I realize at the beginning of this chapter and several more times since, I emphasized that this portion of my book is most definitely not primarily about cracked eggs. Not by a long shot. I have tried to be lighthearted and at the same time, reflect on a very special experience with God. I hope I have been able to bring out of this experience some thoughts on what I believe God was saying to me, and hopefully have given the reader some spiritually significant things to think about, regardless whether you are able to believe the story. If I have even just slightly increased someone's awareness and appreciation for a miracle-working God that cares about every detail of their life, then I can rejoice that God has touched someone's life and maybe made their day better. If my story has brought a smile or lightened someone's heart for even just a moment, I have accomplished some of what I hoped to do in writing this chapter. We tend to want to look for God in just the big events of life, but maybe, just maybe sometimes, if we will take time to notice, we may find Him revealing Himself and doing something great in the quieter ways.

GOD'S MESSENGERS

There is the story of an owl that I recently read in a book. The Christian author told of how God had used an owl to help relay to her something she needed to do. No, the owl did not speak audibly to her. Nothing like that happened. But some behavior of this owl which I need not go into detail here, impressed upon her what God wanted her to do. She followed what she believed was the Lord's leading and as things turned out, it became obvious that indeed God had used that owl in leading her to do what He wanted. She talked about how God's messengers are everywhere and they come to us in ways we can accept. For her, it was even a grey owl. For me, it was through some cracked eggs.

The LORD *said, "Go out and stand on the mountain in the presence of the* LORD, *for the* LORD *is about to pass by." Then a great and powerful wind tore the mountains apart and shattered the rocks before the* LORD, *but the* LORD *was not in the wind. After the wind there was an earthquake, but the* LORD *was not in the earthquake. After the earthquake came a fire, but the* LORD *was not in the fire. And after the fire came a gentle whisper.* (1 Kings 19:11-12)

THE HEART OF THE MATTER

The heart of God is what matters, and that is what this chapter has been about. It was about a manifestation of God at work as through this miracle He spoke to me His heart and assured me He was there for me. Maybe the reader of this account of the eggs is left wondering if even I really believe my own story; ...that this cracked egg thing ever really happened. I am OK with leaving a certain degree of mystery for the reader as to where this author really stands on this. Do I believe unequivocally that this literally happened, or have I been all along, telling this story totally *"tongue-in-cheek"* and just having fun with my readers? I assure the reader here that I have only told it as I remember seeing it. I know what my visual senses tell me I *"saw"* that day in my kitchen. I also know that I do not need some cracked eggs to become miraculously un-cracked to believe and know that I serve a miracle-working God and that He gave me the spiritual insights I have shared here regarding the miraculous.

Cracked eggs restored? ...really? ...A reality or a vision? ... or just a good story God gave me through a somewhat inexplicable experience to pass on to others and to bring out some spiritual truths applicable to living out our faith in a good and caring God? God and I have fun and a few laughs together. Sometimes we just try to keep things light. I personally have had some fun with this part of the book. I hope you have too. For those who know me and might have the misperception that I am too serious a guy, you may have a struggle trying to picture this light-hearted side of me who is speaking every word of this chapter with an ear-to-ear grin.

If you have stayed with me thus far, thanks for coming along for the ride with me as I have told my story. If you can conclude this portion of this book with a smile and a light heart, just maybe you have gotten the main point of this story. I would hope what the reader takes away from reading this chapter is that cracked and broken lives can be restored by Almighty God. When all hope seems gone and life seems too broken, the God of the miraculous is able to step into that otherwise impossible situation and make you whole again. I hope you're still smiling. I am.

Blessed are we who can laugh at ourselves, for we shall never cease to be amused.

CLOSING THOUGHTS

13. SOMETIMES A DRY VALLEY; ... SOMETIMES A FLOOD

"No weapon forged against you will prevail."...."Do not fear, for I have redeemed you; I have summoned you by name; you are mine. When you pass through the waters, I will be with you; and when you pass through the rivers, they will not sweep over you. When you walk through the fire, you will not be burned; the flames will not set you ablaze. For I am the LORD your God."
(Isaiah 54:17, 43:1-3)

*I*t is my hope that this book will serve to encourage those who face great hurdles in life. The same God who walked with me through the valley of cancer, is the same God who walked with me in the challenge of the ministry that He called me to, and the same God who has and continues to manifest His love and attention to every detail of my life, sometimes even miraculously. As I speak of the miraculous, I think of the world-renowned Sid Roth, a Jewish believer in Jesus as the Messiah who has spent thirty-five years investigating the supernatural of God and who hosts *It's Supernatural!* TV broadcast. I too have come to know this God of miracles and have attempted to share a little of what God has done in my life. Satan thought he could take my life before my appointed time. When I do pass from this life it will be on God's terms and according to His time-table.

I do not like to hear someone say that *"so and so lost their battle with cancer"*. I was never in jeopardy of *"losing my battle with cancer"* and I never will. Why can I say that? Because there is no cancer or any other disease that can dictate when I will die. When my physical body does die, it will be on God's terms and in His timing. I will leave this world a winner, not a loser in a battle against a disease. Cancer or some other disease might destroy this body I live in, but that does not mean I lost a battle. The Bible says: *"No, in all these things we are more than conquerors through him who loved us."* (Romans 8:37). As I said, I go out a winner no matter what. That old devil has failed in his attempts at every turn as my God has repeatedly dealt him a blow that has sent him fleeing. *"The one who is in you is greater than the one who is in the world."* (1 John 4:4)

The Spirit of God who lives in me is far greater than any devil. One aspect of the gospel's good news is that I do not have to give in to the devil and I am not subject to his power. Christ already defeated him and he has no power in my life. *"By His (Christ's) death He might destroy him who holds the power of death—that is, the devil."* (Hebrews 2:14). *"We know that anyone born of God does not continue to sin; the one who was born of God keeps him safe, and the evil one cannot harm him."* (1 John 5:18) We are told however to *"put on the full armor of God so that you can take your stand against the devil's schemes."* (Ephesians 6:11). *"Submit yourselves, then, to God. Resist the devil, and he will flee from you."* (James 4:7)

My God was there with me as my family and I walked through the valley of the shadow of death in 1987 when my first wife and their mom went home to be with the Lord. My God walked with me when again I went through the valley of the shadow of death via a series of heart attacks and then more recently stared into the face of death in my journey through cancer. My God walked with me in times where I felt my hopes were drying up in a parched and barren desert, and He walked with me when at other times it seemed the floodwaters of adversity were about to pull me under. Sometimes I have felt like I was getting beat up in a dark alley, but in every instance at even my lowest moments, by the grace of God I have gotten back up and re-entered the fight. I like how one singer, Josh Turner, put it when he had gone through a particularly bad day and nothing had gone right. He said something along the line of feeling similar to a punching bag. Life is kind of like absorbing such punches, yet still going forward. That was his story behind his album that is titled 'Punching Bag'.

As I have undertaken the writing of this final chapter, I could not help but be reminded of things recently happening that have profoundly affected others whom I love. It was September of 2011. The eastern seaboard including up my way suffered the double-slam of two tropical storms that unleashed a terrible flood. Another devastating storm, Hurricane Sandy, hit the northeast in October, 2012, disrupting millions of lives. The devastation of those storms was immense and widespread. My original home town where I had been born and raised, Johnson City, NY, was especially hit hard by the 2011 storms as were many other communities. My heart was broken as I heard and watched the reports of flood damage. I saw the devastating aftermath of the flood's rage as I visited the affected residential area of some of my family members who had lost their homes and material possessions. They had escaped the flood waters with their lives but had lost their homes and possessions. It would prove to be a long, arduous ordeal in the coming days and months as they attempted to recover. It frustrated me that my health so severely limits me and I was totally unable to help with the clean-up that family there had to deal with. Countless more such events and tragedies have and continue to occur throughout our land and around the world.

I mention such events as the flood that hit my home town of Johnson City to say this: As bad a time as it was for me to go through my cancer, my troubles did not seem so big anymore as I now turned my heart towards their crisis and heartache. For them, the passage of scripture from Isaiah 59:19 about the enemy coming in like a flood really began to hit home. I knew for certain that some of my family members who had gone through the flood had steadfast faith in the Lord. Surely I know, along with a lot of indescribably very hard work and seemingly insurmountably difficult days, it was primarily their faith in God that saw them through this most difficult time and it would see them through in the days and years ahead. Meanwhile, countless lives throughout the world are facing new crisis on a daily basis. People are hurting and crying out for relief and answers to their dilemmas. If it had not been for the Lord who is at my side, my own crisis of cancer would have claimed my life and I certainly would not have had the courage or stamina to have confronted that demon. I call it a demon in the sense that I see cancer as essentially an evil thing as one of my pastor-friends called it when he prayed for me. Oh, if only more people would realize they have a friend in Jesus who is only too willing to walk with them through their valleys or even the floodwaters. But it seems many choose to go it alone and leave God out of their lives. Some just flat out do not believe in God. That is sad and the Bible says a fool says there is no God. I agree. Nothing is more foolish than to say there is no God or to leave Him out of one's life.

NOT ALWAYS STRONG *(...and we don't have to be)*

For me, the time since first being diagnosed with cancer was filled with one great painful challenge after another and it seemed like the enemy had opened the floodgates of assault on us. I sincerely hope I have not sounded like a man describing life as one big journey of struggles, suffering and heartache. Far be it from me to want to come across like that. Quite the opposite, I view life in a very positive light, something wonderful to be enjoyed and lived to the fullest. But in this book, I have of necessity needed to tell it as it was, especially with the cancer. There is no way to wrap up life's severest challenges such as cancer, and tie a pretty bow on it. The cancer was ugly and at times tormenting. Yet if you are reading these pages, you know by now this author loves life and maintains a bright outlook on each new day that God gives. Admittedly my wife and I on many occasions found ourselves wondering if we could get through another day. It took a toll on us.

There may be some reading this who are even right now facing their own great difficulty and I pray you find encouragement in these pages. Throughout the ordeal, I had always tried to present myself as unwaveringly strong in the Lord. I did my best to carry myself in such a way as to have family and friends and church family see me as having unshakable faith and God-given courage. Most of the time I did a fairly good job of it too. But truth be known, there were times the emotions of it all got the best of me and I crumbled. My body was weakened by the constant pain and frequent times of sickness. My insides had been permanently and irreversibly altered barring a miraculous reconstruction by God. By the way, He can do that too if He wants to. It's not unheard of. I was not always able to look like the strong, positive man that I wanted so desperately to maintain. I had to admit on more than one occasion that I needed encouragement and help. To have such times where the challenges seem like too much to bear is not a failure of faith. It is OK to admit to times of such weakness. But always sooner or later, I would recover from those more difficult moments and between family, friends and God being there for me, I would live to fight another day. In the Bible we read about the man named Job. He was a righteous man, yet through tragedy, he lost his family, his possessions and his health went horribly bad. It has been said of him that he had staying power, and when all was said and done, God brought things together for him. That is because Job served and loved God who cares so much, even about the smallest detail.

A RUGGED CROSS AND GOD'S LOVE

I have not looked at my cancer or any other hurdles I have faced as unfair or *"why me?"*. That is not how I live life. Jesus, as He faced the horror of a cruel death on a cross could have said *"why me?"*, but instead moved ever forward towards the eventuality of going to the cross to pay the price for our sins. *"God demonstrates his own love for us in this: While we were still sinners, Christ died for us."* (Romans 5:8) God has made it quite clear and simple. We

257

have all sinned. If we refuse to accept what Christ did for us on the cross, and knowingly and willfully reject Christ, we will die in our sins and be lost for eternity. One Christian writer I read somewhere has correctly stated that each person can choose God or reject God's offer of salvation. That is a basic, clear Biblical principle that runs throughout the Holy Scriptures.

I think of Joshua in the Bible who said we must choose whom we will serve. He chose to serve God. I gave my life to Christ many years ago. God gave me a free will to accept His offer of salvation. Receiving that salvation of course hinged on whether or not I put my faith in Him and accepted His offer. I could have rejected that offer but as the Heavenly Father drew me to Christ, I chose to believe in and receive Him as my Savior. It reminds me of my upbringing and Christmas. I was raised with six siblings. Our parents bought us gifts every December and placed them under the Christmas tree. They chose for us to have those gifts, and they were already ours to have but we had to exercise our will to choose to accept them. Of course no sane kid was about to turn down those gifts with his or her name on it. Once we accepted the gifts, those gifts that mom and dad chose for us to have became ours to enjoy.

I see that being very much like what God has done for us. Amazingly millions choose to turn down Christ's free gift of eternal life through faith in Him. Those Christmas gifts filled my young heart full to the brim. Far greater than those childhood gifts, my life as a Christian is an abundant life. That does not mean my life is trouble-free. It does not mean I am rich in worldly wealth or that I am exempt from illness. It does mean I have the promises of God in the Bible and living for Him results in a far better life here. As we trust Him with our lives He begins to subdue our enemies and eases life's frustrations. He turns things around and begins pouring out His blessings. He strengthens us to face whatever life throws at us. This has been my experience, and it is founded upon God's promises. His promises were no less true in that time I was in the midst of facing my worst moments with cancer. I have the joy of the Lord. Jesus is my God, my Savior, my Lord, and even my friend. He has seen me through every aspect of my life. I have loved ones who have died and gone on to heaven. I will see them again when I get there. God invites whosoever will to call upon the Lord and be saved. *"Everyone who calls on the name of the Lord will be saved."* (Romans 10:13). *"The Lord is not slow in keeping his promise, as some understand slowness. He is patient with you, not wanting anyone to perish, but everyone to come to repentance."* (2 Peter 3:9)

WHAT MUST YOU DO TO BE SAVED?

In response to the Holy Spirit's leading, admit you are a sinner and with a repentant heart, ask God's forgiveness. *"There is no one righteous, not even one ... for all have sinned and fall short of the glory of God."* (Romans 3:10,23). *"In him we have redemption through his blood, the forgiveness of sins, in accordance with the riches of God's grace."* (Ephesians 1:7) Believe in and receive Jesus. *"For God so loved the world that he gave his one and only Son, that whoever believes in him shall not perish but have eternal life."* (John 3:16) *"Everyone who calls on the name of the Lord will be saved."* (Romans 10:13) *"To all who receive him, to those who believed in his name, he gave the right to become children of God."* (John 1:12) Confess that Jesus is your Lord. *"If you confess with your mouth, 'Jesus is Lord,' and believe in your heart that God raised him from the dead, you will be saved."* Romans 10:9 If you have taken these steps of faith and commitment, you are saved. It is really one step. It does include repentance however, an aspect of salvation that a lot of people these days like to try to leave out of the equation. Place your faith in Christ, and by God's grace through faith alone, you will be saved.

FINAL THOUGHTS

Just as I finished typing that sub-heading *'Final Thoughts'*, a special moment happened. I turned to my wife who was at her computer next to me, and I simply said to her that I had now arrived at the end of my book and was getting ready to write my *'Final Thoughts'* as I drew her attention to that heading. She simply responded with the words *"I am proud of you."* It may not sound like all that special of a moment as I recall it here, but it was for us. Her tears came in that moment, and yes, I admit to mine too. I am reminded of her tears back there on February 1, 2010 when I wrote the word *"Cancer"* on my legal pad as the doctor told me my diagnosis. Now a few years later, her tears flow again as she hears me say I am writing my final thoughts for this book. Like Jeremiah the prophet, I guess I am sometimes a *"weeping prophet"*. I literally weep for America's soul, for lost family members, for the hurting and for humanity in general.

Yes, Sharon said *"I am proud of you."* It had been a long, at times, heartbreaking journey since the day we received my diagnosis of cancer and finding out that it could very possibly be that we would have only months or a handful of years left together. We started on a journey and an ordeal that we were not at all familiar with or sure about what all would happen in the days ahead. It did look very bleak. Most definitely there was a high probability that I might not have been here by now typing this book. But as God would have it, by His grace I am still here. It is in fact, miraculous that I survived cancer. God willing, I may yet stick around a lot longer, but it is all in His hands and I am ready for whatever God decides. He already knows the number of my days. I hope by writing this book, my words of encouragement will live on past my earthly days and lighten someone's heart as they face their own challenges. If I have left something of myself through this book, I can leave this world knowing that just maybe in some small way the life I lived has made a difference for good. May that be my legacy.

WHETHER I LIVE OR I DIE, …I WIN!

The only true winners in this world are those who have placed their faith in Christ. Because my Savior lives and has won the victory, I live and I win. Cancer thought it could have me. But I have news for that cancer …it never did and never could own me. It could never rule the day. It could never have my spirit. As I mentioned earlier in this book sometimes obituaries will say something along the line that someone *"died after losing a long battle with cancer".* I would never want such a statement written about me. When I pass on from this life, it will not be that I lost any battle, but rather because God chose to take me home in His own good time. God has me. He did throughout the ordeal and He always will. Illness may take lives in the sense it may destroy the physical body, but we are so much more than just flesh and blood. We humans are living souls.

My heart goes out to a broken world that is full of humanity crying out for answers and hope. Wars, terrorism, hate and troubles that seem insurmountable plague our planet. As I write, we are witnessing many in our own nation here in America racing down a path of destruction with many of its citizens determined to forsake all forms of decency and morality. A new generation is quickly assuming the controls and direction of America. Many, but not all, these days lack much sense of morality or right versus wrong. Cursing has become the accepted norm. Immoral sexual relationships are becoming all too common. The sanctity of marriage between a man and a woman is being treated as no longer important. Men and women are living in sexual immorality as they live together without being married. The sanctity of life is also falling by the wayside with many people. Lying is considered no big deal. God says all of this is a big deal. Times have changed, but God's standards remain constant. Evil is being called good, and good evil.

Certainly there remains much good and greatness to our nation. But also it is true that many are departing from God's ways and a nation that forsakes God is heading the wrong direction. While much is going sour these days, there still remains a great multitude of our population that holds to its integrity; that still loves God and country and proudly still flies the flag; that still believes in doing the right thing; that still takes a bold stand against evil; that still holds out hope for better days. America is still a great nation. Will it remain so or will it neglect God too long and lose that greatness?

A BRIGHTER DAY

For my wife, my sons and daughters, my grandchildren, and for me, it is a brighter day than it looked like in February of 2010 when I had to tell them the news that I had cancer. God restored our hope and I have a new lease on life. I thank my wife and family, my brothers and sisters, my friends and also my colleagues in ministry, for all the encouragement they gave me along the way. I have spoken about the journeys we find ourselves on in life, about generations that have been a part of my life, and even about cracked eggs whose significance I am still trying to more fully understand. I believe all these things have helped form and affect my own life into what it is today. The bottom line? I said it way back in chapter one and I say it again. It is about trusting God. I trusted God before cancer. I trusted God during cancer. And I trust God for the future. You too, can trust Him.

A HIGH NOTE

I could not write the last word in this book without ending it on another and final high note. Jesus Christ has been there for me at every crossroad I have come to. I can say with Job of the Bible that I know my Redeemer lives and that I will see Him face to face. My time on this earth is getting shorter with each passing moment and in light of eternity it will not be long before I make that final journey to heaven's shores. I cherish every moment, even the difficult ones that my Savior gives me here. I have tried and will continue to try to persuade others to trust Jesus as their Lord and Savior. Neither cancer nor anything else that life ever throws at me can steal my hope or my joy. One day I will enter into the glorious presence of my Lord and I will spend eternity enjoying my God who loved me enough to lay His life down on a cross and pay the price for my sins. He rose from the grave and extended His amazing grace to me. Until that day He takes me home, I will sing praises to Him and walk with the One who is my best friend. This book tells of a lot that I as well as my wife went through. We came through it and at the time of this writing, I have definitely gained the upper hand on the cancer and all the complications.

I feel relatively good now and by God's grace I have been lifted up out of the valleys and find myself on solid ground, ready to once again take on whatever challenges might lie ahead. Sure there remains some chronic pain left over from the cancer experience. Sure there are a few ongoing symptoms I must deal with each day. But those things no longer hold me down. I'm alive and as the saying goes, I have people to see, places to go, and things to do! Today truly is a good day for Sharon and me. We have nothing but praise for our God and an upbeat, positive outlook of where we are today. What a joy life is with Christ in my heart. Thank you Jesus. To all who read these words, I encourage you to trust Jesus and keep that smile going. God is smiling at you. The best is yet to come.

….And as one of my friends and colleagues in ministry Rick always said when he was still on earth:

"Keep it Simple; Keep the Faith" …Thanks Rick.

EPILOGUE

By the time I have finished undertaking the writing of this book I will have been engaged in this project going on two years. I fully realize I am not an established author and it will be a challenge as to what to do next with what I've written. There are many questions that come to mind. Who will want to read it? How will I get it in print and out there available to the public? Is my effort worthy reading and who will its message speak to? I must have edited this work twenty times or more. At some point I had to just conclude that it will never be perfect and it is time to take it to the next step. If anyone is encouraged or ministered to, or in any part of this book been blessed or found in it something that speaks to their situation, I will count that as enough to make it all worth the time and effort I put into it. I've touched on a wide spectrum of subject matter and some of its content is more down-to-earth than some other parts. No doubt I have said some things that some will find questionable and may have some doubts and skepticism in regard to some of my spiritual experiences. Hopefully much of what I have written is simply some helpful, encouraging insights and information others can gain from reading it and maybe prove useful in their own journey.

I've written about journeys. I recently finished reading the book *'Earn the Right to Win'* by NY Giants coach Tom Coughlin. It was a tremendously inspiring book for me. In one place he speaks words in regard to putting off facing a challenge or great undertaking, saying it is easy. He explains that doing that requires simply doing nothing. He then speaks of a journey by talking about taking initial steps on what could be a lengthy journey. You'll likely face many challenges in the process. Patience and courage will be necessary. That really spoke to me and adds to what I've been trying to say in this book. I've written about the cancer. That part of my book is just recounting the journey cancer took us on and I've attempted to share that experience in words from my heart. As I then moved into the subject of ministry, I have tried to share my testimony of what God did in my life. Some of what I've shared is easy to digest as I speak of how God changed my life when I placed my faith in Him, and then heard the divine call of God into the ministry. I've mentioned only a very small sampling of some of our experiences in our travels in an itinerant preaching ministry. It would be my hope that what I've shared in all of that might encourage someone to seek God and to catch a vision for ministry in some mission field God would call them to. Beyond all of this I have shared several experiences where God has moved in the realm of the miraculous and in letting me hear His voice and getting an occasional peek into the dimension of the spiritual realm of divine activity through dreams, visions and special occasions of receiving a Word from God, and I have hoped the reader understands I share those things from a humble heart. While for a lot of people these experiences may not be common daily experiences in their lives, it is no less valid that God does and has spoken to humanity in such ways, not only in the ancient past but in these times we now live. If per chance there be any who conclude in their hearts and minds that this author is off his rocker with some of the things he has shared, that is the risk I have taken. I say that in jest. Some godly men and women of the Bible were thought of as out of their mind at times. I've read a lot of great books, and almost always there are some things said in them that I either disagree with or find hard to swallow. When that happens I try to just smile and move on and receive what is in that writing that I do need to hear and can accept.

I have asked God to direct my thoughts and give me the right words and right attitude for this book. I have set out on this voyage to openly and honestly share my heart and be an encourager which is really my primary calling. I hope I have achieved my goal and that this book will bless someone. Thanks for coming on this journey with me as you've read these pages. Everyone is on a journey. I dare you to keep going forward and do so in partnership with God as you take that journey alongside Him.

With the Apostle Paul of the Bible, so I too continue on in the sentiment of these words:

"...that I may finish my course..." (Acts 20:24)